D0935012

Travels and Archaeology in South Chile

Travels and Archaeology
in South Chile

BY JUNIUS B. BIRD

With journal segments by MARGARET BIRD

Edited by John Hyslop   Biographical Essay by Gordon R. Willey

UNIVERSITY OF IOWA PRESS 𝚿 IOWA CITY

University of Iowa Press, Iowa City 52242
Copyright © 1988 by the University of Iowa
All rights reserved
Printed in the United States of America
First edition, 1988

Typesetting by G&S Typesetters, Austin, Texas
Printing and binding by Edwards Brothers, Ann Arbor, Michigan

No part of this book may be reproduced or utilized in any form or by any means, electronic or mechanical, including photocopying and recording, without permission in writing from the publisher.

The biographical essay by Gordon Willey is reprinted with the kind permission of the author and of Dumbarton Oaks, Washington, D.C.

Library of Congress Cataloging-in-Publication Data

Bird, Junius Bouton, 1907–1982.
  Travels and archaeology in south Chile.

  Bibliography: p.
  1. Indians of South America—Chile—Antiquities.
2. Bird, Junius Bouton, 1907–1982. 3. Chile—
Antiquities. I. Bird, Margaret. II. Hyslop, John,
1945– . III. Title.
F3069.B53 1988   983'.01   87-30245
ISBN 0-87745-202-4

Contents

Acknowledgments

In the 1930s a number of people facilitated the fieldwork in Chile: Ricardo Latcham, Julio Santibañez, Ken Williams, the Ross family, and Lucas Bridges. Very special thanks go to William Fell, his son John, and John's wife Peggy. Bird's assistant at Laguna Blanca was Doug Thompson; his assistant at Fell's and Palli Aike caves was Pedro Ojeda.

The 1969–1970 fieldwork was in collaboration with the National Museum, director Greta Mostny, and the Institute of Patagonia, director Mateo Martinić. Bird's assistants in the field were Patricio Núñez, Hugo Yávar II, Tom Bird, George Duncan, and Patti Fell.

Stephanie Gartner and Harry Bird are thanked for their work organizing the photo archive. Much gratitude goes to Nick Amorosi, who drew the plans and maps, and to Juliet Clutton-Brock (Department of Zoology, British Museum of Natural History) and Vera Markgraf (Institute of Arctic and Alpine Research, University of Colorado), who contributed studies to this volume. We thank Ian Tattersall (Department of Anthropology, AMNH) for his contribution to the descriptions of the human remains and Thomas Amorosi (Hunter College) for classifying the faunal material.

Robert Bird, Peggy Bird, Mateo Martinić, and Thomas Lynch read the manuscript.

JOHN HYSLOP

Preface

This book reports the excavations by Junius B. Bird in Chilean Patagonia in 1936 and 1937. At the time, that investigation yielded evidence for the earliest human occupation of the South American continent. Bird published several articles (1938a, 1938b, 1946a, 1983) on the research, and these investigations have become classic studies, cited in nearly every book on South American prehistory and in most studies on earliest peopling of the Americas. With Bird's passing in 1982, much information from the fieldwork remained unpublished in Bird's files, and the purpose of this book is to make it available.

The preparation of this volume marked the fiftieth anniversary of Bird's early man excavations in Chilean Patagonia. The archaeological work took place under conditions, and with a spirit, considerably different from much research today. This book attempts to convey some of the personal aspects of this truly pioneering investigation by citing segments of the extensive journal kept by Peggy Bird.

Junius Bird was well prepared for work in south Chile. In 1934, at age 27, he had already taken part in six expeditions to various parts of the Arctic, two to South America, and one to the Caribbean Sea. His knowledge of sailing and navigation, essential to the success of the inland channel trip described in chapter 1, was derived from several seasons on the schooner *Morrissey* under Captain Bob Bartlett. Navigating in the Caribbean in 1931, he weathered a severe hurricane in which his vessel was one of two boats out of sixteen in the vicinity which remained afloat.

Bird's earliest interest in south Chile developed after reading J. M. Cooper's book *Analytical and Critical Bibliography of the Tribes of Tierra del Fuego and Adjacent Territory* (1917). In 1932 he proposed to make a six-month trip to south Chile, and Dr. Clark Wissler, chairman of the Department of Anthropology at the American Museum of Natural History (AMNH), agreed that the museum would support the project. In 1932 Bird left for Navarino Island south of Tierra del Fuego and spent several months surveying the entire north shore. He excavated a midden at a site at Puerto

Pescado and then returned to New York just in time to meet Bartlett to go to Southampton Island in the Arctic. Fieldnotes from this first south Chile expedition are at the AMNH in the Junius Bird Laboratory of South American Archaeology.

The expedition to Tierra del Fuego and Navarino Island convinced Bird that additional work in the area would be justified and that he should go there with plenty of time and sufficient financing. "It's an area where everything is in favor of the archaeologist."

Upon Bird's return from the Arctic in the fall of 1933, he accompanied the archaeologist Wendell Bennett on fieldwork in Bolivia (Bennett 1936) for five months. Bird was married to Margaret (Peggy) McKelvy in 1934, and they left for Labrador on the *Morrissey* to dig Eskimo house ruins.

Later in 1934 Junius and Peggy departed for south Chile to pursue anthropological and archaeological work for two and a half years. The second south Chile trip had a number of objectives. One was to survey for archaeological sites in the western channels of south Chile, with a side project of continuing work on a vocabulary of the Alacaluf Indians done by Father John Cooper. A second objective was to continue archaeological work in Tierra del Fuego and Navarino Island, where Bird had worked in 1932 and 1933. An additional goal was to survey and excavate along the north shore of the Straits of Magellan. The research north of the Straits resulted in the landmark early man excavations reported in this volume.

Junius Bird made a black-and-white silent film (16 mm) of the two and a half years in south Chile. That movie is stored at the American Museum of Natural History in New York City.

The text of this book is almost entirely in the words of Junius Bird, except for the diary segments, written mainly by Peggy. Much of the archaeological text here was extracted from Bird's fieldnotes. This material has been edited, often rather heavily, since it was not originally written for publication. Other segments of text, taken from published articles, have been edited only lightly.

This book begins with a chapter which describes Chile's western channels and includes journal excerpts detailing some events of the five-month trip when Junius and Peggy sailed an open cutter through the cold and rainy channels to the Straits of Magellan. This chapter sets the stage for research at several caves/shelters reported in the following chapters. In general, these chapters describe sites in the order that Bird worked them in 1936 and 1937. It should be noted that the excavations at Palli Aike, because they took place at two different times, were begun before, and completed after, the work at Fell's Cave. The chapter describing the work at Fell's Cave in 1936 and 1937 also covers work done there in later years by Bird and others.

During the taping of an oral history in 1969, Junius Bird reminisced:

A thing like Fell's Cave is absolutely fabulous. . . . You have a complete chronological record from the present right back to the extinct animals. . . . I would say on the basis of what I've seen up here [in North America] these little places [his sites in south Chile] are still the best that have been found in the Americas. . . . And what else has been found in South America that is comparable? There are no other sites that have a nicer, long sequence, and with plenty of association with extinct fauna.

Bird was clearly confident and proud of his work in south Chile. This volume will make it possible for other scholars to have more complete access to this information and to evaluate its implications for themselves.

JOHN HYSLOP

Junius Bouton Bird
and American Archaeology

GORDON R. WILLEY

I intend this as an appraisal of Junius Bouton Bird's very substantial con- tributions to the field of American archaeology as seen within the context of that discipline, but my presentation is also a tribute to the man as well as to his achievements in his profession. Indeed, I can think of no other colleague whose accomplishments seem to have flowed more directly and naturally out of his personality and character than did those of Junius Bird. Whether it was exploration at the frozen ends of the earth or micro- scopic study of textile fragments, one always had the feeling that Junius was completely "in character" and supremely well suited to what he was doing. And what he was doing was exactly what he wanted to be doing. He was a truly "inner-directed" man.

In preparing my remarks I have drawn upon the impressive formal record of his career, an outpouring of published statements that have ap- peared in the very short time since his death, and conversations with his many friends and colleagues. Lastly, I have drawn upon a fund of memory of my own associations and friendship with Junius Bird, which go back more than forty years.

THE BIOGRAPHICAL DATA

The simple outlines of biography tend to be routine, but early events often signal a life's direction. This is the case for Junius Bird. From boyhood he was intrigued by adventure and fired by scientific curiosity. He was born and raised in a family of scientific traditions. His father, Henry Bird, was a distinguished entomologist; his mother Harriet was a descendant of Seymour Bouton, a well-known naturalist of his day; and his older brother Roland became a paleontologist. Junius was born on September 21, 1907, in Rye, New York. He went to school there, and he was fascinated by ar- chaeology from the age of 9. In 1925 he matriculated at Columbia Univer- sity, but after two years he was lured away from college by an offer to accompany the famous Captain Bob Bartlett to the Arctic. The adventures and excitements of this trip decided things for Junius. He never returned to Columbia but struck out to become an archaeologist and a scientist by engagement in the field. He made several more trips to the Arctic, which he enjoyed, but he also must have paid attention to business, for years later one of his American Museum publications, on Eskimo culture in Labrador (Bird 1945), was based on this early youthful collecting and note-taking.

The American Museum of Natural History became Junius' base early on. In 1931 the Museum made him a lowly field assistant, probably feeling it could offer him no higher title in view of his lack of a formal academic degree. Junius carried on archaeological research in New York, New Jersey, and Pennsylvania. In 1931 he also did some archaeological survey along the Caribbean coast of Central America. One of his most entrancing tales of this period concerned riding out the 1931 hurricane in a small boat in Belize harbor. But he also attended to archaeological business, for I recall talking with him about Honduran coastal archaeology many years later, after I had visited the region, and he was still very knowledgeable about that part of the world.

Junius had an extraordinarily wide, and at the same time specific, knowledge of archaeology from all over the Americas, and much of this was based on firsthand, on-the-ground information. In this preliminary biographical review, let me run over some of the high spots in his archaeological experience. One of the most prominent, and the one that projected him at the age of 30 into the international archaeological limelight, was southern Chile. The work he did there concerned the problem of early man in the Americas, and his results became an important contribution to that specialty. We will return to all this later. For the moment, in this biographical sketch, this is the place to pick up an important vital statistic in Junius' life. Bird began his work in south Chile in 1932–1933 with a survey in Tierra del Fuego and Navarino Island. The work was resumed in 1934, but before taking off on it he married Margaret McKelvy. I spoke of how Junius' life was closely integrated with his work; he now integrated Margaret, better known as Peggy, into it as well. Both the expedition and the honeymoon were highly successful. Peggy proved herself a formidable ally right from the start, flourishing under the conditions of a 1,300-mile trip in a nineteen-foot sailboat as well as journeying across the flats of far southern South America in a wind-driven Ford car.

Subsequent Bird expeditions and excavations included a long 1941–1942 season along the shore in northern Chile, research that was to prove as innovative as what he had done earlier in the Straits of Magellan. This was followed by his 1946–1947 dig at Huaca Prieta on the north coast of Peru, another landmark in American archaeology. And there was other fieldwork after this, especially his excavations and surveys in Panama directed toward early man problems. In later years, too, he returned to southern Chile, attending conferences, visiting museums, and carrying out additional field surveys. He was at it as late as 1980. From about 1950 on, however, much of Junius' energy went into laboratory analyses, especially of textiles.

During this research career a lot of other things were happening as well. In the Department of Anthropology at the American Museum of Natural History, he was made an assistant curator in 1939, shedding the humble designation of field assistant. In 1946 this was changed to associate curator, and in 1957 he was made a full curator in South American archaeology, a position which he held until he was given emeritus status in 1973. This "emeritus" title, incidentally, did not inhibit Junius Bird any more than his original title of "field assistant" did in 1931. He went right on with active research, without breaking stride, until the last weeks of his life in 1982.

A further discussion of Junius Bird's many activities must be compressed if I am to move on to a more detailed consideration of his research. Among other things, he was a great teacher. One does not think of him primarily in this role, as he did not hold a professorial appointment of any duration in a university; however, he gave special seminars and lectures at a number of institutions, including Yale, Columbia, Harvard, Berkeley, the University of California at Los Angeles, and Rice Institute. In a more informal way he also trained a great many students in the laboratory and in the field. As a curator at the Museum of Natural History he was ever a helpful colleague to those of us who went there to inspect collections or seek advice. He organized at least two major shows there, one, "Art and Life in Old Peru," in 1961, and after that, a Pre-Columbian gold show in 1970. He was a key participant in organizations and institutions other than his own, serving as one of the original trustees of the Textile Museum in Washington, D.C., as an advisory committee member and consultant to Pre-Columbian studies at Dumbarton Oaks, and as a president and long-time member of the Institute of Andean Research.

His major research achievements and his sundry scientific activities were well recognized by honors. These include the Viking Fund Medal for Archaeology for 1956, an honorary Doctor of Science from Wesleyan University in 1958, the presidency of the Society for American Archaeology in 1961, the Order of Merit from the Government of Peru in 1962, the Order "El Sol del Perú" in 1974, and the Explorer's Club Medal in 1975. A more popular sort of award was bestowed even more recently by *New York Magazine*, which listed him among the one hundred "most interesting New Yorkers." Anyone who knew Junius personally would certainly go along with this choice.

On a more personal and private side, Junius and Peggy maintained a home in Riverdale in the Bronx, a hospitable setting for many an archaeo-logical discussion. They were interested in community and civic affairs and members of various clubs and associations, including the Explorers and Century clubs in New York City. Junius is survived by his wife and their three sons, Robert McKelvy, Harry Bouton, and Thomas Lee Bird. His death came, after an illness of a few months, in New York City on April 2, 1982.

Such is the biographical frame of the man; let us now turn to the ways in which Junius Bouton Bird enriched and changed our knowledge of American archaeology.

EARLY MAN IN SOUTH AMERICA

In 1934, when Junius and Peggy Bird set off on their expedition to the Straits of Magellan and Tierra del Fuego, the field of early man studies in the Americas was just beginning to move out of the realm of speculation and conjecture into the domain of fact. In 1927, the same year that Junius had signed on with Captain Bartlett to explore the Arctic, a man named J. D. Figgins published an article in *Natural History*, a magazine of the American Museum, in which he laid out the circumstances of the discov-ery in New Mexico of man-made projectile points in association with ex-tinct Pleistocene fauna (Figgins 1927). The tight geologic-stratigraphic context made the association unassailable, and the geological dating esti-mates were in the range of 15,000 to 10,000 years ago. Although there was some rear-guard wrangling for a time, the dam on early man in the New World had been breached. Shortly afterward, Frank H. H. Roberts (1935) and Edgar B. Howard (1935), respectively, in the Lindenmeier and Clovis sites, brought forth evidence generally comparable to the Folsom results, and the search was on in earnest for early man in the Americas.

Down in South America, the will-o'-the-wisp of Pleistocene, or "Paleo-lithic," man had been pursued unsuccessfully for a long time. Peter Lund's Lagoa Santa finds in interior Brazil had been made in the early part of the nineteenth century (Lacerda 1882); Florentino Ameghino (1911) and Felix F. Outes (1905) had advanced claims for very ancient lithic artifacts from Argentina; and the redoubtable Max Uhle (1919, 1922) argued for a "Paleolithic" horizon in northern Chile. But the evidence for great age for any of these was unconvincing. Ales Hrdlička and his fellow critics (Hrdlička et al. 1912) had torn most of it to shreds, as Hrdlička had simi-larly demolished North American claims of man's great age in the western hemisphere. We know now, looking back on these claims, that some of them did pertain to quite early materials, but as of the mid-1930s there was no substantiation of this. Junius Bird was to be the first to pin down an early man claim in South America and make it stick.

I remember the December 1937 meeting of the American Anthropological Association in New Haven where Junius gave a feature evening lecture presenting the Magellanic results. This was the first time I ever saw him, this lean, lively, and convincing young man. I recall the photographic record of the expedition as excellent. The presentation was direct, simple, and to the point. Junius was never one to use excess words. A year later the definitive article "Antiquity and Migrations of the Early Inhabitants of Patagonia" appeared in the *Geographical Review* (Bird 1938). It was, and still is, a highly informative paper. In a few pages it lays out the geographical and environmental setting, defines what are, in effect, archaeological culture subareas or regions, and goes on to record the excavations. Two principal regions were explored: the Beagle Channel country off the southern edge of Tierra del Fuego and the Straits of Magellan between Tierra del Fuego and the South American mainland.

It was in the Straits of Magellan zone, on the mainland side, that Junius Bird found the earliest cultural remains. These sites were old camping places in rock shelters or caves on the treeless, windswept plains of southern South America. The people who had lived here had been primarily land hunters, pursuing the now extinct native horse and ground sloth as well as the still extant guanaco. Two sites feature in these discoveries: Palli Aike and Fell's Cave. In the lowest refuse levels of both were bifacially flaked, chipped stone projectile points of a distinctive ovate-bladed, stemmed form in which the stem had a "fishtail" appearance and some slight fluting on both faces. While by no means the same as the then newly recognized Folsom and Clovis points of the North American High Plains, these Magellan points were reminiscent of Clovis-like points from the eastern United States, of a type called Cumberland. This typology, the early stratigraphic position in deep refuse, and the associated remains of extinct animals all implied some considerable antiquity.

At that time, Bird was cautious in his age estimates, which he arrived at by following various lines of reasoning, including geological shoreline changes and computations about rates of refuse deposition. He was confident that the early Palli Aike and Fell's Cave complexes, the two principal components of his Magellan I Period, were old but suggested a date of no more than about 4000 B.C. Subsequently, as we now know, the fishtailed fluted point has been found in a number of other South American locations including Ecuador (Bell 1965), Panama (Bird and Cooke 1978), and Argentina (Cardich et al. 1973). In some of these it has been placed stratigraphically and by radiocarbon dating in early contexts. This radiocarbon dating, as well as radiocarbon dates since obtained for the Straits of Magellan contexts, is about 9000 B.C., a time fully consistent with generally similar Paleo-Indian finds in North America.

The relationships of the various Paleo-Indian finds from all over the hemisphere remain a much disputed topic. Are Magellan points and the early lanceolate points of Middle and North America all representatives of a grand big-game hunting tradition that was carried over both continents by early hunters? Or are we dealing with a series of essentially independent traditions? But however one interprets the data, one thing was made certain by Bird's pioneer work in the Straits of Magellan. Man, in his foragings and wanderings, had made his way to the far southern tip of South America by 9000 B.C.—a key fact to be taken into account by anyone addressing the difficult and large subject of the peopling of the New World.

The discovery of this early cultural horizon was not Junius' only achievement in the Magellanic work. Coming at the time that it did, it obviously attracted the most attention, but of equally lasting value was his development of a long five-period sequence which revealed a more or less continuous occupation of that part of the New World, from late Pleistocene until historic times. Subsequent periods in the Palli Aike and Fell's Cave stratigraphies were marked by climatic changes and new artifact inventories. The Magellan Period III features a leaf-shaped point form. Some twenty to thirty years later South American archaeologists were to recognize the affinities of this projectile point—now best known as the Ayampitin point, from González' (1960) excavations in northwestern Argentina—throughout much of Andean South America, where it is the hallmark of the era of 7000 to 4000 B.C. (see Willey 1971: 50–57). Bird's Magellan Period IV, with its short triangular-bladed and stemmed dart points, appears as an outgrowth of Period III, and the final Period V, with its small arrow points and limited presence of pottery, links the Magellanic sequence to the historic Ona tribe.

In the Beagle Channel excavations Bird was investigating another cultural tradition, one associated with the maritime adaptations of the peoples of the Chilean archipelago and expressed on the historic level by the Yahgan and Alacaluf tribes. Bird's "Shell-Knife" culture, the earlier of his two periods in this region, shows the maritime tradition in full force. Bird ascribed no great age to it, but it now seems probable that he was looking at the later prehistoric time ranges of the tradition. More recent excavations in the southern Chilean archipelago, such as at Englefield Island (Emperaire and Laming 1961) and Punta Santa Ana (Ortiz 1979), show a surprising antiquity to this maritime way of life, with radiocarbon dates going back to about 7000 B.C. Bird's later "Pit-House" culture from Beagle Channel might best be described as a modification of the maritime tradition through contacts with the land-hunting Ona tribe and its immediate ancestors.

NORTHERN CHILE

Bird continued archaeology in Chile but transferred his efforts to the northern part of that country in the early 1940s when he took part in a year-long Institute of Andean Research program during 1941–1942. Ten regional projects, dotted throughout Latin America, from Mexico to Chile, were incorporated in this enterprise, which was funded by the Office for the Coordinator of Inter-American Affairs. The late George C. Vaillant, a member of the Institute and at that time a colleague of Junius' at the American Museum of Natural History, was the originator of the idea, and a number of archaeologists participated, including Junius' other American Museum colleague, Gordon Ekholm. I was fortunate enough to be selected by Duncan Strong to accompany him on a Peruvian project unit and to make my first personal acquaintance with Junius. In June 1941 he, Peggy, their very young sons Robert and Harry, my wife Katharine, and I all set sail from New York for South America on the Grace Liner SS *Santa Elena*.

It was a memorable twelve-day voyage down to Callao, Peru. I became aware of, and dazzled by, Junius' wide-ranging interests, which went far beyond the academic boundaries of archaeology. We all disembarked at Callao and spent two weeks in Lima along with the Birds. During this time, Junius and Duncan Strong and I made several trips up and down the Peruvian coast. I was absolutely overwhelmed by the profusion of archaeological materials thrown up by treasure hunters in the ancient Peruvian cemeteries. Junius, even then, was an avid collector of shreds of clothing and textiles strewn about these necropoli; but—and I recalled this later— he was, on frequent occasions, picking up what he claimed were lithic artifacts, bits of broken black rock which Duncan and I, in our pursuit of pottery styles, ignored. I don't know whether or not any of the rock pieces he found on the Peruvian central coast that June were actually artifacts. I remember at the time I didn't think that they were. But five years later, and a few hundred kilometers to the north, in the Chicama Valley, he was to make us all admit that he had abundant evidence of a preceramic lithic complex in which many of the tools looked about as undistinguished as the ones he had shown me in the field in 1941. But this gets me ahead of my story. I want to take up things in order, and to do this we must take Junius and family down to northern Chile in 1941.

Of all of Junius' research achievements, the north Chilean work is my favorite. Perhaps this has something to do with the nostalgia for one's youth, the pleasant memories of the cruise down to South America, the excitement of my own first archaeological research in a foreign field; but it also relates to the nature of the work. It was the first fine-grained archaeological stratigraphy to be done in an area where none had been done before. This was where Max Uhle and Ricardo Latcham had excavated many years before, and now it was to be the place where Junius was to find the beginnings of agriculture in these regions and to specify stratigraphically a preceramic-to-ceramic horizon line.

The Uhle-Latcham background here is of some interest. As is well known, the great German savant Max Uhle was the father of South American archaeological chronology. By 1900 he had established, through excavations and stylistic studies, the major four-period Peruvian chronology, based on horizon-style phenomena, which still stands to this day. It has been added to at the bottom, so to speak, but the upper part of the structure remains firm.

In 1908 Uhle went to Chile to work with Latcham. In the vicinity of Arica and elsewhere in the northern Atacama Desert, Uhle developed another long chronological sequence. He did this through grave-lot excavations, with typological speculation, and with back-referencing to his Peruvian chronology. Uhle began the sequence with a postulated "Paleolithic Period," modeled on Old World archaeology. This was something he had not done in Peru, but it was apparently occasioned by the much more abundant lithic finds in north Chile. Such a period, one would anticipate, would be on a Paleo-Indian level. Junius Bird's work certainly did not substantiate it for the north Chilean coast.

Uhle's second period is characterized rather generally by a continuation of chipped stone tools and weapons, some ground stone, and early pottery. Junius, in effect, verified this general period and refined it considerably. In his *Excavations in Northern Chile*, published by the American Museum in 1943, he detailed two early coastal fishing periods, featuring lithic points, various ground stone items, cordage, textiles, and basketry. These periods were followed by sites with evidence for maize agriculture but without pottery and, subsequently, by early plain pottery complexes. Radiocarbon dating has since revealed that this early sequence spanned a time range from about 4000 to 2000 B.C. and later. Recent digging in the same region has thrown more light on the transition to agriculture and pottery. It would now appear that these traits appear in north Chile at some time between 1000 and 500 B.C. (Núñez 1978).

Uhle's later periods, in continuing chronological order, were designated as Chavín-influenced (which was not verified by Bird or since) and Tiahuanaco-influenced (for which Bird found little evidence but which has subsequently been documented). Following this, Uhle designated a local ceramic period to which he applied the term "Chincha-Atacameño," in the erroneous assumption that it related to a Peruvian south coastal style, a misconception that Bird cleared up with his Arica I and II periods. Finally, Uhle's Inca-Influenced Period was well confirmed by Bird. All of these results, presented in the American Museum monograph and later recapitulated in an article in the *Handbook of South American Indians* (Bird 1946), made the backbone of archaeological chronology for this part of South America—a masterly achievement based on a single season's fieldwork and its rapid publication.

THE PERUVIAN COAST

Moving still farther northward, Junius Bird, again accompanied by Peggy and their boys, joined the Viru Valley Program in 1946. The rest of us in that enterprise were directing our attention to the ceramic cultures of the Viru and the north Peruvian coast. Junius, with his Chilean experience, and, I dare say, with his brief lithic collecting period in Peru in 1941 in mind, decided it was time that Peruvian archaeological chronology be opened up "at the bottom." In 1946 this was pretty much heresy. A well-known Peruvian archaeologist openly expressed a lack of "faith" in the preceramic. But Junius began by selecting a huge black refuse mound, appropriately named Huaca Prieta, in the Chicama Valley, to the north of Viru, for large-scale excavation. The mound was thought to be without ceramics by both Rafael Larco Hoyle and his father. Bird's deep cuts confirmed this, although on its north side he found a surface layer with Gallinazo pottery. In three pits 100 to 150 m north of the mound he found earlier pottery, including pre-Chavinoid ceramics, now assigned to the then unheard of Initial Period of Peruvian chronology. After Huaca Prieta, Junius came down to the Viru Valley and repeated his performance of discoveries in another black refuse hill in that valley, the Cerro Prieto de Guañape (Bird 1948).

The Huaca Prieta and Cerro Prieto findings were another landmark in archaeology for Peru and, in larger perspective, for American prehistory as a whole. The Peruvian chronological structure, which had been begun by Uhle and extended downward by others to include the Chavín horizon, was now shoved backward in time for another millennium or more, with the Initial Period and the preceramic added to the bottom of the time chart. The Huaca Prieta preceramic levels proved not to be of great age when radiocarbon readings were available. Junius had penetrated into the later preceramic phases, dating to the third millennium B.C. These were Peruvian coastal cultures contemporaneous with some of the preceramic complexes he had discovered in northern Chile. Interestingly, however, the lithic assemblages from Huaca Prieta and Cerro Prieto were nothing like the late preceramic materials from north Chile. Instead, they consisted of rough percussion tools, not unlike those Junius had picked up along the strand of the central coast of Peru some years before when I was

entirely unconvinced that they represented a preceramic era. Their affilia-
tions have proved to run toward the north, to Ecuador, Colombia, and
Lower Central America (see Willey 1971: 94, 263).

Huaca Prieta not only yielded information on lithics and early ceramics, but with desert conditions for preservation the site afforded a wealth
of data on food remains and textiles, which included cotton fabrics, some
with intricate twined and woven designs. It was in studying this rich corpus of textile materials from Huaca Prieta that Junius Bird was led into the
complex world of textiles and weaving, a subject that was to interest him
for the rest of his archaeological career. Plant remains found in the preceramic debris included, in addition to cotton, domesticated lima beans,
squash, jack beans, peppers, and gourds. In cuts north of Huaca Prieta
maize came later, being associated with the Chavín horizon. Later research has shown maize to be somewhat earlier than this at some places of
the Peruvian coast although it can be noted that the dating of an earlier
maize horizon, and its importance in the local cultural development, is
still debated in Peruvian archaeology (see Conrad n.d.).

An interesting familial development came from Junius' work on Peruvian archaeological maize. His young son Robert was with Junius and
Peggy at Huaca Prieta, and it seems fair to speculate that he became interested in both archaeology and archaeological botany at that time. In any
event, Robert has gone on to become one of the leading researchers con-
tributing to our understanding of the development of maize agriculture on
the north coast of Peru and co-authored a paper on this with his father
(Bird and Bird 1980).

One very important lead was provided by Junius' Huaca Prieta excavations. This was to turn the attention of other Peruvian investigators
toward early architecture. Until 1946 we had thought that the earliest permanent constructions on the Peruvian coast were those made of the distinctive conical adobes used by the people of the Cupisnique or Chavín
horizon. But Junius carried the whole story of permanent architecture
deeper in time by disclosing a variety of adobe forms, as well as mud-and-
stone constructions, pertaining to the earlier Initial and preceramic periods. There were no big structures dating from these periods at either Huaca
Prieta or Cerro Prieto; but within a few years, sizable adobe and mud-
and-stone buildings, dating from pre-Chavín times, were located at other
places on the Peruvian coast.

Fieldwork for Junius did not end after the Huaca Prieta dig. He pursued
a number of projects in Chile, Peru, and elsewhere. The early man theme
seems to have been uppermost in his mind in much of this research, as in
Panama, where the discovery of surface finds of fishtailed Magellan-like
projectile points led him to initiate and continue surveys there. These Isth-
mian data are obviously crucial to the New World Pleistocene and early

post-Pleistocene picture. Regrettably, repeated searchings and excavations were unable to tie down or place the Panamanian finds in a way Junius would have liked, but he was still at it almost until the time of his death. He also participated in the excavation of a site known as the Cueva de las Ladrones, in Panama, where, with Richard Cooke, he documented a post-Pleistocene sequence running from about 5000 to 300 B.C., one in which early agriculture and ceramics made their appearances. He also returned to far southern South America, and he followed with interest, often critical, the new discoveries in Peru concerned with early man. At the same time, it is probably fair to say that the most consuming interests of his later decades were in technological studies, so let us turn to these.

TECHNOLOGY AND ARCHAEOLOGY

In 1949, three years after the Chicama and Viru fieldwork, Bird published with the late Wendell C. Bennett their general book on Peruvian and Andean archaeology, *Andean Culture History*. The first such book of synthesis and general survey coverage since Philip Means' (1931) *Ancient Civilizations of the Andes*, it enjoyed an immediate success and for almost a decade was without a rival. Bird's part in the book was a separately signed section headed "Techniques." It was concerned with ceramics, metallurgy, and textiles. The first two topics received five pages each, the last, thirty-seven, so it is clear where Junius' focus of interest lay at that time, and textiles continued to be his primary technological interest. He made the observation then that his statements on ceramics and metals were wholly derivative from available published studies but that his section on textiles contained original research information of his own.

On the face of it, one might assume that Junius felt that ceramics already played such an overwhelming part in archaeology that other, less well-studied aspects of material culture deserved their share of concentration. Actually, this is only partly true. Pottery has been intensively studied in the pursuit of cultural and stylistic distributions and in working out chronologies, but we know surprisingly little about its techniques of manufacture, at least in some parts of the world, such as South America. Junius' disclaimer that what he had to say about pottery in his *Handbook* was "wholly derivative" from the published sources is a little too modest. As one reads over the section, it is obvious that the author had looked at a great deal of Peruvian pottery and had examined it closely. Among other things, he was particularly interested in mold-made wares and in the processes that the ancients had followed in their manufacture. This same interest was maintained when he turned to the negative- or resist-painting of vessel surfaces. Complexity in craftsmanship always fascinated Junius. In the metallurgical section, Junius was writing from available source material, but he was aware of how little was really known then and spoke with admirable caution about casting, gilding, alloying, and such matters. His discussions of smelting and of "lost wax" or *cire perdue* casting again reveal his ever-present concern with the details of the way things were done. Thus, in describing a gold beaker of probable Lambayeque provenience, Junius directed his main attention to the types of tools that were used in making such a vessel and to the way in which these were used (Bird 1967–1968). In the scholarly context of Garcilaso's ethnohistoric descriptions of an Andean metalworker's kit, Junius explained how such polished stone anvils, hammers, and other utensils were employed, how the edges and surfaces of these implements imparted such-and-such effects to the final appearance of the gold beaker.

This same interest in the craftsman—his techniques, his possessions, the quality of his life—comes through again in Bird's paper on the "Copper Man" (1979b), the mummy of a prehistoric miner killed in a cave-in in a mine shaft in the Atacama Desert of northern Chile. The accompanying artifacts, including the still hafted, wooden-handled stone hammers, wedges, wooden spades, and other miscellaneous implements, give us an on-the-scene picture of Pre-Columbian copper mining. Baskets, which the miner had with him for collecting the ore, and rawhide llama skin bags for transporting it, are carefully described and illustrated in the article. The entire piece is not only a study in technology but one of empathy, an identification on the part of the archaeologist with the Prehispanic miner—a feeling for his tasks, the difficulties which confronted him, including the dangers of the job, which in this case proved fatal.

Bird's metallurgical interests did not exclude more strictly chemical or technical ones. In a paper published in conjunction with chemist Arnold M. Friedman and geologist Edward Olsen (Friedman et al. 1972), he drew upon their analyses in his discussion of a series of Moche copper pedestal cups, attempting to distinguish which vessels were made from natural "free" copper and which, apparently, from ores that had required smelting. At the time he wrote, our knowledge of such matters in ancient Andean metallurgy was considerably less than it is now; but Heather Lechtman, our current foremost student of the subject, advises me that Junius' early interests in pursuing this line of investigation were a key stimulus to subsequent work on questions of ores and smelting.

One final item concerning Junius Bird's interests in Pre-Columbian metallurgy is worth recounting. For the most part, one does not think of Junius as an archaeologist given to generalizations or statements of synthesis. One remembers instead his pragmatic, no-nonsense attention to detail. And yet Junius had the ability to step back in the midst of a concern for the trees and tell you about the forest. This brings me to the case of the stingless bee. Junius observed that the very finest and most delicate lost-wax casting in native America came from Colombia and Lower Central America and not from Peru-Bolivia where metallurgical techniques were also well developed. He explained this high-level craftsmanship in Colombia–Lower Central America by the natural presence there of the most suitable kind of native wax for this kind of casting—the wax of a stingless bee, a tropical forest insect not found farther south on the Peruvian coastal deserts or in the Peru-Bolivian high Andes (Bird 1979a). In spite of the sweep of the pronouncement, there is a very Junius-like quality about it— eminently sensible and grounded in his characteristic observations of the ordinary and the humble as well as the exotic and spectacular.

This down-to-earth kindredness, this ability and desire to empathize with the ordinary person in his or her ordinary tasks, was the quality, I am sure, which led the quite extraordinary Junius Bird into the study of textiles. If one follows metallurgy one is forced to dwell, at least a large part of the time, in the highly specialized realms of chemistry. Ceramics, too, can lead in similar directions in the chemical and physical sciences. Textiles, in contrast, while complex, do not demand such training. The ancient weaver was confronted with a task, and he or she went about solving it in a manner that literally could be unraveled and reduplicated by the investigator. In a manner of speaking, as the ancient craftsmen or craftswomen grew more skilled and more given to virtuoso performances so, too, could the diligent researcher become more knowledgeable and adept at understanding, recreating, and reliving the products and experiences of the original makers. At least this is the way I interpret Junius' enthusiasm for his Peruvian textile research. In recent years I do not think I ever visited Junius' office on the fifth floor of the American Museum when he failed to take me by the arm, lead me over to a table with textile fragments spread out upon it, and explain to my faltering comprehension some technical trick or twist that he had just discovered. It was always phrased as: "Look at what the weaver did on this one; look at how ingeniously she solved this problem." Junius, with eyes aglow, was right back there with the ancients, applauding their successes.

It is with some trepidation that I set about trying to tell you about Junius Bird's contributions to the study of American archaeological textiles. I am, at best, "all thumbs" with textiles. My wife has often told me that I don't know the difference between weaving and knitting. I know that Junius was very disgusted with my behavior with textiles in the field. I suppose I was always a little afraid of them. In 1941, at Puerto de Supe, on the Peruvian coast, we came across some textile bits in our excavation of a Chavín horizon site. I remember stuffing a number of filthy-looking fragments into specimen bags, with the rationale that this would be evidence that the old boys of this period knew how to weave and that we could probably tell whether it was wool or cotton by due analysis. The collections were shipped to the American Museum for study, as I was then a graduate student at nearby Columbia University. Junius asked me, upon my return to the States, if I had found anything interesting in the way of textile material. I said no, not really, a few nasty-looking scraps which I didn't think amounted to much. Junius helped me unpack the collections. I guess he wanted to see for himself. Anyhow, a few days later, when I went down to the Museum, I was confronted by both an indignant and an elated Junius. "Good God, man," he exploded, "do you realize that two of those 'nasty scraps' of yours from Supe, which you never even bothered to look at, are the finest pieces of Chavín-style tapestry weaving that anybody has ever seen?" These now well-known pieces, with their fascinating condor/feline inwoven designs, were later described and illustrated by Lila M. O'Neale in our Ancon-Supe report (Willey and Corbett 1954).

When Junius Bird launched into the study of textiles, stimulated by his experiences in north Chilean and, later, Chicama-Viru archaeology, there were few serious students of the subject, at least in the Americanist field. The late Lila M. O'Neale, to whom I have just referred, was certainly foremost in Peruvian archaeological textiles, and Junius recommended her to us to do the Supe materials. With her untimely death soon afterward, Junius pretty much had the field to himself; indeed, over the next score of years, he, more than any other person, was to train and inspire a host of co-workers in the study of archaeological textiles. His first serious beginning, at least as far as publication goes, was the *Andean Culture History* article of 1949 already alluded to. Junius' attitude toward the Peruvian textile arts is revealed in one of the opening sentences of that article when he states: "The fact that some of them [textiles] rank high among the finest fabrics ever produced should lead us, in all humility, to seek not only a knowledge of their origin and development, but also a better understanding of what they actually represent in terms of human accomplishment" (Bennett and Bird 1949: 256).

In another essay, published two years later, Junius enlarged on this same theme and answered my questions as to why, when he turned to technological studies, he chose textiles. He felt that they provided, in his words, "a surprising range of information about the people who made them, probably more than can be derived from any other of the commonly associated artifacts" (Bird 1951: 51). He went on to explain this by saying that such things as plant and animal domestication may be reflected in the fibers used, chemical knowledge detected in dyes, mathematical calculations implied in the constructions, and even insights into the individual personalities of the weavers obtained from a close inspection of their products.

After the Chicama-Viru work, and the discovery of so many textile specimens, Bird set about his study of them with intensity. He visited museums, such as the Textile Museum in Washington, D.C., and consulted widely with textile experts familiar with the products of other world areas. In typical Junius Bird fashion, he learned how to weave himself. The body of Chicama-Viru cloth revealed things about Peruvian textiles that others had missed. Shreds and fragments that had appeared as plain revealed on closer inspection some amazing warp designs. This was done through an analysis of the yarn elements themselves, their compositional, textural, and color differences. Such elements were then plotted, strand by strand, on graph paper and the graph checked back against the textile (Bird 1963). In this way the Peruvian interlocking-crab or interlocking-fish motif was eventually revealed on some of the earliest of the coastal textiles. This is a motif that has a long history in ancient Peruvian art and culture, reappearing in various styles and in various periods—as, for example, in the Interlocking or Early Lima pottery painting style dating many centuries after the Preceramic Period textile occurrences of the motif. One result of this research, as Junius was to point out, was that much of Peruvian art, with its characteristic rectilinearity, was seen to have its beginnings in weaving technology, with designs and motifs so originating being later transferred to other media.

How, in a few words, can we set down Junius Bird's contributions to the study of textiles? I have tried to summarize this by reading his papers and by consulting with his former colleagues. To be sure, one could draw up a list, such as his definition of the changeover from twining to weaving techniques on the Peruvian coast, his pointing out of the great step-up in cloth production with the appearances of the loom in Peruvian sequences, or his discoveries of design and weaving technique to which I have just referred. But all of his colleagues with whom I have consulted have repeatedly made clear to me that Junius' greatest impact on the field was that of an inspirational leader who trained, encouraged, and stimulated others to pursue Peruvian, and other, textile studies. His students, however formally or informally instructed by him, did him honor in *The Junius B. Bird Pre-Columbian Textile Conference*, the proceedings of which were published in a handsome volume brought out a little less than a decade ago (Rowe et al. 1979).

A SUMMING UP

In retrospect, Junius Bird's three great archaeological field achievements—at the Straits of Magellan, in the Atacama coastal desert of northern Chile, and in the sites of the early coastal dwellers in northern Peru—are the "dirt archaeological" pillars of his reputation as a New World prehistorian. They bring together key data on early man in the Americas, on the early hunting-fishing-collecting populations of the long Pacific strand of South America, and on the beginnings of native farming life in South

America. It is a total accomplishment difficult to match. The distinguished British prehistorian Grahame Clark once said to me: "You know this man Junius Bird always seems to be digging at just the right time and in the right place to provide the answers for some of the most important questions." Junius, I am sure, if he had overheard this, would have demurred; but Clark was at that time preparing a book on world prehistory, and I think his praise can be taken seriously.

To this superlative record in the field, we can add Junius Bird's accomplishments in technological studies, especially in the textile arts, where, with his Peruvian data, he opened up a whole new perspective upon the intricacies and the sophistication of an ancient craft and its craftsmen and craftswomen.

But such a summing up, however impressive its listing and content, is only a part of the story. I said at the beginning of my remarks that Junius was always fully "in character" in his work. It was a part of him. It cannot be detached from him. Because of this, we all recognize and pay special tribute to some character and personality traits which, I am sure, gave his work the distinguished quality which it possessed.

The first of these traits was Junius' adventurousness, his desire to explore and to innovate. We see it in the boy and his interests back in Rye, New York. It takes over fully when it leads him to join expeditions to the Arctic.

But this adventurousness never became aimless. It was circumscribed by a second trait, a quiet inner discipline. It was this discipline that organized and carried out the Magellanic voyages and research; and it was the discipline that, in a quite different way, led him to learn how to weave, to pick out the thousand threads in a textile design.

His self-discipline was closely allied to a third trait that he had in good measure—a sense of practicality, a pragmatic approach to problems. It is a quality that makes innovative vision pay off. Genius, to be effective, needs a balance wheel somewhere in the mechanism.

A fourth quality, to which those of us who knew Junius will attest, was his modesty. There was nothing false about it. He knew what he knew, and he was not hesitant in letting you know about it in no uncertain terms. But he did not feel that he had the answer to everything, and it was not necessary for him to put down others to justify himself.

A fifth and most salient quality was Junius' openness and generosity. I cannot count the number of people who have stressed this in talking about him. He shared his information and his insights with anyone who evidenced an interest in the things that he was doing, and he was not only willing to do this but was excited and enthused about it.

This brings us to a sixth trait, Junius' never-failing enthusiasm. He pursued his studies of the past for the sheer enjoyment of it, entering into them wholly and unself-consciously, and this enthusiasm carried others with him.

Seventh, and finally, Junius was blessed with a sense of humor. This infused all of his other qualities. It made him a joy to be around. Many great men—God help us—are bores. No one could ever accuse Junius of being dull.

What I have had to say here, however much couched in terms of praise, still falls short, somehow, of capturing the full spirit of Junius Bird. In searching for a final line of summation, I can do no better than to quote what William Conklin said of him, in an appreciation of the man and the scientist: "[His] special ability, to read artifacts the way mortals read books, was like the ability of the genius naturalists—of men like Darwin—who looked at the objects and life of our world and used that visual data to produce entirely new conclusions about the events and laws of the past" (Conklin in Rowe et al. 1979: 9).

BIBLIOGRAPHY

AMEGHINO, FLORENTINO
1911 "Une nouvelle industrie lithique: L'industrie de la pierre fendue dans le Tertiare de la région littorale au sud de Mar del Plata." *Anales del Museo Nacional de Buenos Aires* 20: 189–204.
BELL, ROBERT E.
1965 *Archaeological Investigations at the Site of El Inga, Ecuador.* (Bound together with Spanish version.) Quito: Casa de la Cultura Ecuatoriana.
BENNETT, WENDELL C., AND JUNIUS B. BIRD
1949 *Andean Culture History.* American Museum of Natural History, Handbook Series 15. New York: AMNH.
BIRD, JUNIUS B.
1938 "Antiquity and Migrations of the Early Inhabitants of Patagonia." *Geographical Review* 28(2): 250–275.
1943 *Excavations in Northern Chile.* Anthropological Papers, American Museum of Natural History 38(4). New York: AMNH.
1945 *Archaeology of the Hopedale Area, Labrador.* Anthropological Papers, American Museum of Natural History 39(2). New York: AMNH.
1946 "The Cultural Sequence of the North Chilean Coast." In *Handbook of South American Indians,* ed. Julian H. Steward, I: 587–594. Bulletin 143, Bureau of American Ethnology. Washington, D.C.: Smithsonian Institution.
1948 "Preceramic Cultures in Chicama and Viru." In *A Reappraisal of Peruvian Archaeology,* ed. W. C. Bennett, 21–29. Memoir 4. Menasha, Wis.: Society for American Archaeology.
1951 "Recent Developments in the Treatment of Archaeological Textiles."

In *Essays on Archaeological Methods*, ed. James B. Griffin, 51–56. Anthropological Papers, Museum of Anthropology 8. Ann Arbor: University of Michigan.

1963   "Pre-Ceramic Art from Huaca Prieta, Chicama Valley." *Ñawpa Pacha* I: 29–34.

1967–1968   "Treasures from the Land of Gold." *Arts in Virginia* 8(1–2): 20–23. Richmond: Virginia Museum of Fine Arts.

1979a   "Legacy of the Stingless Bee." *Natural History* 88(9): 49–51. New York: American Museum of Natural History.

1979b   "The 'Copper Man': A Prehistoric Miner and His Tools from Northern Chile." In *Pre-Columbian Metallurgy of South America*, ed. Elizabeth P. Benson, 105–132. Washington, D.C.: Dumbarton Oaks.

BIRD, JUNIUS B., AND RICHARD COOKE

1978   The Occurrence in Panama of Two Types of Paleo-Indian Projectile Points." In *Early Man in America—from a Circum-Pacific Perspective*, ed. A. L. Bryan, 263–272. Occasional Papers No. 1, Department of Anthropology, Edmonton: University of Alberta.

BIRD, ROBERT M., AND JUNIUS B. BIRD

1980   "Gallinazo Maize from the Chicama Valley, Peru." *American Antiquity* 45: 325–333.

CARDICH, AUGUSTO, LUCIO ADOLFO CARDICH, AND ADAM HAJDUK

1973   "Secuencia arqueológica y cronología radiocarbónica de la cueva 3 de Los Toldos (Santa Cruz, Argentina)." *Separatas Relaciones* nueva serie 7. Buenos Aires.

CONRAD, GEOFFREY W.

n.d.   "The Central Andes (Peru-Bolivia)." In *Archaeological Chronologies in South America*, ed. C. W. Meighan. (Forthcoming.)

EMPERAIRE, JOSÉ, AND ANNETTE LAMING

1961   "Les gisements des Iles Englefield et Vivian dans la Mer D'Otway, Patagonia Australie." *Journal de la Société des Américanistes* 50: 7–75.

FIGGINS, JESSE D.

1927   "The Antiquity of Man in America." *Natural History* 27(3): 229–239. New York: American Museum of Natural History.

FRIEDMAN, ARNOLD M., EDWARD OLSEN, AND JUNIUS B. BIRD

1972   "Moche Copper Analysis: Early New World Metal Technology." *American Antiquity* 37: 254–258.

GONZÁLEZ, ALBERTO REX

1960   *La estratigrafía de la Gruta de Intihuasi (Prov. de San Luís, R. A.) y sus relaciones con otros sitios precerámicos de Sudamérica.* Revista del Instituto de Antropología I. Córdoba, Argentina: Universidad Nacional.

HOWARD, EDGAR B.

1935   "Occurrence of Flints and Extinct Animals in Pluvial Deposits near Clovis, New Mexico, Pt. 1, Introduction." *Proceedings, Philadelphia Academy of Natural Sciences* 87: 299–303.

HRDLIČKA, ALES, WILLIAM H. HOLMES, BAILEY WILLIS, FRED E. WRIGHT, AND CHARLES N. FENNER
1912 *Early Man in South America*. Bulletin 52, Bureau of American Ethnology. Washington, D.C.: Smithsonian Institution.

LACERDA, AUGUSTO
1882 "Documents pour servir à l'histoire de l'homme fossil du Brésil." *Mémoires de la Société d'Anthropologie de Paris* 2nd series, 2(4).

MEANS, PHILIP A.
1931 *Ancient Civilizations of the Andes*. New York: Charles Scribners Sons.

NÚÑEZ, LAUTARO
1978 "Northern Chile." In *Chronologies in New World Archaeology*, ed. R. E. Taylor and C. W. Meighan, 483–512. New York: Academic Press.

ORTIZ, OMAR R.
1979 "Punta Santa Ana et Bahia Buena: Deux gisements sur une ancienne ligne de rivage dans le détroit de Magellan." *Journal de la Société des Américanistes* 66: 132–204.

OUTES, FELIX F.
1905 "La edad de la piedra en Patagonia." *Anales del Museo Nacional de Buenos Aires* 12: 203–575.

ROBERTS, FRANK H. H., JR.
1935 *A Folsom Complex*. Smithsonian Miscellaneous Collections 94(4). Washington, D.C.: Smithsonian Institution.

ROWE, ANN P., ELIZABETH P. BENSON, AND ANNE L. SCHAFFER (EDS.)
1979 *The Junius B. Bird Pre-Columbian Textile Conference*. Washington, D.C.: Textile Museum and Dumbarton Oaks.

UHLE, MAX
1919 "La arqueología de Arica y Tacna." *Boletín de la Sociedad Ecuatoriana de Estudios Históricos Americanos* 3(7–8): 1–48. Quito.
1922 *Fundamentos étnicos y arqueología de Arica y Tacna*. 2nd edition. Quito: n.p.

WILLEY, GORDON R.
1971 *An Introduction to American Archaeology: Vol. 2, South America*. Englewood Cliffs, N.J.: Prentice-Hall.

WILLEY, GORDON R., AND JOHN M. CORBETT
1954 *Early Ancón and Early Supe Culture: Chavín Horizon Sites of the Central Peruvian Coast*. Columbia Studies in Archaeology and Ethnology 3. New York: Columbia University Press.

Travels and Archaeology in South Chile

Fig. I. Map of southern South America with routes traveled by Junius and Peggy Bird from 1935 to 1937.

1. Background and Departure

OVERVIEW

I planned the work in south Chile with the conviction that the prehistoric record was an important part of the story of the human occupation of the Americas. The first trip, lasting six months in 1932–1933, was by way of Buenos Aires to Punta Arenas. From there I went by launch to Porvenir in western Tierra del Fuego; then by mail car to Río Grande on the east coast, and from there with three horses to Lago Fagñano and to Harberton on Beagle Channel (fig. 1). I crossed this by rowboat, and spent the next three months excavating shell mounds on the north shore of Navarino Island. Then I retraced the same route on the return trip, reaching New York in May. Total cost, $750.00. The excavations and survey on Navarino Island revealed a long and extensive occupation, broken into two distinctive cultural divisions. While there was no means at that time of measuring age, it was found that there had been a coastal uplift of 15 ft. since the start of the first occupation, and 2½ ft. since the appearance of artifacts identifiable as Yahgan (the historically known Indians). A subsequent radiocarbon measurement indicates that this occurred a thousand years ago.

With this as the basis, further work was planned, and in 1934 I returned, this time with my wife Peggy. Traveling by way of Santiago, Chile, we went to Puerto Montt, where we bought a 19-ft. locally made cutter and installed a marine engine. In this we traveled down the coast, stopping at Puerto Aysén, the last place where gasoline and supplies could be obtained. A little over five months were spent aboard this boat seeking and checking archaeological sites among the islands down to the Straits of Magellan. We had planned to spend part of the winter working on Elizabeth Island in the Straits, but the amount of material available there did not justify the effort [Bird 1980]. Instead we went south and spent the winter months working three rock shelter–middens, one on the west side of Navarino Island, one on the north side, and one on Tierra del Fuego in Yendagaia Bay just west of Ushuaia.

Returning to Punta Arenas in the spring, we bought a 1917 Model T Ford for $27.00 and made a survey of sites along the north side of Magellan Strait east of Punta Arenas (Magallanes) and at Laguna Blanca. This was a large glacial lake maintained at a high level before the recession of the glacial ice. Work there showed that the region was occupied before the lake dropped to its present level. At the beginning of winter we drove north through the Argentine to Comodoro Rivadavia, and from there across the Andes to Puerto Aysén.

That winter was spent on the island of Chiloé, and in the spring we returned to Puerto Aysén and drove back south as we had come, checking archaeological collections on the way. We then excavated in three volcanic caves (Palli Aike, Fell's, and Cerro Sota), the first of which we had tested on our way north in the fall. In these we found stratified cultural material extending the human record back to the late Pleistocene, before extinction of the native horse and giant ground sloth [*Mylodon*]. On completion of this work we sold the Ford ($27.50), and returned to Puerto Montt by steamer, visiting the Mylodon Cave in Ultima Esperanza before leaving the south. The little cutter was sold to the Chilean hydrographic office. We returned to New York after our departure, having made the trip for a total cost averaging out at about $65.00 a month.

In 1968 I returned with an NBC television crew to the volcanic caves mentioned earlier, filming one, Fell's Cave, for inclusion in a documentary film, *The First Americans.*

In December 1969 we went back to Fell's Cave for work in cooperation with the National Museum of Chile to recover organic material for radiocarbon dating. Twenty-nine carbon samples were secured, and age measurements were obtained for the major cultural divisions. The earliest occupation according to these measurements began 11,000 years ago.

In December 1973 Peggy and I returned briefly to this southern area on board the cruise ship *Vistafjord* and in 1978 on the Lindblad *Explorer.*

Artifacts collected in the course of these trips have been on exhibition at the American Museum of Natural History (AMNH), to illustrate the cultural record of that region. They will be featured in the new hall of the Native Peoples of South America, especially the material relating to the Paleo-Indians.   *(from Bird 1975)*

SOUTH CHILE AND THE CANOE INDIANS

For the present purpose the picture to be kept in mind is that the end of South America is not only divided between Chile and Argentina but is also divided roughly along the same line into two regions as different from each other as Norway and our western plains (fig. 1). The basic material cultures of the primitive peoples inhabiting these regions reflect the profound differences in physical structure, climate, floras and faunas.

The Western Channels

The shoreline at the western base of the mountains is well described as one of the most irregular and broken in the world. It is only 870 statute miles in a straight line from Puerto Montt to Cape Froward, yet the shore measures 4,500 miles according to existing surveys, which are incomplete and lacking in detail. It would be useless, if not impossible, to measure the shoreline of the offshore islands; but if we include western Tierra del Fuego, and the mainland, we obtain a rough estimate of 12,000 miles of shore on a direct line of 1,000 miles. In all this distance there is no place where one can walk along or near the shore without the greatest difficulty. The reason lies not only in the densely tangled forest that clings wherever it can secure foothold, but also in the rough nature of the country—mountains and hills that drop precipitously beneath the sea with little or no foreshore. Beaches are few and widely separated. Glaciers and swift-flowing rivers offer further obstacles.

It is clear, then, that occupation of this territory must have depended on the development of an adequate boat or canoe. . . .

For food the natives on the Pacific side necessarily depended almost entirely on what the sea had to offer—a large variety of excellent shellfish, seals, otters, porpoises, and, occasionally, whales. Fish, however, seem to have formed a surprisingly small part of their diet. Oceanic birds of several species are found in large numbers throughout the year in certain parts. On land it is a different story. . . . Vegetable foods, such as berries, wild celery, and, in the north, the *pangue* [*Gunnera tinctorea*] stems, are seasonal and are sometimes found in large quantities. The slight use made of these may well be due to the medicinal qualities of most of them.

In seeming recompense for the unpleasant climate, nature has provided several items whose importance has not been fully appreciated. One of these is the *tepu* tree [*Tepualia stipularis*]. Its habitat is confined to the area with the greatest rainfall—exactly the region where its qualities are most needed. The wood can be cut green and, even in heavy rain, with its fine, dense twigs an excellent fire can quickly be made. Unlike most of the fast-burning woods with which we are familiar in this country, the *tepu* produces a good bed of long-lived coals. Its position in the economy of the people is rivaled only by the beech tree, which provided bark for the canoes, and the tough vines used in their construction.

The knife made from the shell of a single species of mussel, the giant *choro* [*Mytilus chilensis*], has likewise played a unique role. It is almost as effective as a knife of iron, and is certainly superior to one made from the available stones. Only where *choro* shell was difficult to obtain, at the margin of its habitat south of the Straits, did the canoe people eventually utilize stone for knives.

Hence, in a region where excessive rain and wind and rough topography combined to discourage primitive occupation, the fundamental necessities were at hand for overcoming the difficulties presented.

Chiloé Island to the Gulf of Peñas

To avoid confusion, what was found and observed will be presented not in the order of our fieldwork but as it appears in retrospect. The starting point is Puerto Montt, latitude 41° 30'S. There are numerous large middens around the Gulf of Reloncaví and down the east side of Chiloé Island. This area is favored in that the westerly winds are not so constant and strong as they are farther south and much of the moisture they bring is precipitated on the west coast of Chiloé. Protected water and abundant seafood make the situation so favorable that the coastal culture which eventually spread south could easily have developed here.

In most of the oldest shell heaps there was a disconcerting lack of artifacts. About all that has survived of the things that the people used are rough, unilaterally flaked hand axes and unretouched stone flakes. At what may have been only a few centuries before the arrival of the Spaniards, stone spear or knife points, made with pressure flaking, were introduced. With points of this kind were found hafted drill points and polished stone celts, but no potsherds. Sherds were found only on the surface, with glazed European ware; hence they can be at the most only slightly Pre-Columbian.

A rare find that we were fortunate enough to be able to examine was a section of one of the old plank boats, a *dalca* which had been washed out of a bog by the sea in 1935. There are good historical descriptions of this type of boat, which was found in 1553 in extensive use around Chiloé (Lothrop 1932), but this is the only known surviving section, and it is evident that some type of rotary drill was used in its manufacture. It makes one wonder whether the plank boat antedated the tools adequate for its construction. Coppinger (1883: 43, 44, 51, 52) describes one in which the lashing holes must have been cut by chopping; if so, its owner was familiar with the use of iron tools and may have used a chisel.

Our work here did not yield any scale by which we might estimate the age of the oldest occupation. Clean beach gravel beneath the middens some feet above the present beach level suggests rising of the land. But this upward movement seems to have ceased, as is evidenced by the undermining of middens located at the heads of protected inlets, where they are not exposed to waves or currents or subject to slipping of the surface soil. One cannot be too critical regarding such phenomena, especially if the shore consists of clay and gravel with little or no outcropping of rock. The settling must be recent, since some of the large middens are only slightly affected.

South of the Gulf of Corcovado, throughout the Chono Archipelago, conditions are such that no serious attempt at land settlement has ever been made, not even today, when the population of Chiloé is overflowing to other parts of Chile. The islands are, on the whole, low and there are many east–west passages, so that excessive rain falls over the whole group. Beaches and landing places are very rare, and we failed to find a single midden.

It may be well to remind the reader—it has been noted before (Darwin 1886: 212)—of one valuable clue in the locating of old camping places. Normally the boggy soil of the zone of heavy rains is highly acid. At the camping places this acidity is neutralized by the shell refuse to such an extent that plants and shrubs which prefer acid soil do poorly, whereas forms which tolerate limy soil thrive. The resultant growth is discernible at some distance, and the effect holds for sites abandoned for more than a century, and probably longer.

As no traces of Indian camps could be found around the few harbors on the outer side of the Taitao Peninsula, a search was made about the reputed mouth of the San Tadeo River, on the south side of the Isthmus of Ofqui. But there we found a submerged forest (fig. 2) which may indicate subsidence of the land. Otter hunters told us later that boats drawing less than 3 ft. can get through at high tide into a channel running back through an extensive swamp. As there was no dry ground, this site was a total loss archaeologically. Perhaps the condition has resulted from local shoreline changes, but, as indications of submergence were noted around the Gulf of Reloncaví, it may be that the coast between Puerto Montt and the Gulf of Peñas is sinking at the present time. No similar evidence was found farther south.

Peñas to the Straits of Magellan

Between the gulfs of Peñas and Trinidad is a broad band of islands whose principal channels run north and south. As some of the islands are high enough to have snow the year around, the rainfall along the inner channels is probably less than it might otherwise be. We have no records to substantiate this, however, unless we interpret the presence of the shell mounds along the inner channels as a reflection of this more favorable condition. Here also are found the purest remnants of the Alacaluf tribe, living almost as their ancestors did when first seen by whites (Bird 1946b).

In the middens we found evidence of a simple, primitive, shell-knife

culture. There was also the same coarse percussion stonework found near Puerto Montt, and, in addition, there were small, single-barbed harpoons for seals, bone awls, and evidence of the use of bark canoes. We found no proof that the later stonework of the north reached this latitude. A single example of pressure work, of late manufacture, is of a pattern found farther south, but not in the north. Here also there was no scale for an age estimate. In areas now heavily forested several of the largest middens had begun on bare rock or gravel. This need not mean any great age, since the progressive spread of vegetation can be observed as one travels back in the fiords toward the icecap. It is impossible to do more than generalize regarding the interpretation of the increasing vegetation. It is clear that in places the ice has retreated faster than mosses and lichens can spread over the exposed rocks, and this shows that the climate has swung away from the conditions of temperature and precipitation necessary to maintain the ice at static limits. We cannot say how long this change has been in effect or how constant it has been. All that is certain is that because of it considerable change has occurred in the vegetation since people first occupied the region.

Fig. 2. A submerged forest at the mouth of the San Tadeo River near the Isthmus of Ofqui.

From Trinidad Gulf to the islands west of Tierra del Fuego there was very little refuse and none of the middens seen were large. This may possibly be attributed to the large extent of territory, in which a small population could exist for a long time without leaving much evidence of occupation on any one spot.

In the Straits of Magellan, Elizabeth Island [see Bird 1980 for his archaeological work there—ed.], opposite the eastern limit of the forest, seems to mark the eastern boundary of the canoe people's travels. Canoe runways were seen at Fenton Station, at the entrance to Oazy Harbor, but no midden refuse was found. Here, at the edge of the forest, at the eastern ends of Skyway and Otway sounds, and perhaps in the Ultima Esperanza district, the canoe people had opportunity to observe the hunting equipment of the foot Indians and to have cultural exchanges with them.

Brecknock Peninsula, at the west end of Beagle Channel, has been mentioned as a barrier to migration between the western islands and those south of Beagle Channel, but it is no worse than similar exposed passages farther north that are crossed whenever occasion demands. It is true that it probably marks the boundary between Alacaluf [of the western channels] and Yahgan territory [of Tierra del Fuego]; but Yahgan house sites and implements are found on Elizabeth Island, and Alacaluf have been down to Navarino Island in recent years.   *(from Bird 1938a: 251–260)*

DAILY LIFE SAILING THE CHANNELS

Santiago

Wednesday, December 12, 1934

Went to National Museum of Natural History in afternoon. Had a letter from Dr. Lothrop to Sr. Latcham, the head of the Museum, an English-Chilean. Very cordial—said no permission to dig was necessary. The Museum gets equivalent of $500 per year from the government, for upkeep; most of the few employees are volunteers, and any fieldwork must come out of their own pockets.

Puerto Montt

Sunday, December 16

In A.M. to look over available boats. Apparently the only type used here is a kind of cutter; square stem, square stern, straight keel—solidly built, 20–40 ft. long. Did not see any boat at all suitable for us.

Monday, December 17

Found a suitable boat, belonging to a fisherman, Tomás, from the island of Maillén, beyond Tenglo Is. Newly built; decked over forward, about 19 ft. long, with a sloop rig. Will take a good deal of fixing up, of course, but is strong and in good condition.

Thursday, December 20

Walking through outskirts of town met a very "brava" little terrier puppy—white with tan markings—very short stub of a tail. Bought her from the children for 40¢. Her name is Muñeca.

Isla Maillén

Friday, December 21

Tomás came in about 10:00 and we left for Maillén Island, taking along our Palmer engine and fittings. Very light wind, so took about three hrs. to get there. Hired a team of oxen and hauled the cutter ashore at Tomás'. The hole through the forward part of the keel is used when beaching or launching the boats. A chain is passed through it, fastened to a stick so it cannot pull out, then the other end of the chain is fastened to the ox yoke.

Fig. 3. Hauling the cutter, the *Hesperus*, ashore on Maillén Island.

Sent for the carpenter who built the boat, and arranged to have him make the necessary alterations.

Thursday, January 3

The old woman from next door came to call on us in the evening; her mother lived to be 105, always on the island, and there were Indians here when she (the mother) was young. According to our friend, everyone is pure Chilean now—her aunt was the last Indian!

Sunday, January 6

In the P.M. an old man, with a fine long, white beard came with two oxen to pull the boat down the hill and into the water (fig. 3). He guided them just by touching a long stick to the yoke and talking to them.

Isla Capera Guapi–Gulf of Reloncaví

Thursday, January 10

Went across to the small island of Capera Guapi, just a few minutes away by boat, where there is a shell mound extending some 1,600 ft. along the beach.

Fig. 4. Excavating the midden, a shell mound, on Capera Guapi Island.

Monday, January 14

Four more men helping on mound (fig. 4). Found two skeletons, a man and a child.

Tuesday, January 15

Shell knives, stone hammers, a bone awl, etc., from the midden [details and description of this mound are preserved in Bird's fieldnotes at the AMNH—ed.].

Wednesday, January 16

Last day of work on mound. Made a plan of the cut; 16 ft. deep, down to old beach level.

Hesperus—*Western Channels, January 22–June 20*

Tuesday, January 22

Finished loading and under way at 1:45 P.M.

Isla Refugio

Thursday, January 31

The sun came out at 1; as the fog lifted, we saw the peak of Volcán

Corcovado looming high above us, sharp and snow-covered, a grand sight. Anchored along east side of Refugio Island.

Friday, February 1

Woke at 3:40 A.M. to find sea running in from a tide eddy, making off the point. Boat anchored fore and aft—when we tried to get up the bow anchor, to turn her head into the waves, found it would not come. Tried to hold on till daylight and change of tide, but it became too rough. Left the anchor, tied to an oar. Dinghy broke rudder by bumping against it, and we had to use an oar to steer. Hoisted the mainsail and ran thru the tickle to a better situation in a small bay with a river at the head. Just before high water rowed out near last night's anchorage to look for oar and anchor, but water too rough to round point. Junius tried to go overland, but could not get past the crevasses. The woods are the most impassable I have ever seen—living trees lying on their sides and on one another in a jackstraw mess which must be seen to be believed. All the trunks are thickly covered with mosses, lichens, and ferns, and among the trees is a great variety of undergrowth. Saw several steamer ducks, one quite close "steamed" with his bill open. Also two kelp geese, male and female. The males swim in the white surf along edge of rocks, the only place in the whole surrounding where their white plumage is an asset. The females, dark plumage with a few white feathers, are inconspicuous on the rocks. Also a pair of oyster catchers. Picked wild celery for soup.

Sunday, February 3

6:30 P.M. moved out to bay where we lost our anchor. Oar it was buoyed to was lodged in rocks—also found, and took, oar lost by someone else. Too rough to look for anchor.

Tuesday, February 5

Over to Refugio Island. Tide slack about 8:40 and water calm—first time in five days. Caught chain on grapnel in a few minutes and had no trouble raising anchor.

Isla Canale

Thursday, February 7

We anchored in a lovely little bay at east end of Isla Canale. Glorious sunset—blue, yellow, and gold with purple mountains all around and everything reflected in the calm water. Much phosphorescence in the water that night. A gray heron on shore, very near us.

Aysén

Monday, February 11

Underway at 5:50 A.M. and proceeded up Aysén River. The town is stretched out on a plain, and is larger than we'd expected. In 1928 there were two houses; now there are 2,000 people. Most of the houses are hurriedly constructed—the streets are wide, with large logged-over ditches on either side.

San Esteban Inlet, Rescue Point

Tuesday, February 26

5:30 A.M. sunrise, and sun actually visible! Underway at 8:35 A.M., hatches battened down and set for rough going. No wind, but sea very rough and uneven. Increasing wind and tide against swell made the going bad. Stopped at a little bay on south side of San Esteban Inlet (north side of Rescue Pt.) at 2:30 and cooked lunch (fig. 5). Then went on up inlet under sail, examining all the coves on south side, but found no traces of ancient or modern occupation. Cut over to north side of inlet and found narrow bay with grass-lined shore. Found a good campsite in the woods—unusual in this land of thick underbrush—set up our tent and made a bough bed.

Taitao Peninsula

Wednesday, March 6

Hard rain, very poor visibility, but little wind; by noon calm, with improving conditions. At 2 P.M. wind beginning southerly; thought it might smooth the effect of the westerly winds and be fairly calm along shore. Underway 2:20 P.M. with hatches battened and sail up. Outside found wind too much alongshore to be of help to the sails, so lowered them just off Rescue Point. 3:00, wind increasing, very rough, hard going. Off the point the tiller stick broke, giving us a few exciting minutes while splicing it. Sun out from about 3:30 on, with fine colorful sunset. Ran into Cliff Cove and anchored 7:20 P.M. (ten miles in five hours!).

Thursday, March 7

Underway: outside, hoisted jib, which was all the sail she could carry. Stopped at 6:30 in Christmas Cove, San Andreas Bay, and glad to be in.

Sunday, March 10

A gale blowing from the north, with much heavier and more constant rain than is usual here, continuing all night. The evening before it had been apparent what was coming, so felled a tree to windward of the tent, and were very glad of the protection. Also had a small drainage ditch around

Fig. 5. Junius Bird holding a steamer duck he shot, at San Estebán Inlet, Rescue Point.

tent which took off most of the water. The river which had appeared to be such a good anchorage, barring the shoal at the entrance, was a proper torrent and would have given the boat a hard time. The anchorage selected in the lee of the small island proved the best in the bay for a northerly wind. Conditions continued bad all day, with barometer steadily falling. The strong current of the river running against wind made it almost impossible to get to the boat in the punt. With sufficient provisions ashore, we did not risk it, but spent day reading, sewing, oiling oil skins, etc. Have almost finished Capt. Cook's *Voyages*.

Cape Rapier Lighthouse, Tres Montes Peninsula

Monday, March 11

Day began overcast with light rain squalls from west. Blue sky showing through about 10:00 A.M., turning into best day we have had here. Broke camp. Set the sails at 1:00 P.M.; wind favorable, sea still rough from northerly blow. Passed Cape Rapier at 3:25—the lighthouse and keeper's house on a narrow ledge of rock, high above water. They raised the flag as we went by. Around famous Tres Montes Peninsula 5:50. Continued on toward Punta Barroso, anchoring just south of entrance, off a sandy beach, by moonlight. Our best run—slightly over sixty miles in nine hours.

Gulf of Peñas, Río San Tadeo, Isthmus of Ofqui

Monday, March 18

Up at 5:00 A.M. to look at bottom, finding no damage; struck squarely on keel. Conditions favorable in late P.M.; underway at 5:05. Ran up into river to where all the open water shown on charts is filled with standing trees, in 2–3 ft. water at low tide. Could not find any opening into river. Anchored 5:40 P.M. on edge of sunken forest. Calm, lovely evening. Rowed around among trees in the punt—a strange, desolate scene, the black, bare trunks sticking up in the twilight.

San Pedro Lighthouse

Thursday, March 21

A lovely sunny morning. Underway 11:50 A.M. 2:40, arrived off San Pedro Island lighthouse. The chief was away—three young men, a sailor, the cook, and one Indian boy, Alejandro, were the only people there.

Saturday, March 23

Went to lighthouse, and checked over Dr. Cooper's vocabulary with the Indian boy, as far as possible.

Wager Island

Wednesday, March 27

In P.M. crossed to Wager Island due west from anchorage at San Pedro. Found two huts, unoccupied for perhaps two years, and small shell deposit a foot thick. Dug test pits finding deposit so small as not to be worth digging. Continued south along coast of Wager Island.

Fatal Bay

Wednesday, April 3

Around the point of the cove where we'd first anchored to another cove beside Indian campsite—light drizzling rain continuing all day. Ashore, digging a trench into north side of deposit. Upper 2 ft. loose crumbly "cholga" and limpet shells mixed with light brown humus and many roots; evidently a relatively late deposit, containing no artifacts. Below this, black bog-like layer. This was saturated with water, evidently quite acid, as all the lime in the shells had dissolved, leaving only the brown outer skins of the mussels, as in Labrador deposits. Bones of birds, seals(?), deer(?), and porpoise scattered occasionally through this. No chips. Found a harpoon point with rounded shank, of early Navarino type, bone basket, awl, split and ground sea lion tooth, and ground mica schist implement, use and type unknown.

Friday, April 5

Weather improved—occasional bits of sunlight. Made contour survey across point from trench. All finds, except a bit of worked whalebone, were from lowest stratum. Absolutely no stone chips—only three rough percussion chipped blanks of grayish-gray stone. Left anchorage and sailed down with light northerly breeze to unnamed island just west of Schafer Island.

Thursday, April 11

Rowed all around the shores of Lucas Cove. On NE side of the island in the center of entrance there was abundant grass; possible indication of presence of old campsite, so dug a test pit about 15 ft. in from edge of shore where surface was about 7 ft. above HWM. Scattered ashes and shells down to rock at 44 in.; no finds.

Puerto Edén, English Narrows

Moved on south to islands on east side of Eden Harbor, just beyond the Narrows. This is by far the best section we have seen south of the Gulf of Ancud; plenty of low islands and bays, many lobos, some porpoises, many white-breasted shags, steamer ducks, gulls, a few grebes and harrier hawks. There is considerable open land, with bunch grass.

Friday, April 12

Fine morning, scattered clouds, sunlight, calm. Headed for camp seen yesterday on Level Bay, but noticed another camp on SW side of an island, so ran in there. An Indian camp, two huts, two canoes—a third was over on

Fig. 6. An Alacaluf camp on the east side of Eden Harbor, English Narrows. The women are preparing for shellfishing.

the east side of the channel (fig. 6). The men stood with hands in pockets all the time we were approaching, looking very glum. In response to our use of their greeting, "lowél," they said nothing. Asked where Pedro was, they said they did not know (Pedro, a brother of Alejandro of San Pedro Light, is supposed to speak good Spanish). As soon as we ran in through kelp to the shore, men, women, and children swarmed aboard, and those who could not get on the *Hesperus* sat in the punt. Five women, six men, two young boys of 15 or 16, four young children under 5, seventeen in all, and eleven dogs, who sat on the nearest rocks and stared. One man looked old, may have been about 50—the rest, 25–35; all the women, 20–30. It is very difficult to tell age—have found boys who looked 9 or 10 often were 14 or 15, and men and women who looked very old were about 50; the same must be true here.

One, José, spoke some Spanish, though all knew the names of things they wanted. We were immediately asked for tobacco, thread, needles, files, skirts, pants, kerosene, rope, cloth for sails, etc. All were well-clothed except two youngest children who were running about naked. José's little girl had a red cotton string around her neck, with one of the purple snail shells [*Chlosostoma atrum laron*] common around Puerto Montt hanging from it. The clothing, however, was very ragged and dirty; most of it seemed to have been secured from naval ships, consisting of parts of old uniforms.

They squatted about on the boat, apparently feeling the cold, although it was a warm day for these parts—smoking cigarettes and short-stemmed pipes of their own manufacture, made from any short piece of wood, with a wooden or bird bone stem—very crude affairs. They said they were the only outfit in the Narrows—that the other camp was Chilotan. Played our tiny phonograph for them, and negro spirituals seemed to be the favorites. It was difficult to tell which they preferred, but with the spirituals they made a kind of hissing noise and hummed the melodies while they were being played. They mellowed up quite soon after our arrival, laughed and smiled—but they have such ugly faces that a smile is little improvement. The men wear their hair quite long—the women "haggle" it off at the shoulder—on both, it is uncombed, often falling over their faces.

Showed José pictures in Dr. Lothrop's book, and he checked names with those given by Alejandro, adding those of some of the spear types which Alejandro said he had never seen. The only harpoons here were the double-barbed ones, 5 in. to 9 in. long—none of the saw-toothed fish spears. The shafts are poles with the bark still on, 7–8 ft. long and about 1¼ in. in diameter. Saw three well-made coils of lobo-skin line identical in size with the coils of harpoon line used by the Eskimos.

They showed us an iron knife which they said they used in cutting it. It was well-rounded, like line which has been worked with a line-working tool—the kind which has two or three holes of different sizes, but they denied using any such tool for making it. These lines had harpoon points attached to them by what looked like a hangman's knot, but was made by looping the end of the line about the shank, and whipping with a separate thong which is kept from slipping by a slit in the end of the main line. The point is wedged in the split at end of shaft, and line and shaft are grasped together. The line is long enough to reach as far as the weapon can be thrown, and the end must be secured to the canoe or held by the thrower.

The harpoon as shown by Dr. Lothrop and others, with a short line at-tached to the shaft, may be used at times, but is a very ineffective system, as anyone who has ever harpooned a seal can easily testify—while the use of the long line is a different matter. Taking up a harpoon point that was not fastened to a line, asked one of the men to show me how to rig it. He reached over, took a thin, braided sinew line from around his wife's (?) waist and attached it in a way somewhat similar to that shown by Dr. Lothrop. The seal-skin line he pictures, made by the Yahgans, may have been for the same purpose and the example of a complete harpoon was per-

Fig. 7. An Alacaluf house on the east side of Puerto Edén, English Narrows.

haps given him as in the above case. Saw six unattached harpoon points and two on lines. The Indians made no attempt to barter, but asked for things without offering anything in exchange. Presents of tobacco and thread and two shags were received without any expression of gratitude or even pleasure. When we went ashore, most of them remained on the boat until we returned, at least an hour later.

We asked José if we could enter his hut and received an indifferent "sí." The whole structure was covered with many lobo skins, tied and laid over the framework in irregular fashion, and the interior was dry and comfortable (fig. 7). This hut was slightly larger than any we had seen before. The floor on either side of the fire was spread with thin layers of fine branches with some seal skins and two deer skins spread over them. A great quantity of roasted seal or lobo meat lay about the bed of coals and was tended by a woman nursing a child of at least 2 years. She did not offer us any meat, but readily gave us permission to help ourselves when we asked; it was rather tough, but quite good. Three or four more seals were tucked under the hut covering just outside the base of the framework. Five small puppies lay on the floor. A grown dog came in and helped himself to a bone and was allowed to chew it awhile before having it taken from him, but was not scolded for taking it. All dogs seen were well-fed and were about the size of most of the Labrador Eskimo dogs. Many baskets lay about the hut—about twenty-five—most of them empty and all of the same weave as seen before. They are knotted by hand without the use of an awl, and the Indians denied knowledge of the other weaves shown by Dr. Lothrop. Watched them working on two unfinished ones, which were suspended by a piece of grass from the hut frame.

A quantity of old coats were scattered about. Their complete outfit consists of a few things of their own manufacture: dug-out canoes, cut very thin, the sides raised with roughly attached boards, the same as shown by Dr. Lothrop; short light oars; 4-pronged shellfish spears, identical with Yahgan spears; harpoon points with 2-barbed heads; poles for dislodging limpets, about 4½ ft. long, 2–3 in. thick, with flattened ends; baskets; and a bucket. The rest of their outfits, clothing, knives, etc., comes from the whites.

The women especially were quite interested in me, asking my name as soon as they came aboard, patting my cheeks, and smiling in quite a friendly manner. One of them, unnoticed, took a button out of my pocket, put it in her mouth, where she left it, showing it off with great glee. The children are attractive, pretty, vivacious, and laugh easily; their parents are the exact opposite.

Saumárez Island

Saturday, April 20

At daybreak a canoe full of Indians appeared (fig. 8). Two men, three women (two with nursing babies, one boy and one girl), one boy, 2 or 3 years old, one boy of 7 or 8—twelve in all. They were a better outfit than those at English Narrows, more friendly and not quite as beggarly. Checked over names of things illustrated in Dr. Lothrop's book with the two men and with identical results as before. I played the phonograph and again they sang an accompaniment to the spirituals. Also made a ball out of tinfoil and played with the children, who threw it remarkably well, but caught it extremely poorly.

Moved around to their camp and went ashore. They had finished the birds we'd given the old woman yesterday and apparently had not been successful last night when they were off trying to snare shags. Pablo, demonstrating use of snare, made a continuous soft "tsch, tsch" noises, blowing air out, with tongue against roof of mouth—a noise which will wake the bird and make it put its head up, but will not frighten it; he also mimicked the sound roosting shags make. I could not learn if they get

Fig. 8. Alacaluf Indians near Saumárez Island.

more than one bird at each roost; they had five or six of the snares in the canoe and probably make a concerted attack, but as soon as one bird is fast, the rest must take to the water. Showed Pablo how to put boric solution on girl's inflamed eyelid. Before treating her, gave the old woman scissors to cut the child's hair, which hung down over her forehead, and she was very careful to gather all the hair cut off, then threw it into the fire. Also showed them how to put solution on another child with purplish birthmarks (?) on bridge of nose, which had been recently scratched. Took stills and movies of children; the sun came out for a while and they played about naked, climbing among the bushes, gathering the reddish seed pods of the fuchsia, ⅝ in. long, with insipid flavor. Saw one child take a handful to his father, who ate them without any expression of thanks. They shivered practically all the time they were out in the canoe, showing little of the hardiness you might expect, and it was not an especially cold day!

Tuesday, April 23

The coldest night we have had, with heavy frost. Off Cascade Cove met broken drift ice which extended across channel, up into Penguin Inlet. Just west of Wilson Island, near Wellington Island, is a conspicuous cliff about 70 ft. high, sheltering a large-mouthed cave, in the rear of which found scattered vertebrae and ribs of a single human body; no skull or long bones; had apparently been disturbed a long time ago. About halfway up cliff, a narrow cleft, extending back into rock about 10 ft. with level floor; contained remains of four adults, child and baby burial made at different times. Worked here till evening, securing two fair skulls and some bones, but no grave goods.

Gage Inlet

Wednesday, April 24

After lunch sea was calmer and wind still good, so went on. Found a well-made hut, recently occupied, near the beach. About 100 ft. back from the water, under a ledge of the cliff, was a fine rock shelter, about 40 ft. long, 17 ft. wide, at the center tapering off at the sides, 9 ft. high at front and some 3 ft. at rear, the whole floor buried in shells. We moved our air mattresses and sleeping bags right in, built a fire, and were very dry and comfortable.

Monday, April 29

Having dug up most of the floor, had to move our bedding out, although there was still room for the fire, and we continued cooking in cave. Took over the hut: cleaned the branches off the floor, cut and laid new ones; put our two tents over the ends, in place of seal skins, filling in the spaces with branches in true Alacaluf style.

Friday, May 10

Fine sunny A.M.—scattered clouds over sky—cloudy about noon with occasional showers during P.M. Temperature 34° when we got up. Ran along between Newton and Hunter Island—a beautiful section—took a panorama. Saw about fifteen kelp geese, but few shags. Penguins seen only very rarely between Gulf of Peñas and here. Shot three steamer ducks. Saw a whale sound east of Cutter Island, throwing his flukes high into air before he dove. Saw him blow again later, and thought at first it was smoke from fires on shore—then heard the noise and saw him dive; could not tell what kind of whale he was. Opposite north end of Muñoz Gamera Bay on Long Island, was an encampment, two huts, three small canoes, one dory, and about twenty Indians. Spoke with them asking one, who replied in good Spanish, if we could get any gasoline over at the government coal shed in the bay. He said there was nothing over there, a little kerosene but no gas. They wanted us to land, but it was almost dark so we left and crossed to Ramírez Point, anchoring off Dolores point where a settler has a corrugated iron shack and is clearing land. Landed and had some cocoa with the family—they have been here seven months. Gave them a steamer duck.

Saturday, May 11

Ashore to settler's house, Louis ——, for coffee, and while there a canoe with three men, one woman, and a girl of 2–3 years came over from camp on Long Island. One of the men, José, about 28 years old, husband of the woman, Rosa, who is quite pretty. Their little girl, Berte, is a darling child, very pretty, well-mannered, intelligent, with a spotless white dress on. José is to work for Louis and they were moving their things into a new hut next to the shack. José speaks very good Spanish, best of any Indian we have seen, and has spent some time in Magallanes. His father, another José, is, according to Louis, 95 years old. Louis, speaking of the Indian canoes, said that they were made of bark before, and José corrected him saying "también de tablas [planks]," not like the plank boat they have now (dory) but quite different—"pero yo no he visto—mi papá, sí—él sabe cómo haces." Said his father could make a model, so offered him 150 pesos for one about 2½ ft. long, if well made, 100 pesos if inferior; a high price, and perhaps enough to prove an incentive. Went through Dr. Cooper's vocabulary with him, getting much closer agreement between words than in north. José says language of northern group "different idioma."

There are among the Indians in this vicinity three men from the north, one of whom, Santiago, was with José. The former speaks very poor Spanish and a few words of English; he was present during questioning of José, who, when asked a word from the northern dialect, different from the term in use here, would point to Santiago and say, "lengua de él, nosotros así." Covered only part of names of things illustrated in Dr. Lothrop's book, José leaving before we'd finished. He knew about bola: said it was used for guanaco and deer—that he had never seen one but that his father knew how to make and use them. There are no longer guanaco on the peninsula, but he said there'd been plenty before. José claimed to have forgotten many words and it apparently is so, as for some he hesitated a considerable time before replying. He recognized the feather head band and plume and admitted having been through an initiation ceremony similar to the Yahgan—boys and men staying together in the hut for some days with much singing and story telling—but said they no longer do it—only singing the songs when drunk.

Tempano Narrows—Skyring Sound

Friday, May 17

At the glacier before Tempano Narrows, took pictures of the boat among the small icebergs, from the punt. Found Tempano Narrows much worse to pass than Pilot Book intimates. A strong current running through to northwards at about five knots. Were almost carried through before realizing the risk involved; anchored in lee of some boulders just at entrance. Landed on east side and climbed hill above to survey the situation before proceeding. Deer droppings—first we have seen. The Narrows are rather impressive. Surrounded by snow-capped mountains (fig. 9); the glacier just west of Rengo Pt. feeding ice into the swift current; almost constant avalanches of ice blocks from the edge of the ice cap down the precipitous sides of the mountain forming the west shore, falling a couple of thousand feet. The glacial ice drifts close along south side of Rengo Pt., swings out into the swift current of the Narrows, gathers speed and dashes itself against the boulders in the stream, most pieces shattering to fragments, but an occasional well-built growler, as big as a two-car garage, will go rolling over and over until it brings up on some rock.

    Spent some time watching where the ice struck rocks, laying out a course through; took pictures and decided to wait for high water (fig. 10). On our arrival, tide was still about 2½ ft. below mark of highest water tide, but showed no apparent rise during the first hour after tying fast. Thought this perhaps due to proximity of Narrows, so cooked lunch and waited. About 2:30 P.M. noticed that water was falling, but there was no slackening of the current to the north. 3:15, water was a foot below HWM and falling fast; no sign of slack water, so decided to run through. Ran engine about half speed and passed through without difficulty, but could not avoid whirlpool at other end. The bottom at center was about 2½ ft.

Fig. 9. Junius Bird resting on shore before entering Tempano Narrows in Gajardo Channel.

Fig. 10. The *Hesperus* and its punt tied up at the entrance to Tempano Narrows, Gajardo Channel.

below surface of surrounding water, but we headed off just before reaching it, so got clear. The whirlpool turns clockwise and as all the ice collects to the right side of it, one must clear it to the left, and in so doing cannot avoid being drawn into it. The punt, which can carry six men in smooth water, was apparently pulled down for half her freeboard; a canoe would have a gay time. Continued on out inlet; anchored for night along shore almost abreast Frontón Pt.

Tuesday, May 21

Stopped at Juan Island; found a woman, her two sons and daughter, apparently of Scandinavian or German descent. Have been here going on three years; all hands at work and place shows they have been at it hard since they came. Could not sell us any meat, as they have only 150 sheep and are not killing any yet, but did give us a drink of milk, and cabbages, onion, and carrots out of their fine garden—*very* welcome to us! Said four canoes and one boat of Indians were in the vicinity for a while during the past summer.

Hotel Río Verde—Fitzroy Channel—between Skyring and Otway Sounds

Thursday, May 23

Across the channel in a motor boat to the little hotel: it was clean and pleasant and we decided to stay there. Our mail came out from town—thirty very welcome letters. There was great excitement at the hotel when we asked for a bath; we finally got a big wooden tub and lots of hot water. Then a most excellent dinner and a bottle of wine. We sat by the stove, reading and re-reading our letters until almost midnight. It was good to be inside and hear the wind blowing! Sun all day.

Riesco Island—Otway Sound

Wednesday, June 5, 1935

Stopped at a point a short way south—good site and some shells, but only one scraper. Further on, stopped at a point covered with great sandstone boulders, all over the beach; many worn absolutely round by the water (?) and others still partly surrounded by the rock from which they had been "carved." Very curious. You'd think the Indians would have a legend of a War of the Giants, with their huge bolas! Took movies and stills.

Fortescue Bay

Tuesday, June 11

As we came into Fortescue Bay, we saw an "escampavía" [government patrol and survey boat], manned by naval officers—at anchor. Tied up alongside and went aboard. We had a most welcome bath and dinner. Spent night alongside.

Straits of Magellan

Thursday, June 20

Left at 7 A.M. in bright moonlight. Wind strong. Started with jib alone, then with a reef in mainsail, and as wind lessened, we let it out almost entirely; it looked as though we wouldn't reach Magallanes today. We were saving some gasoline to maneuver in the harbor. Houses along the shore, and a road with a number of cars, but water too shoal for us to get near enough to stop any of them to ask for gas. We drifted very slowly, and just as we were in sight of Magallanes, the wind freshened. As we came up to the dock an "escampavía" signaled to us to come alongside and tie up. It was about 3:00 P.M. and what was our horror to find a crowd of people to greet us! We later found it was Corpus Christi Day and they had nothing better to do. We were certainly glad to see Sr. Limacher, however. The officer in charge of the "escampavía" took us below, and Captain Arroyo, port captain, came to us instead of our going to him with our papers! There was no customs inspection at all, and everyone was fine to us. They had us leave our boat where she was, so we didn't even have to unload her! After having our pictures taken, went with Sr. Limacher to the pension where Junius stayed before—the Casa Detleff, or Trocadero, and where they had a room, our trunks, tea, and a bath waiting for us. Junius had his beard shaved off. It seems very nice indeed to be here.

Friday, June 21

Took our boat to the shipyard and had her put into "drydock." Unloaded her.

(We later sold the *Hesperus* to the Chilean navy for use in survey work. At some point she was sent north in the hold of a naval vessel, which sank. An inglorious end!)   *(from M. Bird 1934–1937)*

2. Chronological Synthesis and Dating

The stratigraphic excavations of four caves/shelters north of the Straits of Magellan (Cañadon Leona, Palli Aike, Fell's, and Cerro Sota; see fig. 11) provided Bird with the evidence for a long sequence. He summarized it as follows.

THE PERIODS

There were five prehistoric periods of the inland culture. The oldest consists of remains of people who hunted the ground sloth and the native American horse; the latest is identifiable with the culture of the Ona of Tierra del Fuego. The periods are distinguished by the types of projectile points and by the presence or absence of certain other artifacts. All lack pottery, which is found only rarely in this region on historic Tehuelche camps, associated with modern horse bones and trade beads. All have in common simple stone scrapers for working wood and bone. Blades [stone scrapers] for scraping skin, however, show an abrupt change in pattern and are an important diagnostic trait. The first three periods used large blades [scrapers] which varied in size and proportions, while the fourth had the small "thumbnail" type which, because of the manner of hafting, is much more uniform in size. The last is used to the present day.

First Period

The oldest culture can be most readily recognized by the projectile points— barbless blades with tapering stems [fishtails] expanded at the base. The few associated artifacts are: bone flaking tools, bone awls, scrapers, rough chopping tools, and flat lava disks of unknown use (fig. 12). At this time cremation burial was practiced.

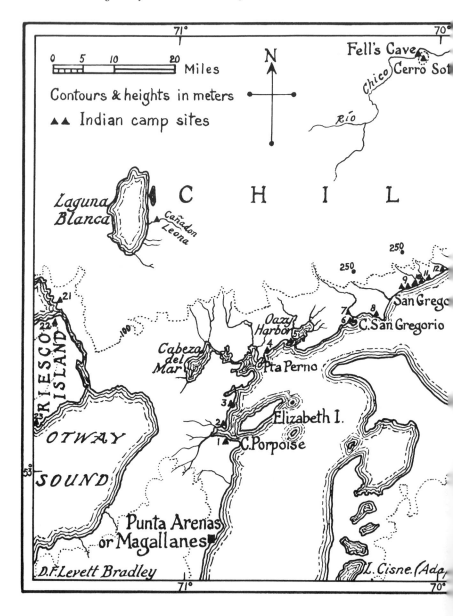

Fig. 11. Map of Straits of Magellan area locating the archaeological sites Cañadon Leona, Fell's Cave, Cerro Sota Cave, and Palli Aike Cave.

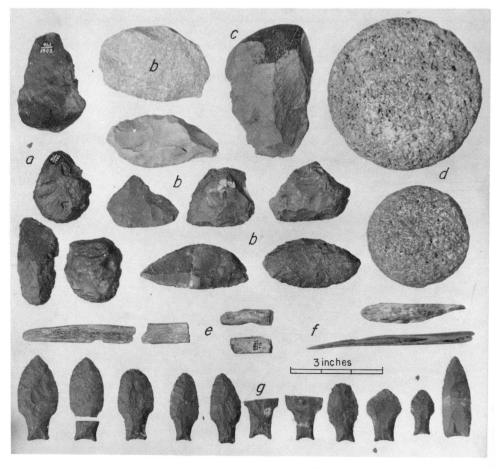

Fig. 12. Period I artifacts: (a) endscrapers; (b) sidescrapers; (c) chopping stone; (d) discoidal stones; (e) fragments of bone chipping/flaking tools; (f) bone awls; (g) bone points.

Second Period

The second cultural level yields bone projectile points of varying form and size, two types of awls which seem to be confined to this level, and numerous scraping tools (fig. 13).

Third Period

The third period produces stemless stone points, the majority of which are triangular in outline with rounded bases; awls; scrapers; and bola stones. These stones are mainly small ones for taking birds, a significant fact in view of the use of bird bolas elsewhere in America (fig. 14).

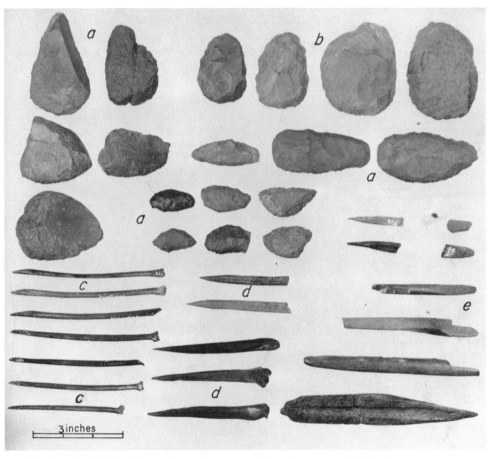

Fig. 13. Period II artifacts: (a) sidescrapers; (b) endscrapers; (c) bird bone awls; (d) bone awls; (e) bone points.

Fourth Period

In the fourth period, stemmed knife and projectile points replace the stemless types and are accompanied by the small hafted scrapers already mentioned. There are also simple beads and ornaments, awls, and large bola stones of various forms (fig. 15). Burials thought to be of this period are found in stone cairns, the body extended.

Fifth Period

Although artifacts of the fourth period may have been in use until the historic period, the presence of a fifth cultural group is evident. Small arrow

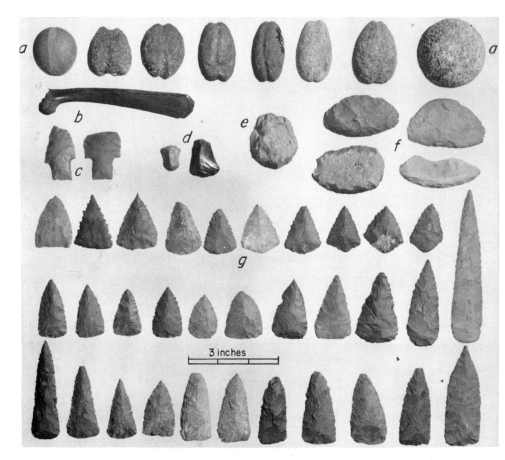

Fig. 14. Period III artifacts: (a) bolas; (b) bone scraper; (c) straight-stemmed projectile points (very rare); (d) hafted scrapers (very rare); (e) endscrapers; (f) sidescrapers; (g) stemless projectile and knife points.

points of a type characteristic of the Ona (fig. 16) associated with other typical Ona artifacts such as combs, beads, and rough bone tools show the relatively late presence of this tribe on the mainland.

Historic Period

The only evidence of white contact at the Straits is the material on Tehuelche campsites. The abundance of modern horse bones probably dates them at about the middle of the eighteenth century. Plain undecorated sherds, pipes, hammered copper ornaments, and sometimes glass trade beads are found.   *(from Bird 1946a: 19–20)*

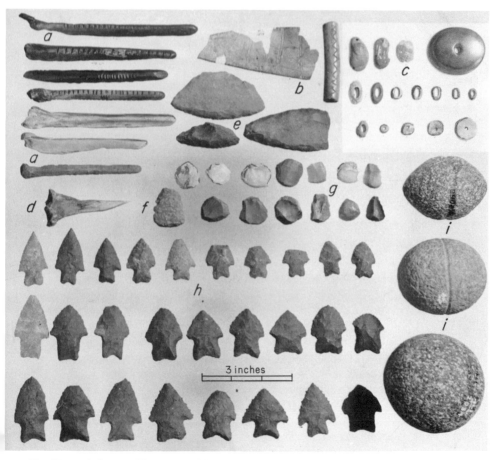

Fig. 15. Period IV artifacts: (a) chipping tools; (b) incised bone; (c) beads and ornaments; (d) bone awl; (e) sidescrapers; (f) endscrapers; (g) hafted scrapers; (h) stemmed (Patagonian) points and knives; (i) bolas.

THE RADIOCARBON DATES

The sequence above was created before the invention of carbon-14 dating. In 1950, soon after Willard Libby announced the technique, Bird submitted a sample of burned sloth and horse bones from Palli Aike Cave, and sloth dung from the Mylodon Cave, to Libby's laboratory in Chicago (Bird 1951: 44–46). The dates of 8639 ± (C 485) for the Palli Aike sample and 10,832 ± 400 for the sloth dung are discussed in chapter 4, Possible Age of Deposit, and chapter 7, Age of Remains.

Soon thereafter Bird requested John Fell to secure a sample from the lowest level of the debris in Fell's Cave. Samples were removed in 1952 and sent to Bird

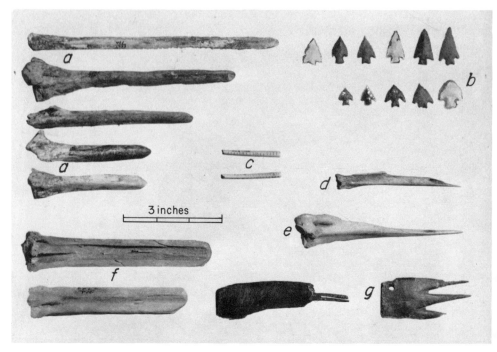

Fig. 16. Period IV (Ona) artifacts: (a) chipping tools; (b) Ona projectile points; (c) beads and/or ornaments; (d) bird bone awl; (e) bone awl; (f) bark removers; (g) combs.

with an oilfield worker, Mr. Dudley Frazier, who was traveling from Patagonia to the United States. He never forwarded them to Bird, despite attempts to contact him.

In February 1960 Fell extracted another sample from the cave and sent it to Bird. Fell removed carbonized material from the lowest layer by the back of the cave, and 1.5 m east of Bird's trench. Fell wrote (1960): "[It came] from a very big fire three and a half feet across, but [it] contained no big bits of burnt wood, [and] only very compressed ashes."

That sample was submitted to the Geological Survey of the Department of the Interior in March 1960, and in November the date was ready. The sample (W-915) had an age of 10,720 ± 300, or a date of about 8760 B.C. Bird noted that if the 5,730-year half-life figure had been used, the age would have been 11,041 years.

In November 1968 Bird returned briefly to Fell's Cave with an NBC film crew. He removed another carbon sample from a hearth in the southeast corner (2 ft. from rear wall) of the lowest layer. It was assigned number I-3988 by the

Teledyne Isotopes Laboratory, and the analysis of it produced an age of 11,000 ± 700 years, or a date of about 9050 B.C.

A primary objective of Bird's return to Fell's Cave in 1969 was to obtain samples for radiocarbon dating. A sequence of nine new dates was prepared (table 17 in chapter 5), and Bird gave approximate absolute dates to the five periods established by the work in 1936–1937. The dates of the periods are:

Period V—700 yrs. to present (Ona)
Period IV—6,500 yrs. to present
Period III—8,500 to 6,500 yrs.
Period II—10,000 to 8,500 yrs.
Period I—11,000 (or earlier) to 10,000 yrs.

3. Cañadon Leona

GENERAL DESCRIPTION

The Cañadon Leona site, lat. 52° 26' S, long. 72° 05' W, lies at the distance of a fifteen-minute walk up from the eastern shore of Laguna Blanca, a very shallow lake without an outlet. The shore here follows the base of a clay *barranca* [cliff] 30 to 40 ft. high which is cut by a number of gullies and ravines. From the top of this [cliff] the land rises with a rolling slope to the low hills to the east where a conspicuous beach terrace (230 ft. above the lake) shows the extent and height reached by the lake at one time. No rock formation can be seen anywhere, and except directly in front of the mouth of the canyon, its walls are invisible, and one could pass very close by without suspecting its existence.

The walls of the canyon, averaging about 40 ft. in height, are of a very soft stone containing a few fossilized bones. In all fairly protected parts the rock is surfaced with a thin, hard coating like glaze on chinaware. Where this has flaked or weathered off the wind and rain have cut the softer under part into intricate and interesting forms (fig. 17). The fact that the glaze is found evenly distributed, as much at the head as at the mouth of the canyon, and that broken places show no tendency to glaze over again, indicates that whatever caused this feature affected the entire surface of the canyon walls uniformly and at one period. This was, of course, after the canyon had been cut in the rock. At the east end, where the canyon is little more than a gully, the rock disappears beneath coarse gravel, and is filled level with the surrounding plain. As this gravel is washed away by occasional freshets, more of the old canyon is exposed.

I believe the above is evidence that the lake rose to the level of the beach terrace on the hillside to the east, 60 ft. above the top of the canyon walls, after the canyon was formed. While submerged, the rock developed the hard, glazed surface. The recession of the lake must have been rather rapid as there is no evidence of the effect of waves, nor intermediate beach terraces. This left the bottom of the canyon and the surrounding land bare and free from vegetation, and it was at this stage that the Indians first made use of the place.

The foregoing has its significance archaeologically as it shows that the earliest material here does not necessarily belong to the first inhabitants of the region. . . .

In the main canyon there were, up to within six or seven years ago, four separate places where the cliff overhung sufficiently to provide good shelter (fig. 18). One (no. 1), under the north wall on the west, is well protected from all winds, but the floor, composed of gravel and dirt washed down from above, is flooded with every severe rain or freshet. Further down the opposite side another shelter (no. 2), or more properly cave, 40 ft. deep with sufficient room to stand in, is cut under the base of the cliff. Water from a spring runs in under the cliff and has washed away part of the dirt floor, but no trace of occupation is visible.

Further to the east along the same cliff is another shelter (no. 3) with a level floor 95 ft. long, averaging 12 ft. in width. The rock underlying the floor for most of its length is slightly concave and is filled with dry earth mixed with charcoal, bones, and artifacts not exceeding a foot in thick-

Fig. 17. Cañadon Leona shelter no. 5 before excavation.

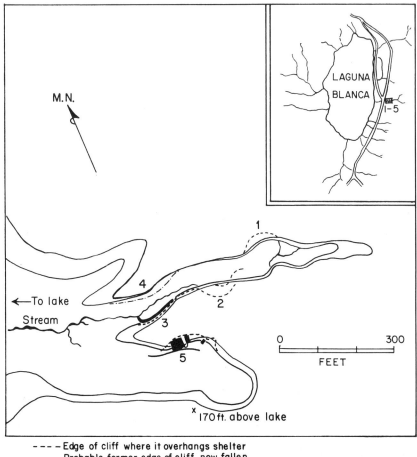

M.N.

LAGUNA
BLANCA

1-5

1

4

←To lake

Stream

2

3

5

0   300

FEET

x
170 ft. above lake

- - - - Edge of cliff where it overhangs shelter
—·—· Probable former edge of cliff, now fallen
———— Outer line-edge of sloping land surrounding canyon
⌣⌣⌣⌣ Inner line – floor of canyon

Fig. 18. Map of shelters on east side of Laguna Blanca. The principal excavations took place at shelter no. 5.

ness until near the western end. There the rock dips steeply and about 5 ft. of dirt, containing very few artifacts, is piled against it. In front, the deposit has been so disturbed and washed by the water as to be useless for systematic excavation. Between twelve and sixteen hundred cubic ft. of debris were examined [Bird left no further notes on this excavation, which he considered useless, although he made some comments on its implements; see The Artifacts, below—ed.].

On the rear wall of this shelter there are rock paintings. These have endured only where applied on the hard surface, and even on this are poorly preserved. With but two exceptions they had been put on with little care, and subsequent scratching with charcoal makes it more difficult to determine the original outlines. Only black and red were used, unless some [lines] which now appear a dirty buff were originally that color and not a poorly prepared black.

Along the northern side of the canyon across from the third shelter there was, until six or seven years ago, a similar overhang (no. 4), but this has since broken off. That part of the floor now visible beneath the fallen rock is uneven and the lack of debris shows that it was not used much. This, like shelter 3, must have been a very drafty place with westerly winds. Of the two, no. 3 on the sunny side must have been preferred.

As shown on the map (fig. 18) there are smaller branches or arms at either side of the entrance of the canyon. The northern branch is small, offers little shelter, and shows no evidence of having been used.

EXCAVATION INFORMATION

In the southern [branch] a vertical cliff forms the northeastern wall and overhangs at one point forming what was once a good shelter, no. 5. At one end of the shelter there are two small caves, one above the other. These were used as [our] kitchen and bedroom while working here (fig. 27), and found to be very satisfactory, but as the floors of both were free of dirt, and as no more bones or specimens were found in the ground in front than elsewhere, it is apparent that they could not have been used much.

The floor of the canyon is a smooth, grass-covered slope. Its surface is undisturbed by erosion, as never more than a slight seepage of water enters from above, but a fast-flowing spring at the mouth shows that considerable water enters the basin through the rock somewhere beneath the surface of the soil. In the shelter, water level was found to be only about 30 in. below the surface. With about a 4 percent gradient it was necessary to cut a 125 ft. drainage trench, but as the soil below water level was only soft mud, it was impossible to cut this much below 5 ft. until it had drained

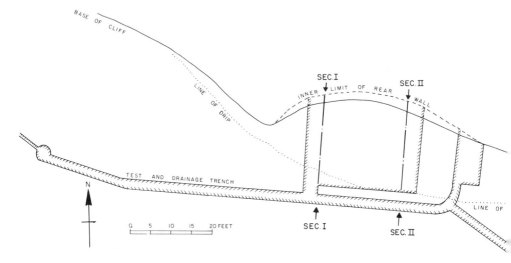

Fig. 19. Plan view of Cañadon Leona rock shelter no. 5.

for some time (figs. 19, 20). This wet condition, though retarding the work, at least minimized the chance of specimens being out of position because of the burrowing of foxes, skunks, or *coruros* [*Ctenomys magellánicus*]. This is a factor which must not be overlooked, as such situations in southern Patagonia, when dry, have usually been honeycombed by these animals.

In order to secure specimens with reasonably accurate data, the dirt from the main part of the floor of shelter no. 5 was excavated in even layers 9 in. in thickness (fig. 21). The system used in segregating specimens in levels parallel to the surface was unsatisfactory near the bottom, because the underlying sand was so far from parallel that a level which touched it at one end was 2 ft. above it at the other. Hence the specimens from [levels] 9, 10, and 11 may include some from the surface of 12 which rightly belong with the latter. For example, the [stemless] triangular point found near the outer edge of the main pit at a depth of 7 ft. 3 in. was practically touching the sand. This must be remembered when considering the things from these three divisions [Bird pioneered in the excavation of natural stratigraphic layers throughout his life—ed.].

The wet condition made it necessary to work down from the surface of the layer being removed, using planks to stand on, and allowing the freshly exposed mud to drain undisturbed for several days. By having several layers started and working a large enough area, this could be managed without loss of time. As nothing could be recognized when it came from the mud, all chips, flakes, and stones were saved and later washed and sorted.

Fig. 20. Drainage trench and excavation unit.

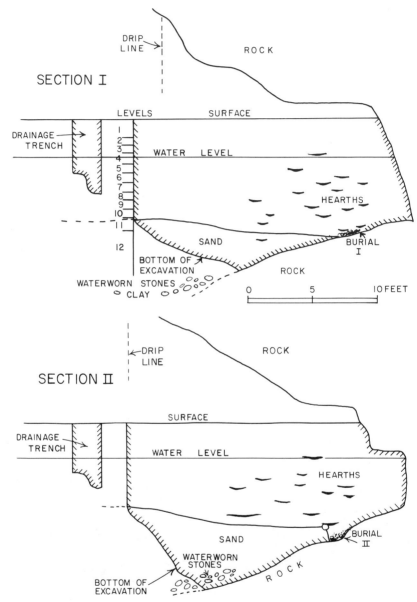

Fig. 21. Two section drawings of Cañadon Leona (shelter no. 5) excavation.

When the excavation was too deep for the trench to carry off the water, it was necessary to bail by hand, and the flow was found to be over forty gal. per hour.

The earth from the surface down to a depth varying from 7 to 9 ft. was of uniform color and texture: fine, brown, windblown soil. The fact that there is no darker topsoil layer indicates that the deposit has accumulated at a nearly constant rate up to the present, and is still being built up. Above the level of the last [lowest] of the material were two groups of burials, containing eight individuals, men and women. The graves were lined with red clay, with which the bodies had also been daubed.

Beneath this is a whitish, clayey sand composed of disintegrated tufa. Further down, the sand is clearly water-deposited and mixed with many pieces of tufa and waterworn stones. Small fire hearths, with thin streaks of ash, occur from 2 ft. below the surface down into the sand to a depth of 11 ft. 6 in., almost at the level of the water-laid sand. Bones were found from the surface down, but never in sufficient quantity to form an appreciable percentage of the total volume.

THE ARTIFACTS

For a complete list of the tool types, see tables 1 and 2. Grouping the specimens from both excavations, we have a fairly uniform culture from top to bottom, with certain changes indicated by the occurrence of a few items. From about 7,500 cubic ft. of earth removed from this shelter [approximately] 4,400 artifacts were recovered, among which are more than 580 broken and unfinished bolas, but only 48 arrow and knife points. It is difficult to understand why some of the wind-eroded camps [where we collected artifacts] had many arrow points but no bolas, although they are contemporaneous.

Junius Bird provided small drawings (fig. 22) to help identify the tool types in his field artifact classifications. These drawings are useful when reading any of the numerous artifact tables reproduced in the following three chapters. Because Cañadon Leona was the first site excavated north of the Straits of Magellan, Bird left more written comment about the artifacts excavated there than for any other subsequent site.

Points

From the floor of shelter 3 we have five of the small-stemmed, well-made Ona type arrow points. From there and from the main excavation [shelter 5] down to level 6, we have fifteen of the much broader-stemmed, more roughly made [Patagonian] points which may have been either for arrows

POINTS

    ONA - SMALL AND BARBED

    SMALL TRIANGULAR

    SMALL RUDIMENTARY STEM

    PATAGONIAN - STEMMED

    SPEAR

    OLD-TYPE - STEMLESS, TRIANGULAR

    FISHTAIL

KNIVES

    HAFTED

    KNIFE OR SPEAR

    SMALL, LEAF-SHAPED

    SINGLE-EDGE (FROM FLAKE)

    3-EDGE

    COMBINATION KNIFE-SCRAPER

SCRAPERS (HAND)

    ROUGH, SINGLE-EDGE FLAKE

    2-EDGE, LARGE

    2-EDGE, NARROW (PARALLEL)

    2 POINTS

    2 SIDES TO POINT

    ONE-EDGE (LIKE 2-EDGE)

    ONE-SIDED WITH ROUNDED END

    LARGE CIRCULAR

    END

    REVERSED 2-END

    REVERSED 2-EDGE

SCRAPERS (HAFTED)

    CIRCULAR EDGE

    END OR ONE SIDE

    END AND SIDES

BOLAS

    SPHERICAL, LARGE

    SPHERICAL, SMALL

    LEMON - SHAPED

    EGG - SHAPED

    PLUM - SHAPED

    IRREGULAR AND WATERWORN

    FLATTENED (DISK-SHAPED)

    SMALL, GROOVED LONG AXIS

    SMALL, NOTCHED LONG AXIS

    SMALL, GROOVED SHORT AXIS

    SMALL, NOTCHED SHORT AXIS

    UNFINISHED, LARGE UNBROKEN

    UNFINISHED, SMALL

    DUMBBELL

FLAKE FOR GROOVING BOLA

RUBBING STONE, CIRCULAR

LARGE GROOVED (HAFTED HAMMER?)

STONE BEAD

BONE

    CHIPPING TOOL

    BIRD BONE AWL

    SOLID POINT AWL

    BONE LANCE POINT

Fig. 22. Junius Bird's small drawings depicting stone and bone artifacts found in south Chile excavations.

Table 1. Artifacts from Cañadon Leona (Points, Knives, Scrapers, Bone)

Group	Category	Shelter 5 Levels					
		1	2	3	4	5	6
Points	Small, Ona	1	1	–	–	–	–
	Small, triangular Ona	–	–	–	–	–	
	Patagonian knife or arrow	2	1	3	2	3	
	Old-type (stemless)	–	–	–	–	–	–
Knives	Hafted	–	1	–	2	4	
	Knife or spear	1	–	–	1	2	
	Long, thin	–	–	–	–	–	
	Small, leaf-shape	–	–	3	3	2	
	Flake, single-edge	–	–	–	1	2	
Scrapers / Hand Scrapers	Rough, single-edge flake	37	74	174	274	396	35
	(Above, but discarded to limit weight)	(5)	(25)	(55)	(114)	(200)	(18
	Flake, 2 sides to point	–	8	9	8	10	
	Flake, 1 side with rounded end	2	–	2	7	1	
	Large, circular edge	–	3	5	–	5	
	Long, narrow, 2 sides to point	4	7	5	8	21	▶
	2-edge, narrow	–	1	2	2	4	
	2-edge, large	5	4	12	5	10	
	2-edge, reversed	–	–	–	–	–	–
	1-edge (like 2-sided)	2	3	8	11	12	▶
	Chipped both sides along top	–	–	–	–	–	
	End	–	–	2	2	3	
	Reversed, 2-end	–	–	–	–	–	
Small Hafted	Circular edge	3	3	3	27	38	3
	End, or 1 side	8	11	48	40	118	1(
	End and sides	2	5	6	32	39	2
	Unfinished, uncertain	2	10	5	7	3	

Shelter 5 Levels								Shelter 3		
7	8	9	10	11	12	60–90″	Position Uncertain	Below	Surface	Total
–	–	–	–	–	–	–	–	6	–	8
–	–	–	1	–	–	–	–	–	–	2
–	–	–	–	–	–	–	–	2	1	15
–	–	–	1	–	3	–	–	–	–	4
–	–	–	–	–	–	–	–	9	14	32
–	–	–	–	–	–	–	1	–	–	8
–	–	–	–	–	–	–	–	–	–	1
–	–	–	–	–	–	–	–	–	1	10
–	–	–	–	–	–	–	–	2	1	10
263	149	147	67	16	10	36	18	58	36	2,113
(119)	(16)	(25)	(13)	(2)	(–)	(10)	(18)	(1)	(28)	(820)
12	23	18	5	2	1	3	–	2	4	111
3	6	5	2	–	–	–	–	–	2	36
3	–	–	–	–	–	–	–	–	2	23
19	8	6	2	–	–	–	1	1	–	101
1	4	2	5	1	1	1	–	–	1	27
11	17	22	–	–	–	1	–	2	1	96
–	–	–	–	–	–	–	–	1	–	1
7	13	6	–	–	–	–	2	1	7	88
–	–	–	–	1	1	–	–	5	–	8
6	3	2	1	1	–	1	–	1	–	24
–	–	–	–	–	–	–	–	–	–	1
22	7	9	4	–	–	1	–	–	–	148
108	49	52	31	2	2	9	11	13	3	610
7	15	12	3	–	–	2	2	2	–	147
8	11	7	–	–	–	–	–	5	–	60

Table I. *(continued)*

Group	Category	Shelter 5 Levels					
		1	*2*	*3*	*4*	*5*	
Bone Implements	Guanaco chipping tool	–	–	2	1	1	
	Tool, use unknown	–	–	1	1	–	
	Guanaco wedge	–	1	–	–	–	
	Bird bone awl	–	1	1	–	1	
	Solid bone awl	–	–	–	–	–	
	Totals	69	134	291	434	675	5

( ) = Not included in totals.
Total stone artifacts (excluding bolas and miscellaneous) = 3,683.
Total bone artifacts = 25.

or knives. From levels 10 and 12 [we have] two small [stemless] triangular points, probably for arrows. This is the total evidence for the use of bows and arrows. If bows and arrows were in use during the total period represented, why is there not more proof of it? Note also that not a single example of the grooved arrow-shaft polisher was found.

Knives

As knives, we are considering only such types as have chipping on both faces. Of the knives, twenty-five are [suitable] for hafting, twenty-eight are of other shapes, not suited for hafting. Just as we have a small number of knives in proportion to bolas and skin-working tools, we also have proportionately few arrow points. We might assume that each family, if using bows and arrows, would probably possess at least six arrows to each knife, and as breakage and replacement would be more frequent for the arrow points, we should find considerably more points than knives on such a site. Here, using our sum totals, there are less than half as many arrow points as knives.

Bolas

We have 579 bolas in all stages of manufacture (table 2). Bolas are divided into three main groups according to their outline (fig. 23). Commonest are the spherical, made in large and small sizes. Next are the lemon-shaped bolas, grooved about the short axis. No small examples of these were

Shelter 5 Levels								Shelter 3		
7	8	9	10	11	12	60–90″	Position Uncertain	Below	Surface	Total
–	1	–	–	–	1	–	–	3	–	11
–	–	–	–	–	1	–	–	3	–	6
1	–	–	–	–	–	–	–	–	–	2
–	–	–	–	–	–	–	–	1	–	5
–	–	–	–	–	–	–	–	1	–	1
471	306	288	122	23	20	54	35	118	73	3,709

found. The third group are the egg-shaped ones, grooved about the long axis, and made in large and small sizes. In addition to these there are occasional variations, represented here by one flat-sided, disk-shaped form, grooved about the edge of the disk, and a surface find [that was] very deeply grooved, with flattened ends, slightly resembling an ordinary thread spool. Some naturally shaped waterworn stones of suitable size and weight have also been used [as bolas].

Although the oldest bola found is a small egg-shaped one, the three main types have all been in use a long time. The lemon shape seems to have become more popular as time passed. The smaller bolas were probably all used for the *manija*, the ball retained in the hand while whirling the *boleadora*. This explains the absence of the small lemon-shaped ones, which would be harder to hold. According to the natives, the rhea [or bird] bolas are smaller than those for guanaco, which may account for the intermediate sizes of the spherical type.

The table shows that the period of greatest use of the bola was that represented by levels 2, 3, 4, 5, 6, and 7. In the recent debris of shelter 3 there was 1 bola to 10 other specimens; in levels 4, 5, and 6, 1 to every 6.6; in levels 8, 9, and 10, 1 to 19.8; in level 12, 1 to 24.

Among the bolas found [there] are a number made from the soft tufa or sandstone. The workmanship on most of these is such as to indicate that they were the work of children and were probably used as toys.

For cutting the groove on the bolas, stone flakes or old scrapers were

Table 2. Artifacts from Cañadon Leona (Bolas and Miscellaneous)

Group	Category	Shelter 5 Levels					
		1	2	3	4	5	6
Bolas	Spherical						
	Large, perfect	–	–	–	–	–	–
	Large, perfect, sandstone	–	–	–	–	2	1
	Grooved fragment	–	3	5	3	5	4
	Grooved fragment, sandstone	1	2	–	3	3	2
	Unfinished	5	23	25	20	21	17
	Small	–	–	–	–	1	1
	Small, sandstone	–	–	–	1	1	2
	Lemon-Shaped						
	Perfect	–	–	–	–	–	–
	Perfect, sandstone	–	–	–	1	–	1
	Grooved fragment	–	–	–	1	–	–
	Unfinished piece	–	20	10	16	12	7
	Egg-Shaped						
	Large, perfect	–	–	–	–	–	1
	Grooved fragment	–	–	–	–	1	–
	Unfinished, large	–	–	–	–	1	–
	Unfinished, small	–	–	–	1	–	–
	Small, perfect	–	–	1	–	–	–
	Irregular Shape						
	Large, waterworn	1	–	1	–	1	2
	Large, sandstone lump	–	–	3	–	2	–
	Small, sandstone lump	–	–	1	–	–	1
	Small, waterworn	–	–	–	–	–	1

Shelter 5 Levels								Shelter 3		
7	8	9	10	11	12	60–90″	Position Uncertain	Below	Surface	Total
–	1	–	–	–	–	–	–	–	1	2
–	–	–	–	–	–	–	–	–	–	3
3	1	–	–	–	–	1	–	–	1	26
1	1	–	–	–	–	–	–	1	–	14
11	5	7	2	2	–	4	–	6	2	150
–	–	–	–	–	–	–	–	2	–	4
–	2	1	–	–	–	–	–	–	–	7
–	–	–	–	–	–	–	–	–	1	1
–	–	–	–	–	–	–	–	–	–	2
–	–	–	–	–	–	–	–	–	1	2
4	1	1	–	–	–	–	7	–	–	78
–	–	–	–	–	–	–	–	–	1	2
–	–	–	–	–	–	–	–	–	–	1
–	–	–	–	–	–	–	–	–	–	1
1	–	–	–	–	–	–	–	–	–	2
–	–	–	–	–	1	–	–	–	–	2
1	–	–	–	–	–	–	1	2	–	9
4	–	–	–	–	–	–	1	–	–	10
–	–	–	–	–	–	–	–	–	–	2
–	1	1	–	–	–	–	–	–	–	3

Table 2. *(continued)*

Group	Category	Shelter 5 Levels					
		1	*2*	*3*	*4*	*5*	*6*
Bolas	Small, Oval, Waterworn Pebbles						
	Grooved, long axis	–	–	–	–	–	1
	Notched, long axis	–	–	–	2	–	–
	Grooved, short axis	–	–	–	–	–	–
	Notched, short axis	1	–	–	–	–	–
	Rough, Unfinished						
	Large, unbroken	–	3	3	1	–	–
	Small, unbroken	1	–	–	–	–	–
	Large, fragment	2	35	27	43	35	40
	Small, fragment	–	3	4	1	–	–
	Large, dumbbell-shape (bola?)	–	–	–	–	–	–
	Disk-shaped bola, sandstone only	–	–	–	–	1	1
	Totals	11	89	80	93	86	82
Miscel-laneous	Flake for grooving bola	–	–	–	–	1	–
	Large, grooved stone, perhaps hafted hammer	–	1	1	1	–	–
	Oval pitted hammerstone	–	1	–	–	–	–
	Rough hammerstone	1	1	6	4	4	–
	Circular flat rubbing stone	–	–	–	–	1	–
	Irregular flat rubbing, or whetstone	–	–	–	1	1	–
	Fragment, flat paint mortar	–	–	–	–	–	–
	Totals	1	3	7	6	7	–

Total bolas and miscellaneous artifacts = 649.

		Shelter 5 Levels						Shelter 3		
7	8	9	10	11	12	60–90″	Position Uncertain	Below	Surface	Total
2	2	–	2	–	–	–	–	–	–	7
–	1	–	–	–	–	–	–	–	–	3
–	–	–	1	–	–	–	–	–	–	1
–	–	–	–	–	–	–	–	–	–	1
1	–	–	–	–	–	–	–	3	–	11
–	–	2	3	–	–	–	–	1	–	7
34	–	6	–	–	–	1	–	1	–	224
–	–	–	–	–	–	–	–	–	–	8
–	–	–	–	–	–	–	–	–	1	1
–	–	1	–	–	–	–	–	–	–	3
62	15	19	8	2	1	6	9	16	8	587
–	–	–	–	1	1	–	–	–	–	3
–	–	–	–	–	–	–	–	–	–	3
–	–	1	1	–	–	–	–	–	–	3
10	2	7	4	–	–	–	4	–	–	43
–	–	–	–	–	–	–	–	1	–	2
1	–	–	–	–	–	–	2	2	–	7
–	–	1	–	–	–	–	–	–	–	1
11	2	9	5	1	1	–	6	3	–	62

Fig. 23. Bolas of various shapes and sizes from Cañadon Leona and other sites north of the Straits of Magellan: (1) nearly spherical with greatest axis in plane of groove; (2) rare—excessively grooved form with flattened ends; (3) polished spherical with broad shallow groove (all polished bolas are very late, perhaps historical); (4) elongated spherical grooved around short diameter; (5) spherical with small knobs or projections to prevent ball from turning in loop; (6–8) nearly egg-shaped—perhaps a *manija* (hand) weight; (9–14) bird bolas (12 to 14 are grooved waterworn pebbles).

used as saws, and several of these were found, with well-worn edges. Wide grooves may have been cut by pecking. In the Beagle Channel region the most recent bolas have a very fine groove, the older ones a much wider one. Here [in shelters 3 and 5] are none of the very fine grooves, but [there is] a considerable variation [in grooves], large and small, with no obvious preference at any one period. The oldest bola does, however, have a wide, deep groove.

For breaking up rocks into blanks for the bolas and shaping them, any other hard stone which would stand the strain was used as a hammer. They are usually no larger than can be conveniently held in one hand and have not been worked in any way to make them more suitable. A number of these were discarded without being counted, so the figures in table 2 are less than the total seen.

Hammerstones

Three large, grooved stones, unsuitable for bolas, may have been hafted for hammers, but they are crudely made. Oval, pitted hammerstones were possibly used for producing flakes for scrapers and knives, as they do not show the effects of very heavy pounding.

Scrapers

The scraping tools divide into two main groups, hafted and unhafted. We have 965 hafted-type scrapers for skin-working, and 2,629 other scrapers of various types suitable for skin- and woodworking. The relative abundance of these seems to be fairly constant through all levels, averaging one hafted one to approximately three unhafted, with the latter showing increased use in the later years. The average [proportion] of levels 2 and 3 and of shelter 3 is 1 to 3.55; of levels 7, 8, 9, and 10, 1 to 2.42.

The unhafted scrapers (thumbnail or snub-nose) vary greatly in size and shape but can be classified according to outline, and the shape and number of the edges. By far the most common are those made from any large flake, sometimes with secondary chipping along one edge only. The outline of this edge is nearly always slightly convex, sometimes straight, and rarely concave. As variants of this we find that flakes, which happen to be thin on two sides, have two edges. If these meet, they usually come to a point instead of being rounded off. If the flake was suitable, the chipping was sometimes continued around one end; with others, the end may be semicircular. It is uncertain if these different forms were made intentionally or served different purposes.

In contrast to these very roughly made scrapers we have others which show more careful workmanship, and a similarity of outline which conforms to a definite pattern. These are made from long narrow flakes, the simplest of which were worked along one side only. Other have two more or less parallel edges. With the most carefully made, two slightly curved edges come together to a sharp point. For finishing these, pressure flaking must have been employed, while the edges of many of the simpler ones look as though they were produced by percussion chipping.

The hafted scraper blades are all more or less alike. The majority are chipped along one side only. Others, circular in outline, are chipped all the way around, and a third group are chipped across one end and up the two adjoining sides. Because many of these are about the same size and might be used interchangeably, it may be that the amount of edge chipped depended only on the suitability of the original flake. For these, the hardest stones available were preferred—jasper, chalcedony, and flint, which are found in this region only in the form of small pebbles.

In addition to the scrapers already mentioned, there are some made from narrow flakes with a chipped edge across one end, about the width of the average hafted blade.   *(from Bird 1936–1937)*

The following text was probably written by Bird after the excavation at Cañadon Leona, but before the return to excavate at Palli Aike and Fell's Cave in 1937. It was probably never intended for publication since it presents ideas in formation. Nevertheless, it is a useful document showing how Bird was approaching the classification of scrapers in 1936.

The problem of classifying the large number of unilaterally flaked stone tools is both difficult and unsatisfactory. If the results are to be tabulated and presented in simplified form, how positive will they be? Will the distinctions made be sufficient to ensure the same analysis by another observer? What data will prove useful for future comparative work? These are but a few of the considerations with which one is confronted at the start.

One has, however, a basic division to work from: (1) tools used in cleaning and preparing skins [with steeply beveled edge], and (2) those used for woodworking and perhaps as knives [with sharp cutting edge]. Beyond that, one almost immediately encounters trouble.

In any complete series, such as removed from a single excavation, certain examples stand out as possible types. Closer examination reveals intermediate forms, so that instead of fixed groups or types, we have such a blending of patterns that even the division between seemingly unrelated tools becomes purely arbitrary.

The task then is to decide which if any are really specialized types or desired patterns, and which ones represent utilization of the accidents of manufacture, or are the result of continued use and reshaping. Adding to the confusion is the impossibility of segregating specimens that may have been rejected by their makers and never used.

In an effort to clarify this last case, the infrequent examples with worn edges have been studied. The results show that our opinion as to which are good and which are second-rate tools is of no value, for what might be classed as undesirable specimens occur with even a higher ratio among those showing worn edges.

As a typical example we may take the sidescrapers recovered at the Laguna Blanca excavations. Roughly 80 percent are irregular flakes some-times retouched on one edge only. The balance present a variety of forms worked on two edges or on the entire circumference.

When the rough-flake single-edge scrapers are arranged as they occurred stratigraphically, we see that they consistently fall within certain limits of size and that with the great majority, the sharpened edge coincides with their longest dimension. These can be considered as group characteristics and an average specimen can be determined which should be useful for comparative studies. But what of the differences? Should they be sub-divided as to curvature and thickness of edge? If they are separated into those with concave, straight, and convex edges, we find the majority fall-ing between the extreme examples, and the proportions of these in the various strata are fairly constant. The only conclusion to be drawn from these facts is that the use to which they were put did not require a close adherence to a fixed pattern. Also, because many examples could not be used for skin-working, the group must have been used principally for woodworking, or as knives.

Their use as knives depends on what we accept as the definition of a knife. An attempt to segregate tools which have sharply beveled edges, and those which would serve as knives, meets with just as little success. Nearly 11 of them can be duplicated by others having edges of the same length and curvature which are too steeply beveled to be of any use except as scrapers. We are forced to admit that some differences must be due to the impossibility of producing the same size and type of flake from mate-rial which varies so much in texture and form.

When we come to the remainder of the sidescrapers there is even greater confusion. At first there seem to be several clear-cut types: those with bi-lateral flaking on the edge opposite the scraper edge; those with roughly oval outline having two edges retouched; those with two adjoining edges forming a point; others high-backed and parallel-sided—all apparently distinct types, perhaps for specialized use. But when the limits of each group are sought, again there is a disconcerting lack of clear division. This makes the selection of what may have been the normal, desired patterns so difficult that it is unlikely that two independent observers could secure the same tabulated results unless the problems involved are clearly understood.

Scraper-Knives

[There is] a rather interesting tool which is usually oval in outline, about twice as long as wide, with an ordinary scraping edge along one side and a knife edge (two-way chipping) opposite it. With some of these the knife edge is well finished, while others are so poorly done that they could not have been used for cutting. From the latter it might be concluded that the two-way chipping has been done merely to give the scraper the desired shape, but why should some have well-finished knife edges? Examination of a sufficient number of these will settle the question.

The few examples of the scraper-knife are so distributed as to suggest that they were known at the beginning and end of the period represented here, but are so rare in between as to make their occurrence there seem almost accidental. From levels 11 and 12 there are 2 among a total of 49 specimens—a proportion of 1 to every 24.5. From the most recent debris in shelter 3 we have 5—1 to every 23.5 specimens. Between these levels we have only 1 scraper-knife to over 4,000 other specimens. This suggests a close relationship between the first and last people to use this place.

Broken Guanaco Leg Bones

Only a few bone tools were found, perhaps because of the wet conditions which made all the bones soft and friable. Guanaco leg bones broken off squarely 3 to 5 in. from the joint are the commonest bone artifacts (fig. 24). Their splintered ends show that they have been used as hammers. Over 200 of these were found but, as many broke on being disturbed, an accurate count was impossible. They were found in both shelters and in all levels down to the underlying sand (level 12). As far as I know, these [tools] have never been described before. It may be suggested that they are not tools, merely the ends of the long bones as left after the removal of marrow. Experiment shows that when breaking these bones for marrow a squared end is the least likely to be produced. Moreover, the splintered ends can only be duplicated when the piece is used to pound harder than is necessary to dislodge any marrow which might have remained within.

Accepting these as tools, it is still necessary to explain their use. As bolas and scrapers are the only other things found in abundance, they may have been used in the manufacture of one or the other. For putting the edge on scrapers they seem so ill-suited that there is little likelihood that they were ever used for that. Bola making has been briefly described by Darwin, who mentions only a stone hammer. However, after a blank has

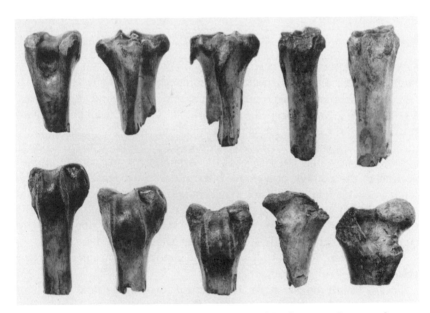

Fig. 24. Broken guanaco leg bones, probably used in the manufacture of stone bolas.

been roughed out a number of small projections are left which, it was found, are more easily removed with one of these bones than with another stone. Once these are off, the surfacing has to be continued with the stone, so that most of the work is really done with that. A fresh bone used in this way reproduces the edges of those found.

Chipping Tools, Awls, Wedges

The next most frequent bone tool, but far from plentiful, are the ordinary guanaco bone chipping tools distributed evenly through all levels. The bird bone awls, the commonest tool in the middens of the canoe-using people in the south, are rare here, only six having been found. Two guanaco bone wedges were uncovered, but had flaked and checked so much as they dried as to be almost unrecognizable. While wet, they resembled very closely the guanaco bone wedges found in rock shelter 3 at Yendagaia on the south side of Tierra del Fuego.

It is noteworthy that amongst the artifacts at Cañadon Leona there are no potsherds. Earthen pots were reported in the region over two centuries ago, about 1720. Also, there was not a single ornament or bead.

FAUNAL REMAINS

Comment

Knowing that horses have been in this region in abundance for at least two hundred years, a careful check of all bones was made with the hope of determining the rate of accumulation, but none were found. A bone from a cow's foreleg was imbedded just below the surface. Sheep bones, plentiful at the surface, were found down only 3 in.

Beneath this, the majority of bones were broken guanaco marrow (long) bones. Vertebrae and other parts of the animal are scarce, out of all proportion to the number of legs. In order to check the possible use of the foreleg knuckle bone for a game played in late years, all of these were laid aside and later cleaned and examined. The number of these, 135 from the right leg, 120 from the left, gives a minimum figure for the number of guanaco killed. Incidentally, none had been smoothed for use.

Fox jaws were found at all levels, but almost no other parts of their skeletons.

Coruro (small rodent) skulls are plentiful down to the sand, and in all cases appear to have been broken open to remove the brains.

Parts of two puma jaws complete the list of mammals (a few skunk bones were found, but only in shelter no. 3).

Rhea (ostrich-like birds) bones were almost lacking down to the white sand; pieces in this [sand] show that the rhea was at least available in the early days. In marked contrast, there was an abundance of these bones in shelter no. 3 in the recent [upper] debris. A few bird bones scattered through different levels look like upland geese.

Eight or ten limpet shells were found in the main canyon, but as it is twenty-five miles to the nearest place where these can be secured, they can scarcely be included in a list of food available at this camp.

Classifications

The faunal material from Cañadon Leona has AMNH catalogue number 41.1/2216. The specimens are marked CL with numbers 1 to 12 representing the levels in the excavation. The faunal specialist Thomas Amorosi has tentatively classified the faunal remains as follows.

Aves

Material: 5 humeri, 1 radius, 1 ulna, 1 femur, 1 tibiotarsus, 1 tarsometatarsus. Distribution: CL12—1 humerus, 1 ulna, 1 femur, 1 tibiotarsus, all from medium-sized birds. CL12—4 humeri, 1 radius, 1 tarsometatarsus, all from large-sized birds.

Rodentia

Material: I incisor, 2 mandibles.
Distribution: CL12—2 mandibles. No provenience for I incisor.

Canidae

Material: I skull, 3 maxillae, 13 mandibles.
Distribution: CL3—I skull. CL6—2 maxillae, 3 mandibles. CL8—2 mandibles.
CL12—I maxilla, 8 mandibles.

Camelidae (Guanaco)

Material: 6 humeri, 10 radii, 2 metapodial, 20 femora, 6 tibiae.
Distribution: Camelid remains are found in all levels from I to 12. Several score
of bola makers from camelid bone are not listed here, but rather dealt with in
the discussion of artifacts (Broken Guanaco Leg Bones).

Fragmentary Material Attributed to Class

Mammalia, large-sized: 3 long bones.
Mammalia, medium-sized. 3 cranial fragments, I thoracic vertebra.

Bird's mention of the foreleg knuckle bones may refer to several skeletal elements. The most likely candidates are the carpals/tarsals or the astragali. Both
types have been used as gaming pieces, but none are present in this collection at
the AMNH.

POSSIBLE AGE OF DEPOSIT

The sheep bones provide the only means of computing the length of occupation. Sheep were first placed on this camp in 1890 or 1891 and have
been kept there ever since. Sick or weak animals seek shelter in the canyon
and often die there. In all the shelters there are bodies, and it seems safe to
assume that within five years after they were introduced they began to die
there. Bones are common just beneath the surface, but none were seen
with more than 3 in. of soil over them.

Since sheep have been introduced to southern Patagonia the surface of
the country has undergone the usual changes which occur when new land
is turned into pasture. Small ponds and swampy land have dried up and
erosion has been increased in many places. Sheepmen who have grown up
there agree that in the country as a whole there is probably more soil
blown about by the wind now than there was before, in spite of the sowing
of grass and the near extinction of the *coruro*. This animal formerly
riddled large areas with its burrows and must have been a factor in the

movement of soil by the wind. So if we take 3 in. as the amount of soil blown into the shelter in the south arm during the past forty or forty-five years and use this as an average for the whole period, we cannot be far wrong. The chance for error lies in the age given to the lowest [sheep] bones, but the increased amount of dirt carried by the wind should counterbalance that. Also, there has been the manure dropped by the animals, and that must make up a certain portion of the upper 3 in.

Naturally, this can be used only for estimating the age of the dirt down to the underlying sand [level 12]. If we take the maximum depth, 9 ft. 3 in., we have a possible age of 1,480 to 1,655 years, which does not seem excessive. Beyond [or below] that we have no means of judging the rate of accumulation and can say only that it must have been much more rapid.

Bird published another estimate of 960 to 1,080 years (1938a: 268). The difference apparently rests in whether one considers the end of the stemless points to occur in level 12 (9 ft. 3 in.), where they are found, or in level 7 (at 4 ft. 6 in.), below which stemmed points no longer occur. Several decades later, with carbon dates, Bird was able to place the lower end of the stemless points (Period III) at about 8,500 years ago.

BURIALS

The description of burial no. 1 at Cañadon Leona cannot be located in Junius Bird's fieldnotes. Burial no. 2 was described as follows.

Burial No. 2

Eighteen ft. further along the base of the cliff from the first burial, a second group of skeletons was found (figs. 25 and 26). Like the first, these lie at the dividing line between the underlying sand and rock and the dark soil, so both graves must have been made about, if not at, the same time. Again, the grave is very shallow: 20 in. deep, 5 ft. long, by 3 ft. 3 in. wide. It contains parts of seven adults and one baby.

Before the bodies were placed in the grave, it was lined with red clay (red paint mixed with clay?). Bits of this clay, on and among the bones, suggest that the bodies may also have been daubed with it. In order to avoid missing any artifacts, this clay was salvaged, and filled two five-gallon tins. The drawing (fig. 26) shows how the bodies were piled up on top of each other. In each case the lower legs have been doubled in underneath, with the ankles together. The arms are extended with the wrists coming together at the pelvis. This position suggests that the wrists and ankles may have been tied together with a thong passing about the hips.

Fig. 25. Burial no. 2 in shelter no. 5 at Cañadon Leona.

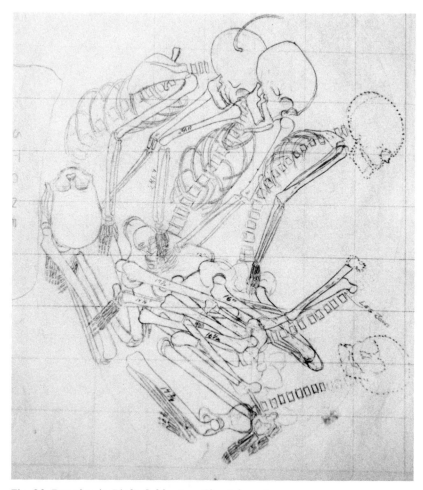

Fig. 26. Drawing in Bird's fieldnotes of burial no. 2.

One side of the grave is formed by the inclined base of the cliff, causing a certain amount of slippage, and is probably responsible for the misplaced bones. Only the two lowest skeletons were complete. Skull no. 3 had rolled slightly from above. The rest of the skeletons are very incomplete. Of the body which was placed on top of the pile, only the legs remain. The next has the legs and pelvis; the other two have legs, pelvis, and sections of the backbone. Three skulls had collapsed and all the other bones were cracked [the skeletal material has AMNH catalogue numbers 99.1/768 to 99.1/771—ed.].

Resting in the pelvis cavity of skeleton no. 1 were pieces of a small infant's skull and bits of ribs and other bones. Possibly [we have] a pregnant mother.

The simplest explanation of the incomplete skeletons and misplaced bones may be that the bodies were piled up with perhaps no more covering than a few skins or robes. By the time the remains had partially decomposed these may have loosened sufficiently for foxes or pumas to get at and carry off pieces.

On top of the bones is the same kind of brown earth found elsewhere above the whitish sand. In this, nearly over the center of the grave and extending off to one side, was a fire hearth. As this could not have been used until after the bones were covered, it shows that the surface at the time of burial must have been very close to the dividing line between the sand and the soil.

The removal of these bones was rather difficult as water was entering the pit, above the level of the burial, at the base of the cliff—more than forty gallons an hour. This required constant bailing, day and night, at not more than three-hour intervals, to prevent it from flooding. After uncovering [the burial], it was allowed to drain for two days and then removed piecemeal. Some of the best-preserved long bones were measured as they lay.

The red clay and the dirt in contact with the bones were carefully washed without producing a single artifact. Nor was anything found nearby which could be associated with either burial.

The artifacts in the surrounding dirt were typical of the third cultural period (III), in which stemless knife and projectile points were used. In the dirt immediately over the burials were the artifacts of the fourth period (IV) which were sufficiently distinct to indicate that a new group of nomadic hunters had moved into the area. My impression is that the burials relate to the Period III people and that they were buried at the close of that period.   *(from Bird 1936–1937)*

SUMMARY

We may read the history [of the shelter] thus. The Indians availed themselves of the canyon shortly after the lake receded. The first occupants used stemless spear or arrow points and small bolas. Subsequently, wind-blown soil accumulated in the shelter; during this period stemmed arrow points and knives were in use, together with various types of bolas. Shortly before the beginning of the historical period a new type of arrow point, identical with those used by the Ona Indians of Tierra del Fuego, came into use. As this was found with the earlier stemmed form, we must conclude that the two types are contemporaneous. We occasionally found these small Ona-type points by themselves, on the wind-eroded sites. Hence, instead of being a cultural introduction or development, they seem to belong to a distinct group.   *(from Bird 1938a: 265–268)*

DAILY LIFE

Saturday, November 30, 1935

Got off shortly after breakfast, after procuring a sheep. The *estancia* (sheep farm) is at the northwest end of the lake—we continued on around to the southeast end. We were met partway by a shepherd on horseback, to show us the track. It was extremely windy and just as we were beginning to get discouraged at the flatness of the country, no shelter anywhere, our guide turned off the road and led us to the edge of a little canyon cut right down in the pampa, with walls of yellowish-white mudstone. Quite sheltered, bushes, green grass, and a little stream—a very welcome sight. The rock overhangs on one side forming two long shallow caves; in the one nearer the entrance to the valley are the cave paintings. There was a similar cave on the other side, but the roof fell down a few years ago. They say this is the most sheltered place for miles. We left the truck at the top of the cliff and unloaded, setting up camp at the head of the canyon—two tents, as before. Collected firewood in the truck—dead *calafate* [*Berberis buxifolia*] branches and old fence posts—and made a fire and cooked a late luncheon. Went to look more carefully at the paintings; they are almost obliterated— most are very crude designs in black or red; two or three seem older, are more carefully done—red, outlined with black.

Sunday, December 1

Windy. Started work at east end of outer cave; a deposit of earth, stones, and bones, only some 6 in. deep. Found two small arrowheads and so forth. Took a walk in evening, downstream and then inland. At one place, above the camp, the streambed is full of stones—found a scraper. Saw many hares and three dead rheas.

Monday, December 2

Windy; calm until late P.M.; several short showers. Found two very small arrow points.

Tuesday, December 3

Calm all day; cloudy, one or two showers. Made a tracing of one of the paintings, the best-preserved of the red and black ones; colored it with red paint, having dug up a few pieces, and charcoal. Found some points too heavy and with too thick a butt for arrows—were probably hafted and used as knives. Took pictures of painting with both cameras.

Wednesday, December 4

Cloudy, quite windy. Having finished work in cave, went around to small area of canyon on south side. The rock overhangs and underneath it is a deposit—quite deep, judging from a test pit—but so damp that it was necessary to dig a drainage ditch. After supper went down to the lake, this time on the north side of stream, but found nothing. Saw a large owl, many *caiquenes* [*Chloephaga picta*] and hares.

Friday, December 6

Cloudy and calm. In digging ditch, find it cuts through deposit, beyond shelter or cliff, to a depth of some 5 ft.

Saturday, December 7

Clear and windy. More than thirty fragments of bolas found while digging ditch, most of them broken before groove was started. Two men came over from the *estancia* bringing a new tire to replace one Mr. Ross loaned us.

Sunday, December 8

Cloudy in A.M., sun in P.M.—not much wind. Moved camp to south arm. There are two small caves there, one above the other. The lower one makes a fine kitchen; the upper one, with a piece of canvas stretched part way across, a comfortable bedroom; cut steps in the soft rock leading up to it (fig. 27).

Monday, December 9

Cloudy. The *capataz* (foreman) of this section stopped in. He said one year the lake, which is very shallow, entirely dried up. Also, that bolas can be thrown 25 to 30 m. Walked over to the *puesto* after supper. Thought it was only a short way, but it turned out to be one and three-quarter hour walk! The ground is covered with flowers. The house is in a pretty, green canyon, larger and not as sheltered as ours. The man has a pleasant wife and four small children. Gave us tea, and bread with fine homemade rhubarb preserve. Gave us two rhea eggs—light green and about 6 in. long. They say there are twenty to forty in a nest. Started back at 9:15 just at dusk and reached home after dark—but the nights are quite light at this time of the year.

Tuesday, December 10

Calm in A.M., strong wind all P.M. and hard rain in evening. A flock of sheep was grazing in our valley when we woke up, making an awful noise. Found some fossil bones in the wall of the main canyon; took them out in five chunks; part of a skull, some teeth, and a long bone—perhaps one of

Fig. 27. Two small caves, one above the other, were Peggy and Junius Bird's home while excavating at Cañadon Leona. The lower cave served as a kitchen. Stairs carved in the tufa rock led to the bedroom (upper cave), which is screened off.

the giant rodents. Made scrambled eggs from one rhea egg, with a cupful saved out to use in *tortas,* and still there was plenty! But the egg may not have been as fresh as it once was.

Wednesday, December 11

Sun and strong wind. Temperature 43° at bedtime.

Thursday, December 12

Windy and cold—Junius to *estancia* in A.M. for more meat. He also brought back lettuce, rhubarb, eggs, and a cake from Mrs. Ross. The noted explorer Sir Hubert Wilkins is in Magallanes [Punta Arenas], waiting for a plane from New York. Lincoln Ellsworth is down somewhere about halfway across the Antarctic continent.

Mr. Ross says the last Indians were around here about forty-five years ago; that a stone bola can be thrown about 20 yds. He's seen the Indian women further east catch the *coruros;* they watch the ground, and when they see it move they jump on it with both heels, which kills the animal and then they fish it out [of the ground] with a piece of wire. They get a lot in a short time. There used to be a large number of those rodents around here till the sheep came in and killed them off. A gardener of his used to catch 1,000 foxes a year—now there are hardly any.

Friday, December 13

The ditch drains the water off fairly well, but digging is still pretty difficult. At least there are no *coruro* or skunk burrows to mix up the specimens; they prefer day places.

Saturday, December 14

Calm, warm day.

Sunday, December 15

Fine, calm day. The Rosses came over, bringing a picnic lunch; built a fire on the pampa and roasted a lamb over the coals. With sandwiches, salad, fruit, cake, and so forth it made a meal long to be remembered. They stayed to tea with us in our cave. They also brought some very welcome mail.

Monday, December 16

Very windy. 120 scrapers from one small area!

Tuesday, December 17

Cloudy and showers in A.M. Fair later, with extremely strong wind towards evening. To Carpa Manzana Hotel for a few provisions.

Wednesday, December 18

Somewhat calmer.

Thursday, December 19

The excavation is down 58 in. and digging is very difficult because of the water, in spite of the drain; there is no stream on this side and all the surface water runs down along the cliff. A small pit shows there are specimens down to 7 ft. anyway, and bones down to 8 ft. The small hafted scrapers are made from such pretty stones—smoky white ones, opaque yellow, gray, and so forth, with some jasper and moss agate.

Friday, December 20

Clear, fine day. Mrs. Conroy and Kathleen Detleff from the Trocadero arrived with young Maggie Donaldson, daughter of the manager of one of the sections here. They all stayed to lunch. They had come to bring a letter from Sr. Limacher; the navy is going to buy our boat and there were some papers to sign. Brought us lettuce, spinach, and rhubarb from the *estancia*.

Saturday, December 21

Calm, cloudy day. Last night we heard a noise in the kitchen, and there was a baby hare sitting in the frying pan by the fire! Pop-eyed, with crinkly fur. We hope to keep him as a pet. Made him a little house out of pieces of sod, and tied him to a stake. Longest day of the year; sunset at 9:15 P.M.

Sunday, December 22

Calm and warm. The hare got away last night. Made a fire up on the pampa and roasted three large pieces of meat we had left; it's hard to keep it in this warm weather. In afternoon, walked up towards north end of lake to a sandy windswept place a shepherd had told us of—about one and a quarter hours going. Found many scrapers and four perfect bolas, each one a different type: a rough, very smooth one with a deep narrow groove; one lemon shape with a sort of knob at each end; one oval, with groove running lengthwise; and lastly one made out of volcanic stone, with an *extremely* deep, wide groove—a very queer bola.

Monday, December 23

Calm, sunny and hot in A.M., cloudy in P.M. and a thunderstorm. Rain all evening.

Tuesday, December 24

Light wind, warm. Tried to deflect some of the water at the head of valley, but with no success. Doug killed a hare for our Christmas dinner and Junius, a goose. The latter flew for 40 yds. with a shot right through its heart.

Wednesday, December 25

Christmas Day. Sunny and warm. Just as I was about to bake a rhubarb pie, the Rosses arrived with some guests from town for a picnic; there were eighteen of us in all! Roasted a calf and a lamb and with all the "fixings" including Christmas cake. We had a real feast and they persuaded us to go back with them, leaving poor Doug in charge of the camp. It was a very Christmassy day—a tree, plum pudding that came in blazing, and so forth. Pouring rain all evening [in 1938 Peggy Bird published an article, "Christmas in Patagonia," about this day—ed.].

Thursday, December 26

Still pouring—they haven't seen anything like it for thirty years! They all say this is the most unusual summer for flowers—so very many more than usual. Went to the shed to watch the shearing, which was very interesting. They do about 3,000 sheep a day, with 30 machines. After lunch it cleared and we went on back. Apparently did not rain quite so hard at camp.

Saturday, December 28

Rain all day. Ever since we came there have been two pairs of little russet-throated sparrow-like birds around camp, picking up worms from the excavation, or crumbs from the kitchen. Today one pair brought their big, fat, fluffy greedy babies for the first time.

Sunday, December 29

Fair in A.M. Cloudy later. Roasted the hare and goose we'd had for Xmas.

Tuesday, December 31

Cloudy and rain. A very quiet New Year's Eve!

Wednesday, January 1, 1936

Sunny A.M. Partly cloudy in P.M. The man from the *puesto* came bringing us some pastry his wife had made, and three bottles of beer, as a New Year's present! So after lunch we went over there—in the car this time—and took some pictures of his children. They gave us tea and then insisted on our staying to dinner, and very good it was, too. Had trouble with the clutch on the way back—it kept slipping and we just got here. They had given us a young rooster and a loaf of bread. In the A.M. a shepherd had brought over our mail.

Thursday, January 2

At 9 ft. 1 in. below the surface found a burial with the remains of a skeleton. Spread the bones out to dry; very fragile.

Friday, January 3

Fine day. Lowest part of excavation has to be continually bailed out. The pit goes down in "steps" and each layer has to be left to dry out somewhat before being dug out. Gathered a few mushrooms; they're not very numerous yet. We also had the chicken, pot roasted.

Saturday, January 4

Showers. Below the burial is a layer of fine, clean sand, with a fire pit, bones, scrapers, and so forth.

Sunday, January 5

Fairly calm and clear. Worked on Ford.

Monday, January 6

Calm and sunny in A.M., showers in P.M. Junius worked on the Ford all day while Douglas went on digging. In the evening 6,000 sheep went by on their way to be sheared. They spent the night near us and what a noise. Took pictures of a glorious sunset.

Wednesday, January 8

A few hailstones in P.M. A shepherd brought over our mail.

Thursday, January 9

Cloudy. Mr. Ross and a young Dr. Jepsum came by, bringing us lettuce, radishes, onions, eggs, and bread! Found a fine knife made out of the translucent yellow stone.

Friday, January 10

Very windy with showers in the P.M. A man from the section house came by and said that there was a drought in 1929, and he and some other men dug a well, one m square and 16.3 m deep, and still found no water! We should have been here then. Our job would have been much easier.

Sunday, January 12

Junius was up at 4:30 to finish work on the Ford. We did not get off until about 10:30. When we arrived at the *estancia* we decided to go to the Hotel Rubens, toward Natales, for lunch. On the way we passed Morro Chico, a very striking block of basalt standing up from the plain. A good place for Indians, and they say they find bolas and arrow points there. From there on the country changes, with hills and trees and greenness in place of monotonous yellowish grass. The Rubens is a nice little hotel, with a lovely garden and the largest violets I have ever seen. After lunch we drove on to the top of a hill with a lovely view of Ultima Esperanza Sound and with purple, snow-topped mountains in the distance. Saw an apparent raised beach, about 100 ft. above the water (gauging from a long distance) and extending along it. Went on to visit an old Scotsman at a section of Estancia Tranquillo, which fully lives up to its name. Back to Laguna Blanca about 8:00 P.M. just before a wind and rain storm. It was late and the weather so bad that they didn't have much difficulty in persuading us to spend the night.

Monday, January 13

Strong wind and hard rain, which let up a little soon after breakfast, so we started back, with another sheep and the usual presents of vegetables and bread.

Tuesday, January 14

Found a second burial at same level as other one. Very wet, of course, as there are more than forty gallons of water running every hour! Kept it bailed out and scattered flour over the bones to help dry them so they could be taken out.

Wednesday, January 15

Junius up twice in night bailing the water to keep it from the bones. Worked all day on taking them out; very slow work as they're so fragile. The guanaco bones associated with them are much harder. Cloudy, calm day—some showers. Worked until late, using lantern.

Thursday, January 16

Still taking out bones, with pictures of each step—also drawings. There are apparently seven skeletons. [They] must have been killed in a fight and very hurriedly thrown into a small pit 20 in. by 5 ft. by 3 ft. One was a woman with a baby.

Friday, January 17

Cloudy. A man came by who seemed to be familiar with the Argentine pampa. Said he had seen single bolas used, even on guanaco, but it must, of course, be a crippling blow on the head or else must break a leg. The sheep from this section are back from shearing, looking very bare and funny. The lambs seem almost as big as their mothers, since they still have their wool.

Saturday, January 18

Sun and clouds. Junius took movies of me washing specimens and Doug working.

Sunday, January 19

Sun and wind. Went for mushrooms up a valley inland a ways. Small bushes covered with a daisy-like flower were everywhere—masses of white. Saw a rhea and at least a dozen young in the distance. Showers in evening. Made a map of the canyon (fig. 18).

Monday, January 20

Dug a pit down through sand at bottom of excavation, and found a fire pit 11 ft. below surface, some knives, scrapers, and a combination knife and scraper, like the one we found on Navarino [Island]. Went on to 15 ft., where gravel commenced. Dull and gray; showers passed us to east but we got none until evening.

Tuesday, January 21

Cold; cloudy and showers. Took some measurements: the cliff here is 30 ft. high. In evening walked down to lake and found our camp is 140 ft. above it; "station 1" on the map is 170 ft. and the old beach is 230 ft. Finished digging.

Wednesday, January 22

Sunny and cold. Dug a test pit right in front of the kitchen—no sign of occupation. Classified specimens and packed some. Filled in the trenches and part of the excavation.

Thursday, January 23

Cloudy and showers. Mr. Ross came by and left some mail. Packed up. Could not keep all the fragments of bolas—took pictures of those we discarded. Also, left many of the single-edge flake scrapers behind. The old [Model T] truck will have a load as it is!   *(from M. Bird 1934–1937)*

4. Palli Aike

GENERAL DESCRIPTION

On the pampa between the Straits of Magellan and the Gallegos River, at an elevation of 100 to 200 m above sea level, are numerous small volcanoes and lava flows. The rough, bare lava contrasts so strikingly with the surrounding grass-covered, level ground that the volcanic formations seem new and fresh. Not all the volcanoes have been active at the same time because the lava flows of obviously different ages overlap, and the interiors of the craters also show different degrees of weathering and erosion. There are no historical records, as far as I know, of [volcanic] activity here.

The semicircular lava hill in which Palli Aike Cave is located is beside one of the older craters. The cave is on the north side of the crest, about 168 ft. above the level of the surrounding country, at one end of a cliff which forms the edge of a lava flow about 30 ft. thick (fig. 28). It faces away from the prevailing wind and is very well protected in other directions. The accompanying plans (figs. 29, 30) show its size and shape but hardly do it justice. In every respect it is an ideal shelter, except that there is no water nearby. Sometimes in wet weather a little water can be had in a small crater fifteen minutes' walk to the west, but the nearest permanent supply is a small lagoon several miles away.

Situated as it is, it is easy to see why the accumulation of earth inside has been slow. Wind currents make a strong eddy at the mouth and have prevented the ashes and dirt from piling up there, and as drainage runs off to one side away from the mouth, nothing has ever been washed in.

With such a shelter one would naturally expect considerable midden refuse, and the fact that there is surprisingly little may be due entirely to the scarcity of water. A fair amount of small barberry and other shrubs is available for fuel, and the region abounded with guanaco before the sheep farmers came in. It would seem that it [the cave] has been used only for short stops when traveling through the country.   *(from Bird 1936–1937)*

Fig. 28. Palli Aike during excavation. The site is located in volcanic lava away from the prevailing winds but distant from water.

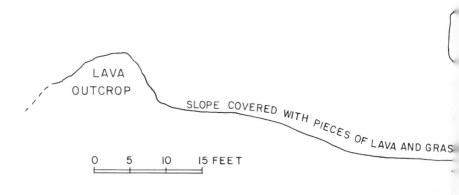

The floor [of Palli Aike Cave] is nearly level, 46 ft. long and about 20 ft. wide, the ceiling 6 ft. high at the rear and 13.5 ft. at the entrance. . . . The accumulation on the floor consisted of extremely fine, dry dust, with less than 10 percent of stones and broken and burnt bones. At a depth of 5 ft. there was a layer of volcanic ash, with a maximum thickness of 2 ft. The floor beneath had been disturbed by large blocks of lava, thrown into the cave at the same time as the ash; 7½ ft. below the surface was the original rock floor of the cave.

In the upper 18 in. we found the same types of things as in the upper 8 ft. of soil at Cañadon Leona. There were no horse bones or other evidence that the present-day Tehuelches had used this place. The finely made Ona-type points were in the upper 6 in. From 18 to 36 in., 319 stemless points were found. From 36 to 60 in., although various types of scrapers were found, there were no stone points, but a few points of bone instead. In the lowest 6 in., over the surface of the underlying volcanic ash, were scattered broken and burnt bones of native American horse, and the ground sloth, and good occupational refuse, yielding stone and bone tools. In all, [approximately] 3,800 artifacts were recovered. On the surface of the volcanic ash, at the base of the wall near the rear of the cave, were three cremation burials, the first human remains accompanied by artifacts in clear association with extinct fauna found in the New World. Embedded

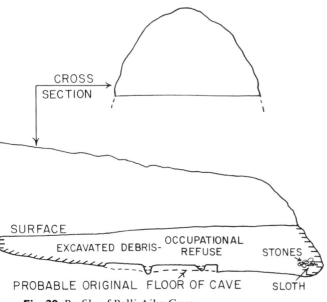

CROSS
SECTION

SURFACE
EXCAVATED DEBRIS-   OCCUPATIONAL
                    REFUSE   STONES
PROBABLE ORIGINAL FLOOR OF CAVE   SLOTH

Fig. 29. Profile of Palli Aike Cave.

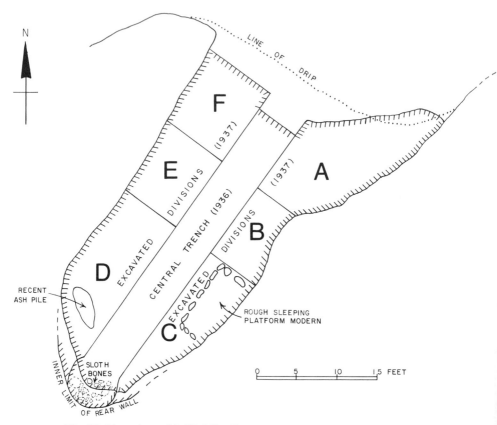

Fig. 30. Plan view of Palli Aike Cave.

in the top part of the volcanic ash was the stem of a type of point not seen previously [later recognized as the stem of a fishtail point—ed.]. A few sloth bones were found mixed with the ash and completely burned. Beneath the ash were parts of at least seven sloth skeletons, with indications that the animals had sheltered and died in the cave. There was nothing to show that the Indians had killed them; but a few stone flakes and some charcoal beneath the volcanic ash down to the original stone floor showed that the Indians had been here. The reason that the cave was not occupied at this early date may be that before the eruption the floor was sloping.

(from Bird 1938a: 268–269)

EXCAVATION IN TWO PHASES

Just before leaving Chilean territory for Argentina in June 1936, we stopped to look at a cave which we had heard of but had not been able to visit before. Known locally as the Palli Aike Cave, it is near the top of an old volcanic crater ridge but is easily accessible. The interior looked promising: a dry, dusty floor about 45 ft. long by 25 ft. wide with plenty of headroom. When, after a few days' digging, it became apparent that we had a deposit dating from at least twice as far back as anything we had found previously, our feelings were a curious mixture of pleasure and despair. Without our regular equipment and with only a few days' supplies left, it was impossible to stay longer. According to the good friend who had been our guide it was questionable how long the track back to Magallanes [Punta Arenas] would be passable. With one assistant it would take at least five weeks to finish the job. More assistants would be impossible without incurring prohibitive expenses. The fine dry dust made the use of masks imperative; a sifter and wheelbarrow would be needed. These and other thoughts came to spoil our pleasure. Moreover, we had not even reached the bottom and there was no telling what might be there. Without the record contained in the dust of this old cave our work would be incomplete. It had to be done somehow.

It was a sad moment when we finally left to continue on through the Argentine, having decided to take a chance on being able to return in the spring. If we had only known how well it would all turn out in the end, how much happier should we have felt [Bird returned the following year and completed the excavation of Palli Aike Cave—ed.].

(from Bird 1938b: 77)

EXCAVATION INFORMATION

In 1936 Bird excavated only the central trench, without removing the cache of sloth bones, in Palli Aike Cave. When he returned the following year he excavated divisions A through F (fig. 30). The following description of the stratigraphy is drawn from Bird's notes (1936–1937) written before he excavated the divisions A to F on the sides of the central trench (fig. 31).

Excepting that part where fires have been made in recent years, the entire surface is covered with dry sheep manure forming a layer about 3 in. thick on the average (fig. 32). Fortunately, sheep are not kept on this part of the farm in winter or there would be more.

Beneath this, to a depth of 2 ft., is what looks like almost pure ashes. This blends into a more brown colored accumulation which extends down to 4½ ft. (fig. 33) containing less ash and more windblown earth. Towards the rear of the cave these divisions cannot be distinguished and the deposit from 3 in. down to 5½ ft. is of uniform structure—ash streaked with windblown earth. For the amount of ash there are surprisingly few bones and

Fig. 31. The beginning of the excavation of the central trench at Palli Aike Cave.

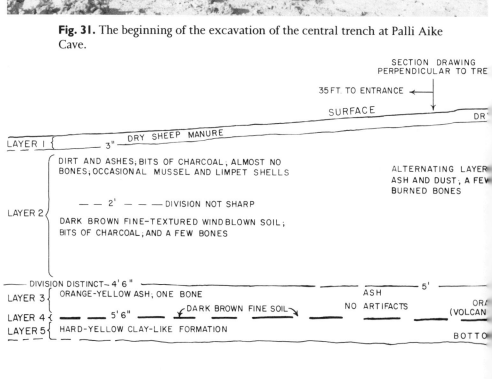

SECTION DRAWING
PERPENDICULAR TO TRE

35 FT. TO ENTRANCE ←

SURFACE

DR

LAYER 1 {   _ 3" DRY SHEEP MANURE

LAYER 2 {

DIRT AND ASHES; BITS OF CHARCOAL; ALMOST NO
BONES; OCCASIONAL MUSSEL AND LIMPET SHELLS

ALTERNATING LAYER
ASH AND DUST; A FEW
BURNED BONES

— — 2' — — —DIVISION NOT SHARP

DARK BROWN FINE-TEXTURED WINDBLOWN SOIL;
BITS OF CHARCOAL; AND A FEW BONES

—— DIVISION DISTINCT— 4' 6" ——   —— 5' ——

LAYER 3 { ORANGE-YELLOW ASH; ONE BONE   ASH

LAYER 4 { — — 5' 6" — — ⟋DARK BROWN FINE SOIL↘   NO ARTIFACTS   OR
                                                                        (VOLCAN

LAYER 5 { HARD-YELLOW CLAY-LIKE FORMATION

BOTTO

bone fragments. As most of those [bones] have been burned it is probable
that the part of the floor excavated had been used as a fire hearth.

For the correct reconstruction of the history of the cave, much depends
upon the exact determination of what the next layer (no. 3, between 4.5
and 5.5 ft.) consists of. At first I thought it was volcanic ash as it apparently covers the entire floor of the cave and is of uniform composition.
However, it has the appearance of having been burned just as it lies, and a
calcined bone imbedded in the center of it favors this suggestion. In this
case might it have been a deposit of dry manure which caught fire and
burned, as happened in the large cave at Estancia Markatch Aike just over
the Argentine border? There the manure was ignited by a shepherd starting
a campfire on the floor and continued to burn about ten days [later, in
publications, Bird always described layer 3 as volcanic ash—ed.].

By washing a sample from layer 3 it was found to contain considerable
sand and a number of small pebbles up to the size of a pea. A slight percentage of it is soluble.

Beneath this there is a streak of soil, varying in thickness from 2 in. to
nothing, and resembling the dirt between 2 and 4.5 ft. in texture. This
covers what seems to have been the original floor of the cave, composed of
pieces of lava imbedded in a yellowish clay (?) which breaks into a powder
when dislodged.

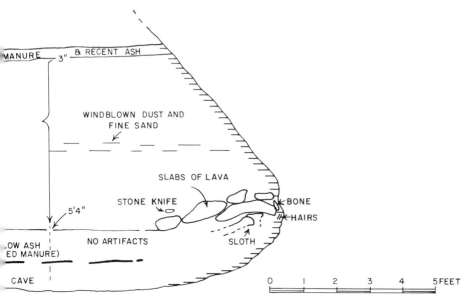

Fig. 32. Section drawing of the central trench at Palli Aike Cave (middle and
inner parts, view to east).

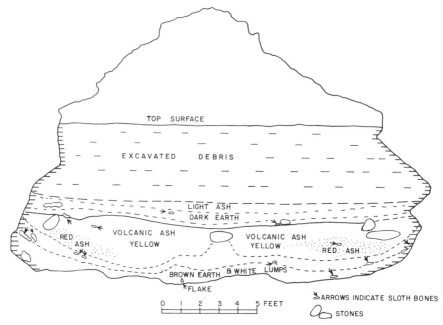

TOP SURFACE

EXCAVATED DEBRIS

LIGHT ASH
DARK EARTH
RED ASH   VOLCANIC ASH   VOLCANIC ASH
                 YELLOW   YELLOW   RED ASH
                      BROWN EARTH & WHITE LUMPS
                         FLAKE

0 1 2 3 4 5 FEET

ARROWS INDICATE SLOTH BONES
STONES

Fig. 33. Section 35 ft. in from entrance of Palli Aike Cave.

For about the first 15 ft. [from the front, or entrance] of the trench, layers 3 and 4 were excavated but as no chips, charcoal, bones, or artifacts were found in them it was concluded that human occupation began at the surface of layer 3. From then on, the bottom of the excavation [of the central] trench followed this with an occasional hole deeper to see what was below.

After the excavations of divisions A through F in 1937, Bird wrote the following notes, giving some special details concerning the composition of the debris at various levels below 24 in.

Divisions C and D—24 to 30 in.

Contained many broken, burned bird bones, fox bones, much less guanaco, many more stone flakes and chips than the ground above. No skunk bones seen.

Division C—30 to 36 in.

Mixture of bones continues the same with bird bones predominating. Many small bits of lava dirt next to wall. Human bones, burned, coming from dirt along wall; small fragments of large bone from dirt along wall, rear of C adjoining B—probably sloth.

Towards rear wall adjoining B, dirt was not removed quite parallel with surface, cutting down 4 or 6 in. deeper than along side of trench, and as volcanic ash is slightly higher against this wall the pieces of sloth bone found were not more than 6 in. at the most from the surface of the volcanic ash.

Division D—30 to 36 in.

Fragment human jaw, center of D, against rear wall, amongst ashes.

Divisions B, C, D, and E—36 to 42 in.

Broken bones continue to come in same proportion to the dirt as in the two levels above; [also] fox, bird, guanaco. A fragment of horse bone in D.

Divisions B, C, D, and E—42 to 48 in.

Avistruce [rhea] bones—first seen since surface layer—but a few.

Division C—42 to 48 in.

The long, perfect spear point and the other point from same division were found almost together between 42 and 45 in. below surface at very rear of cave where there is still over a foot of earth between them and the volcanic ash. Apparently there are no "old-type" points within a foot of the ash, although the material contains a good proportion of scrapers and bones. Practically all of the sloth bones have been coming out of the dirt at the outer ends of C and D, where the level 42 to 48 in. is in contact with the volcanic ash. *(from Bird 1936–1937)*

THE ARTIFACTS

Tables

Tables 3 to 13 list the artifacts found in the various levels at Palli Aike Cave. The central trench was dug in 1-ft. levels, measured from the surface. Divisions A through F were excavated at approximately 6-in. levels. Likewise, the depth measurements were made from the original surface of the cave.

Palli Aike Cave produced more projectile points and small hafted (thumbnail) scrapers than any other cave/shelter excavated by Bird. Figures 34, 35, and 36 depict Period III, IV, and V points. Taken by Bird, these photographs include an occasional specimen from Fell's Cave, or from surface collections made north of the Straits of Magellan. The one fishtail point from Palli Aike, a stem fragment, is depicted in figs. 57 and 58 in chapter 5.

Hafted scrapers are shown in figure 37. Ornaments and beads from the upper layers of Palli Aike appear in figure 16 in chapter 2.

Table 3. Artifacts from Central Trench, Palli Aike Cave

Group	Category	Level						
		Uncer-tain	Surface to 1'	1–2'	2–3'	3–4'	Below 4'	To
Points	Old-type (stemless)	–	1	2	14	–	–	
	Hafted knife	6	3	–	–	–	–	
	Hafted knife or spear point	–	2	–	–	–	–	
	Knife or spear	1	–	–	–	–	–	
	Spear, flat base	1	3	6	9	–	–	
	Spear, rounded base	–	–	–	2	–	–	
Knives	Leaf-shaped	–	1	–	–	–	–	
	Elliptical	–	–	1	–	–	1	
	Blank (of above?)	–	–	7	7	–	–	
Scrapers	Rough, single-edge flake	23	90	61	27	33	1	2:
	2-sided, flake irregular	2	6	12	6	–	–	:
	Rough flake, 2 sides to point	–	6	5	–	–	–	
	Rough flake, rounded edge	–	–	2	4	4	–	
	Well-made, 2 sides	–	7	8	2	1	–	
	Well-made, parallel sides	–	–	3	1	–	–	
	Small, well-made, 2 sides	–	1	–	1	–	2	
	Large, end	–	2	2	3	1	–	
	Small, hafted	19	29	12	3	–	–	
	Combination knife-scraper	–	–	–	4	2	–	
Bolas	Unfinished	–	–	2	–	–	–	
	Large, spherical	–	1	1	–	–	–	
	Flattened	–	–	1	–	–	–	
	Small	–	1	3	3	3	–	
	Plum-shaped	–	2	–	–	–	–	
	Mortar stone fragment	–	2	–	–	–	–	

		Level						
oup	Category	Uncer-tain	Surface to 1'	1-2'	2-3'	3-4'	Below 4'	Total
ɔne ɔols	Awl	1	–	–	–	–	–	1
	Chipping tool	–	1	–	–	–	–	1
	Small, round, flat bead	–	1	–	–	–	–	1
	Totals	53	159	128	86	44	4	474

ɔrtain = From surface about mouth of cave and outer 10' of trench.   Total stone artifacts = 472.
                                                                        Total bone artifacts =   2.

The Stemless Points

The following text (Bird 1960*a*) is a discussion of a set of points which came from Fell's Cave and Palli Aike. The text raises some questions which were answered in part by Don E. Crabtree in a 1970 publication. Portions of Crabtree's article are excerpted following Bird's text.

Period III Points

The projectile and knife points selected for the accompanying photograph (fig. 36) were chosen for various reasons. The upper four rows illustrate the full range in size and all the variations in form and detail present among the recovered specimens. All in the bottom row retain traces of the cement with which they were hafted.

The first four in the top row are of obsidian. That they represent the smallest in size range is due to this fact, and is not a matter of design or preference on the part of the makers. Only small pieces of obsidian seem to be available in this area, for in the collections studied south of Santa Cruz, there were no large points, blades, or implements of this material. All the others, with one exception in the bottom row, are of basalt. Basalt is locally abundant and, judging from associated woodworking sidescrapers, was available in sufficiently large pieces so that if larger points had been desired, they could have been made. Hence the specimen at the right in row 4 is definitely an extreme, and ones like it should not be frequently encountered.

The first specimen at the left in row 2 exhibits the maximum concavity of base line. Such slight incurve occurs rarely, and the majority of the bases are definitely convex in profile. At the opposite extreme is the

Table 4. Artifacts from Divisions A to F, Palli Aike Cave, from Surface to 6 Inches below Surface

Group	Category	Uncertain[a]	Div. A		Div. B		Div. C	
			S–6"	Wall	S–6"	Wall	S–6"	Wall
Points	Ona	2	1	2	–	–	1	–
	Unfinished Ona	2	–	–	–	–	–	–
	Patagonian	11	3	–	–	–	6	–
	Old-type (stemless)	92	–	–	–	1	1	–
	Small, rudimentary stem	–	1	1	–	–	–	–
	Fragment	3	3	–	1	–	–	–
	Unfinished	1	–	–	–	–	3	1
	Spear	10	3	–	1	–	1	–
	Questionable spear	2	–	–	–	–	–	–
Knives	Hafted	37	6	–	5	–	9	–
	"Natural"	–	–	–	–	–	1	1
	Single-edge, leaf-shaped	–	–	–	–	–	–	–
	Combination knife-scraper	4	–	–	–	–	–	–
Scrapers	Rough, single-edge flake	235	15	–	23	7	48	21
	2-sided, narrow	28	–	–	2	1	3	1
	2-sided, large	8	3	–	–	–	–	–
	1-edge (like 2-sided)	14	–	–	–	–	–	–
	2 sides to point	4	–	–	–	1	–	1
	Large, circular edge	4	–	–	–			–
	End	7	–	–	1	–	1	1
	Blank	14	–	–	–	–	3	–
	Small, hafted	174	42	3	31	3	25	25
	Grooving scraper[a]	1	–	–	–	–	–	–
Bolas	Unfinished spherical	7	–	–	–	–	–	–
	Spherical	1	–	–	–	–	–	–
	Fragment, spherical	1	–	–	–	–	–	–

Div. D		Div. E		Div. F		Total
S–6"	Wall	S–6"	Wall	S–6"	Wall	
–	–	–	–	–	–	6
–	–	–	–	–	–	2
3	–	–	–	1	–	24
–	1	1	–	–	–	96
1	–	–	–	–	–	3
–	–	–	–	–	–	7
3	27	–	–	–	–	35
–	–	–	–	1	–	16
–	–	–	–	–	–	2
16	2	3	–	1	–	79
–	–	–	–	–	–	2
–	–	–	1	–	–	1
–	–	–	–	1	1	6
34	16	4	–	7	–	410
5	2	1	1	–	–	44
–	–	–	–	–	–	11
–	–	–	–	–	–	14
–	–	–	–	–	–	6
–	–	–	–	–	–	4
1	1	–	–	–	–	12
3	–	–	–	–	–	20
25	11	2	2	8	1	352
–	–	–	–	–	–	1
–	1	–	–	–	–	8
–	–	–	–	–	–	1
1	–	–	–	–	–	2

Table 4. *(continued)*

Group	Category	Uncer-tain[a]	Div. A S–6"	Div. A Wall	Div. B S–6"	Div. B Wall	Div. C S–6"	Div. C Wall
Bolas	Elliptical, bird	2	–	–	–	–	–	–
	Egg-shaped	4	–	–	–	–	–	–
	Grooved pebble	2	–	–	–	–	–	–
	Rough, irregular, perforated	1	–	–	–	–	–	–
Mortar, Rubbing Stones	Fragment, mortar	–	1	–	–	1	–	–
	Fragment, rubbing	3	–	–	–	–	–	–
Bone Tools	Whale bone	2	–	–	–	–	–	–
	Awl	1	–	–	–	–	–	–
	Chipping tool	6	6	1	–	–	1	–
Ornaments	Bird bone bead	–	–	–	–	–	–	–
	Fissurela shell bead	1	–	–	–	–	–	–
	Unknown bone object	1	–	–	–	–	–	–
	Stone bead	–	–	–	–	–	–	–
	Shell bead	–	–	–	–	–	–	–
	Scratched pebble	1	–	–	2	2	–	1
	Totals	686	91		82		155	

[a]From surface in and near cave.
S = Surface.

Div. D		Div. E		Div. F		Total
S–6"	Wall	S–6"	Wall	S–6"	Wall	
–	–	–	–	–	–	2
–	–	–	–	–	–	4
–	–	–	–	–	–	2
–	–	–	–	–	–	1
–	–	–	–	–	–	2
–	2	–	–	–	–	5
–	1	–	–	–	–	3
1	–	1	–	–	–	3
4	1	1	–	–	–	20
2	–	–	–	–	–	2
–	1	–	–	–	–	2
–	–	–	–	–	–	1
1	–	–	–	–	–	1
2	–	–	–	–	–	2
2	2	–	–	–	–	10
172		17		21		1,224

Total stone artifacts = 1,191.
Total bone artifacts =   29.
Total shell artifacts =   4.

Table 5. Artifacts from Divisions A to F, Palli Aike Cave, from 6 to 10 Inches below Surface

Group	Category	Div. A 6–10″	Div. A Wall	Div. B 6–10″	Div. B Wall	Div. C 6–10″	Div. C W.
Points	Patagonian	–	–	–	1	3	–
	Old-type (stemless)	–	–	–	–	–	
	Fragment	–	–	–	–	1	–
	Unfinished	1	2	–	–	–	–
	Spear	–	–	–	–	1	–
Knives	Hafted	1	–	–	–	10	–
	Fragment of hafted	–	–	–	–	–	–
	Elliptical	1	–	–	–	–	
	Combination knife-scraper	–	–	–	–	2	–
Scrapers	Rough, single-edge flake	18	–	8	4	70	3
	2-sided, narrow	1	–	–	–	3	
	2-sided, large	–	–	–	–	–	
	2 sides to point	1	1	–	–	4	
	End	–	–	–	–	1	
	Blank	–	–	–	–	1	–
	Small, hafted	30	3	17	–	50	
Bolas	Fragment, spherical	1	–	–	–	1	
	Lemon-shaped	1	–	–	–	–	
	Unfinished, spherical	2	–	–	–	–	
Hammer, Mortar, Rubbing Stones	Pitted hammerstone	–	–	–	–	–	
	Fragment, mortar stone	3	–	–	–	–	
	Fragment, rubbing stone	–	–	–	–	1	
Bone Tools	Chipping tool	–	–	–	–	1	
	Awl	1	–	–	–	1	
Ornaments	Bone pendant	–	–	–	–	–	
	Fissurela shell bead	–	–	–	–	–	
	Disk pendant	–	–	–	–	–	
	Fragment, decorated shoulder blade	–	–	–	–	–	
	Totals	67		30		224	

[a]Many fragments.

Div. D		Div. E		Div. F		Total
6–10″	Wall	6–10″	Wall	6–10″	Wall	
–	–	–	–	–	–	4
–	–	–	–	–	–	2
–	–	1	–	–	–	2
–	–	–	–	–	–	3
–	–	–	–	–	–	1
2	–	1	–	3	1	18
1	–	–	–	–	–	1
–	–	–	–	–	–	1
–	–	–	–	2	1	5
45	16	13	2	7	1	222
1	2	–	1	–	–	15
–	–	2	–	–	–	4
1	–	–	–	1	–	9
3	3	–	–	–	–	9
–	–	–	–	–	–	1
37	6	10	2	24	–	195
1	1	1	–	–	–	6
–	–	–	–	–	–	1
–	–	–	–	–	–	4
–	1	1	–	–	–	2
–	–	–	–	–	–	3
–	1	1	–	–	–	3
–	–	–	1	–	–	2
1	–	–	–	–	–	3
–	–	–	–	–	–	1
1	–	–	–	–	–	2
–	1	–	–	–	–	1
–	–	–	–	–	–	1
124		36		40		521

Total stone artifacts = 511. Total bone artifacts = 8.
Total shell artifacts = 2.

Table 6. Artifacts from Divisions A to F, Palli Aike Cave, from 10 to 15 or 17 Inches below Surface

		Div. A		Div. B		Div. C	
Group	Category	10–15"	Wall	10–17"	Wall	10–17"	Wall
Points	Patagonian	–	–	–	–	1	–
	Old-type (stemless)	–	–	–	1	3	–
	Fragment	1	–	2	–	–	–
	Spear	–	–	–	–	–	–
Knives	Hafted	–	–	–	1	1	–
	"Natural"	–	–	–	1	–	–
	Combination knife-scraper	–	–	–	–	1	–
Scrapers	Rough, single-edge flake	9	1	12	6	66	6
	2-sided, narrow	2	–	3	1	9	2
	2-sided, large	–	–	–	–	–	–
	2 sides to point	–	–	–	–	2	1
	End	–	–	–	–	–	–
	Small, hafted	9	–	2	4	36	2
	Blank	–	–	–	3	–	–
Bolas	Fragment, spherical	–	–	–	1	2	–
	Elliptical, bird	2	–	–	–	–	–
	Unfinished elliptical	2	–	–	–	–	–
Mortar, Rubbing Stones	Fragment, mortar	–	–	–	–	–	–
	Cylindrical rubbing stone	1	–	–	–	–	–
Bone Tools	Chipping tool	–	–	–	–	–	–
Ornaments	*Fissurela* shell bead	–	–	–	–	–	–
	Notched shell	–	–	–	–	–	–
	Totals	27		37		132	

Div. D		Div. E		Div. F		Total
10–17"	Wall	10–17"	Wall	10–15"	Wall	
–	–	–	–	–	–	1
3	1	1	–	–	–	9
–	–	–	–	–	–	3
–	–	1	–	–	–	1
–	–	–	–	–	–	2
–	–	–	–	–	–	1
1	–	–	–	–	–	2
46	10	17	3	7	1	184
7	3	–	1	–	–	28
3	–	–	–	–	–	3
2	–	–	–	–	–	5
2	–	–	–	–	–	2
9	5	3	1	11	2	84
–	–	–	–	–	–	3
1	1	–	–	1	–	6
–	–	–	–	–	–	2
–	–	–	–	–	–	2
–	–	–	–	1	–	1
–	–	–	–	–	–	1
–	–	–	–	1	–	1
1	1	–	–	–	–	2
1	–	–	–	–	–	1
97		27		24		344

Total stone artifacts = 340.
Total bone artifacts =   1.
Total shell artifacts =   3.

Table 7. Artifacts from Divisions A to F, Palli Aike Cave, from 15 or 17 to 24 Inches below Surface

Group	Category	Div. A 15–24"	Wall	Div. B 17–24"	Wall	Div. C 17–24"	Wall
Points	Old-type (stemless)	1	–	4	–	18	24
	Fragment	3	–	–	–	–	–
	Unfinished	–	–	–	–	–	1
	Spear	–	–	–	–	–	1
Knives	Hafted	–	–	1	–	–	–
	"Natural"	–	–	1	–	–	–
	Elliptical	–	–	–	–	1	–
	Combination knife-scraper	–	–	1	–	1	–
Scrapers	Rough, single-edge flake	3	–	3	4	49	9
	2-sided, narrow	–	–	3	–	11	1
	2-sided, large	–	–	–	1	3	–
	2 sides to point	–	–	–	–	2	–
	Large, circular edge	–	–	–	–	1	–
	End	–	–	–	–	2	–
	Blank	–	–	–	–	–	2
	Small, hafted	4	–	1	–	8	–
Bolas	Fragment, spherical	–	–	–	–	1	1[a]
	Large, spherical	–	–	–	–	–	–
	Elliptical, bird	–	–	–	–	3	1
	Rough, irregular	–	–	1	–	1	–
	Unfinished	–	–	3	–	2	–
	Grooved pebble	–	–	1	–	–	–
	Small hammerstones	–	–	–	–	–	–
	Flat rubbing stones	–	–	–	–	–	1
	Chisel-like rib bone	–	–	–	–	–	1
	Totals	11		24		145	

[a]All small.

Div. D		Div. E		Div. F		Total
17–24″	Wall	17–24″	Wall	15–24″	Wall	
7	3	3	1	–	–	61
–	–	–	–	–	–	3
–	1	–	–	–	–	2
–	–	–	–	–	–	1
–	–	–	–	–	–	1
–	–	–	–	–	–	1
–	1	–	–	–	–	2
1	–	–	–	–	–	3
41	6	10	–	2	2	129
7	1	4	–	2	–	29
2	–	–	–	–	–	6
2	1	–	–	–	–	5
–	–	–	–	–	–	1
–	–	–	–	–	–	2
–	1	1	–	–	–	4
7	–	–	1	3	1	25
1	–	3[a]	–	1[a]	–	7
1	1	–	–	1	–	3
2	–	–	1	–	–	7
1	1	–	–	–	–	4
1	–	–	–	1	–	7
–	–	–	–	–	–	1
1	–	–	–	–	–	1
–	–	–	–	–	–	1
–	–	–	–	–	–	1
90		24		13		307

Total stone artifacts = 306.
Total bone artifacts =   1.

Table 8. Artifacts from Divisions B to E, Palli Aike Cave, from 24 to 30 Inches below Surface

Group	Category	Div. B 24–30"	Wall	Div. C 24–30"	Wall	Div. D 24–30"	Wall	Div. E 24–30"	Wall	Tot
Points	Old-type (stemless)	1	–	74	4	28	8	1	–	11
	Stemmed	1	–	–	–	–	–	1	–	
	Spear	–	–	–	–	1ª	–	–	–	
Knives	Hafted	–	–	–	–	3ª	1	–	–	
	Combination knife-scraper	–	–	1	–	1	–	–	–	
Scrapers	Rough, single-edge flake	4	–	48	4	30	4	8	3	10
	2-sided, narrow	–	–	9	–	7	2	–	–	1
	2-sided, large	–	–	2	–	2	–	1	–	
	2 sides to point	–	–	2	–	–	–	1	–	
	Circular edge	–	–	2	–	–	–	–	–	
	End	–	–	1	1	–	–	–	–	
	1-edge (like 2-sided)	–	–	16	–	–	–	–	–	1
	Small, hafted	–	–	9	1	5	–	–	–	1
	Blank	–	–	18	1	6	2	1	–	2
Bolas	Unfinished, spherical	1	–	1	–	1	–	2	–	
	Elliptical, bird	–	–	1	–	–	–	–	–	
	Unfinished, elliptical	–	–	–	–	3	–	–	–	
	Fragment, shape uncertain	–	–	5	–	–	–	–	–	
	Fragment, spherical	–	–	–	–	–	–	–	–	
	Irregular shape	–	–	–	–	–	–	1	–	
	Bone chipping tool	–	–	1	–	–	–	–	–	
	Totals	7		201		104		19		33

ªRodent burrow, possibly intrusive.

Total stone artifacts =
Total bone artifacts =

le 9. Artifacts from Divisions B to E, Palli Aike Cave, from 30 to 36 Inches below Surface

Category	Div. B 30–36″	Div. B Wall	Div. C 30–36″	Div. C Wall	Div. D 30–36″	Div. D Wall	Div. E 30–36″	Div. E Wall	Total
Old-type (stemless)	1	–	33	1	38	8	5	–	86
Stemmed	–	–	2	–	–	–	–	–	2
Combination knife-scraper	–	–	2	1	8	1	–	–	12
Rough, single-edge flake	6	–	26	8	26	3	–	–	69
1 edge (like 2-sided)	–	–	6	–	1	–	–	–	7
2-sided, narrow	–	–	3	–	3	–	–	–	6
2-sided, large	–	–	1	–	–	1	–	–	2
2 sides to point	–	–	–	1	–	–	–	–	1
Circular edge	–	–	–	1	1	–	–	–	2
End	1	–	–	–	3	–	–	–	4
Small, hafted	–	–	1	–	2	–	–	–	3
Blank	–	–	6	–	9	2	–	–	17
Fragment, spherical	–	–	–	–	1	–	1	–	2
Elliptical, bird	–	–	1	–	–	–	–	–	1
Fragment, elliptical, bird	–	–	–	–	1	–	–	–	1
Fragment, rough	–	–	1	–	–	–	–	–	1
Grooved pebble	1	–	1	–	–	–	–	–	2
Awl	–	–	–	–	1	–	–	–	1
Chipping tool	–	–	–	–	1	–	–	–	1
Totals	9		95		110		6		220

Total stone artifacts = 218.
Total bone artifacts = 2.

Table 10. Artifacts from Divisions B to E, Palli Aike Cave, from 36 to 42 Inches below Surface

Group	Category	Div. B 36–42"	Wall	Div. C 36–42"	Wall	Div. D 36–42"	Wall	Div. E 36–42"	Wall	Tot.
	Old-type (stemless) point	–	–	2	–	1	–	–	–	
Knives	Single-edge flake	–	–	–	–	1	–	–	–	
	Combination knife-scraper	–	–	–	–	1	–	–	–	
	Blank	–	–	3	–	–	–	–	–	
Scrapers	Rough, single-edge flake	1	–	30	6	35	12	4	–	8.
	2-sided, narrow	–	–	2	–	–	–	2	–	
	2-sided, large	–	–	1	1	–	–	–	–	
	Circular edge	–	–	4	–	3	–	–	–	
	End	–	–	1	–	3	1	–	–	
	Combination side and end	–	–	1	1	2	–	2	–	
	Small, hafted	–	–	–	–	3	–	–	–	
Bolas	Unfinished, small	–	–	–	–	2	–	–	–	
	Small, elliptical	–	–	3	–	–	–	–	–	
	Possible whetstone	–	–	–	2	–	–	–	–	
Bone Tools	Bird bone awl	1	–	1	–	1	–	1	–	
	Solid bone awl	–	–	–	–	1	–	–	–	
	Unknown bone implement	–	–	2	–	–	–	–	–	
	Totals	2		60		66		9		13

Horse and sloth bones appear in B and D at this level.

Total stone artifacts =
Total bone artifacts =

le II. Artifacts from Divisions B, C, and D, Palli Aike Cave, from 42 to 48 Inches below Surface

oup	Category	Div. B		Div. C		Div. D		Total
		42–48″	*Wall*	*42–48″*	*Wall*	*42–48″*	*Wall*	
	Old-type (stemless) point	–	–	–	2	–	–	2
nives	Single-edge flake	–	–	–	–	1	–	1
	Combination knife-scraper	–	–	–	–	1	–	1
apers	Rough, single-edge	3	–	26	6	25	5	65
	2-sided, large	–	–	3	1	3	1	8
	2 sides to point	1	–	–	–	–	–	1
	1-edge (like 2-sided)	–	–	–	–	1	–	1
	Large, circular edge	–	–	2	–	1	–	3
	Combination side and end	–	–	1	–	–	–	1
	End	–	–	–	–	1	–	1
	Blank	–	–	–	–	2	–	2
	Fragment, rubbing stone	–	–	1	–	–	–	1
one ools	Small bird bone awl	–	–	1	–	1	1	3
	Solid bone awl	–	–	–	–	–	1	1
	Unknown bone implement	–	–	1	–	–	–	1
	Totals	4		44		44		92

Total stone artifacts = 87.
Total bone artifacts = 5.

Table 12. Artifacts from Divisions C and D, Palli Aike Cave, from 48 Inches to Surface of Ash or 54 Inches

Group	Category	Div. C 20–25' 48"–S of Ash	Div. C 25–35' 48–54"	Div. C 35'–R 48–54"	Div. D 20–25' 48"–S of Ash	Div. D 25–35' 48–54"	Div. D 35'–R 48–54"	Distance Beginning of Trench Total
Knives	Oval	–	–	1	–	–	–	1
Knives	Small combination knife-scraper	–	1	–	–	1	–	2
Knives	Knife-scraper	–	2	–	–	–	–	2
Scrapers	Rough, single-edge flake	–	4	7	–	5	3	19
Scrapers	Rough, single-edge flake, small	–	1	–	3	–	–	4
Scrapers	2 edges, small	–	3	–	–	–	1	4
Scrapers	2-sided	–	1	1	–	1	1	4
Scrapers	2-sided, variant	–	–	–	–	3	–	3
Scrapers	Circular edge	–	–	1	1	–	–	2
Scrapers	End	–	1	–	–	2	–	3
Scrapers	Flake	–	1	1	1	9	–	12
Scrapers	Core	–	–	–	1	–	–	1
Bone Tools	Small bird bone awl	–	–	–	–	4	1	5
Bone Tools	Fox bone awl	–	–	–	–	3	1	4
Bone Tools	Solid bone awl	1	–	–	–	–	–	1
Bone Tools	Unknown bone implement	–	–	–	1	1	–	2
Bone Tools	Unfinished bone	–	–	–	–	1	–	1
	Totals		26			44		70

R = Rear of cave.   Total stone artifacts = 57.
S = Surface.   Total bone artifacts = 13.

Table 13. Artifacts from Divisions C and D, Palli Aike Cave, from Surface of Ash, into Ash or from 54 Inches to Surface of Ash, or from 54 to 60 Inches

		Div. C		Div. D		
		20–35′	35′–R	20–35′	35′–R	{ Distance to Beginning of Trench
Group	Category	S of Ash into Ash	54–60″	S of Ash	54–60″	Total
	Fishtail point	–	–	1	–	1
	Rough, single-edge flake, small	1	3	5	1[a]	10
Scrapers	2-edges reversed, large	–	–	–	1[a]	1
	2-edges reversed, small	–	1	–	–	1
	Flake	–	1	3	–	4
	Bird bone awl	–	–	–	1	1
	Totals	6		12		18

R = Rear of cave.   Total stone artifacts = 17.
S = Surface.   Total bone artifacts = 1.
Below 60″ but above surface of ash.
A bird bone awl was found in Division F at 54 to 60″ below the top surface.

Fig. 34. Period V Ona points. Top two rows show range of patterns. Bottom row depicts Ona arrows from Tierra del Fuego with the same type of points.

angled base of the first point in row 3. Enough samples of this variation exist—one of them even more sharply angled—to indicate that a few should appear in any good series from the period. They cannot be classed as a type for the variations blend into the convex base form, as shown by the four specimens in row 3.

The photograph shows all the variations present in the side edges. Some are straight, the majority are slightly convex, and some, like the second from the right in row 4, are in part parallel-sided. As all intermediate variations in form exist, there is little basis for assuming that this last-mentioned specimen is a type. Like those with angular bases, it marks another extreme in form variation.

Edges exhibit considerable difference in the nature of the chipping and retouching. Serrated side edges are fairly frequent and, as the base profiles are smoother, we can assume that this serrating was deliberate and inten-

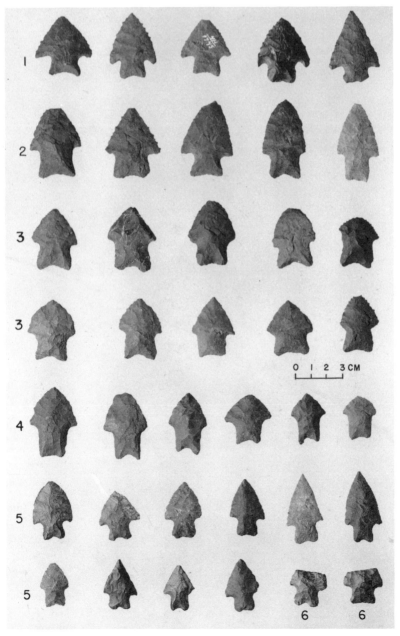

Fig. 35. Period IV stemmed (Patagonian) points. Rows 1 and 2 are knife or spear points. Rows 3 and 4 are hafted knives. No. 5 depicts arrow points. Points marked no. 6 are resharpened.

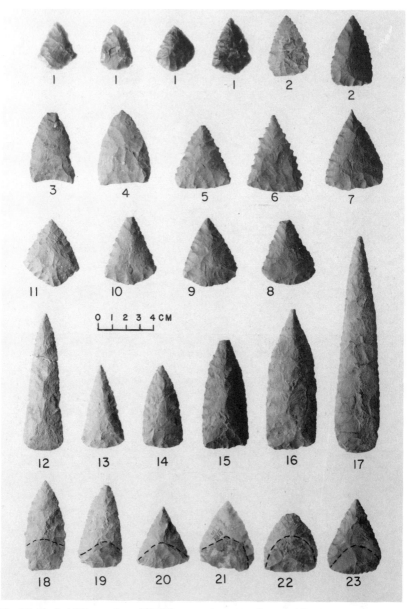

Fig. 36. Period III stemless (Old Type) points: (1) four small, thick, poorly made obsidian points; (2) smallest points made of basalt; (3–17) range of stemless points from the rare concave base (no. 3) through slightly convex and common concave bases (nos. 5 to 9) to no. 11, which has a two-sided base; points 15 and 16 have parallel sides; no. 17 is the largest point found; (18–23) points with traces of hafting cement (below dashed lines).

Fig. 37. Small hafted (thumbnail) scrapers from Period IV and Period V. First left vertical row has flaking on entire circumference. Second vertical row has flaking on end and side. Third and fourth vertical rows (on right) have flaking across one edge. These small tools are often referred to as snub-nose endscrapers.

tional. The fourth specimen in row 2 shows the maximum development of side serration.

Where the tip is intact, it will be noted that they tend to be finished with a very sharp and sometimes quite fine point.

Curiously, not a single chipping tool or flaker was found in association with Period III points, although flakers are abundant in the overlying deposits of Period IV and Period V. What are considered to be broken examples of a distinctly different type occur with Period I [fishtail] points, so their absence in association with the points under discussion is a mystery. Could flakers of wood have been used? This is the one material which has totally disappeared from the Period III levels in the caves. Whatever was used, the chipping seems to have produced a distinctive result, namely, points which have, as a rule, a rather steep edge angle. This is hard to describe or define, but might be a measurable feature.

The points retaining traces of cement fail to show any impression of handles or shafts, and until hafted examples are encountered, it will be difficult to make any decision about function. Among the associated artifacts, there are so few bilaterally chipped flake tools, which might be classified as knives, that some of the points might have been knife blades. If so, some of these must have been resharpened and had their outlines modified in the process. Which these may be cannot yet be decided.

As regards the balance—probably the majority—I am inclined to believe that only spear or dart points are represented, and that none were for arrows. The width of the bases and the pattern of cement distribution suggest attachment to shafts considerably larger than the average for arrows.

Crabtree's Analysis

Bird supplied seven examples of the Period III stemless pressure-flaked points (from Palli Aike) made of basalt and varieties of siliceous stone to D. E. Crabtree, who experimented with the use of wooden flaking implements to make them (Crabtree 1970). Bird also provided a variety of *calafate* hardwood (*Berberis buxifolia*) and a small supply of the native coarse-grained basalt. Crabtree notes that "the use of wooden flaking implements has rarely been considered, because such percussion or pressure-flaking tools do not usually survive in archaeological deposits." He presents a detailed account of his experiment and includes information from Australia, where the use of wooden pressure-flakers is known. He concludes (1970: 153):

> After working with the wooden flaker and producing some acceptable replicas with characteristics similar to aboriginal flake scars, I believe it is entirely possible that the Period III Palli Aike points were pressure-flaked with a wooden tool. I would suggest, therefore, that the geographic range of the wooden pressure-flaker technique should not be confined to Australia.

POSSIBLE AGE OF DEPOSIT

The following paragraph was written by Bird in 1936 or 1937 well before radiocarbon dating had been invented.

If we assume that the cultural change apparent here [in Palli Aike Cave] occurred more or less at the same time as at Cañadon Leona, sixty miles to the west across easily traversed country, we have a basis for computing a possible age for this deposit. There we have a maximum accumulation of 3 in. of soil in forty or forty-five years, giving a minimum of 800 to 900 and a maximum of 1,600 to 1,800 years since the old [stemless point] culture was replaced by the new. Here that same period is represented by a maximum 9-in. layer or one-seventh of the total. If the rate of accumulation has been constant, we have a minimum of 5,600 to 6,300 and a maximum of 10,360 to 11,585 years since the Indians covered the [sloth] skeleton with stones. From this we might take 7,500 years as a fair guess but it is offered only for what it is worth, as something slightly better than mere speculation.

After radiocarbon dating had been developed, Bird selected a sample of burned sloth, horse, and guanaco bones from a few inches above the surface of the thick layer of volcanic ash and from within the ash and submitted them to Willard Libby's Chicago laboratory. They were processed by the solid carbon method and yielded the date (C 485) of 8639 ± 450 B.P. or 6689 ± 450 B.C. (Bird 1951: 44). For that sample Bird submitted 3,252 grams of bone, specimens with field numbers P. 21, 25, 27, 28, 30, and 31. Bird always felt that the date was too recent and noted that Libby had experimented with a new technique when extracting the sample. Subsequent radiocarbon dates of sloth dung (Markgraf 1985) indicate that the 8639 date is probably too young.

FAUNAL REMAINS

Sloth Cache

At the very rear of the cave the debris was so dry that bits of grass and feathers were well preserved all the way down, and it was hoped that some specimens might have been left or lost here which would not have been preserved elsewhere, but nothing we had not already seen was found until we neared the bottom. Here a loose pile of lava rocks was uncovered which attracted attention by the fact that they were smoothed and rounded, either by weathering or more probably worn so at the time of some eruption. As the whole inner surface of the cave is just as it was when the lava cooled, rough and twisted, with no breakage, it was obvious that they had been placed there (fig. 38).

As they [the rocks] were being removed, part of a large bone was dislodged, different from any bones we had seen in this region in association with Indian remains. When the largest slab of stone, about 2 by 2½ ft., was lifted it was found to be concave on the underside. This fitted over, without touching, a section of the skeleton of a large animal. Only a very little dust had gotten into the hollow beneath this stone, so the bones were exposed lying in their relative positions to each other. Where the stones were in contact with them they were slightly crushed. Others were so soft that an ordinary whisk broom destroyed their surface, so we did not attempt to uncover much of the skeleton.

When clearing along the base of the rear wall a bunch of coarse hairs was found at about the position indicated on the drawings. The longest of these measures 5.5 in. No others were seen about the bones, nor any trace of hide.

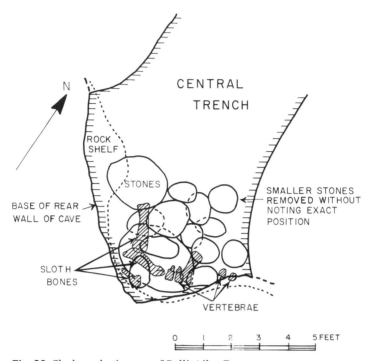

Fig. 38. Sloth cache in rear of Palli Aike Cave.

Spaces between the stones were filled with wood ash, which also forms the covering of the bones not in contact with the stones. Some of these bones are blackened by fire and have been shifted from their natural positions.

At this point the top of layer 3 is not as clearly defined as further out, but it appears that the bones lie on its surface with some of the longer ones imbedded in it.

The nearest artifact, a well-made knife (see fig. 32) was found in the position indicated, and as it was uncovered with a trowel there is no doubt about its position. Other flakes and a scraper were found nearby at about the same level.

Concerning the possible human associations with this animal we can make few positive statements. There is no proof that the Indians killed it, but they did cover it with stones. We do not know whether the flesh was still on it, or if it was merely the dried-up remains like the *Mylodon* [extinct ground sloth] found near Natales [in the Mylodon Cave].

If layer 3 is volcanic ash the animal may have sought shelter here and perished during a nearby eruption. If layer 3 is a mixture of burned manure, windblown dust, and sand then the cave may have been used as shelter for these animals for some time. This one may have died a natural death and the floor burned later, or the Indians may have cornered it in the cave, built a fire at the mouth of the cave to keep it in, and in so doing set fire to the floor and burned the animal to death.

In explanation of why they should have covered it with stones there are two possible suggestions. If they had cornered and killed it there, they may have covered it to keep off foxes and pumas. At the present time some meat would keep in this cave during winter for a month or more, in summer for about ten days. If they had found the dried remains, superstition may have prompted them to cover it.

In the latter case the question is: how much time might have elapsed between its death and the time it was covered? It will be shown later that there is a good basis for assuming a very slow rate of accumulation . . . considerable time may have passed, but even so, it could not have lain indefinitely in this situation without being hidden from view by windblown dust and sand. . . .   *(from Bird 1936–1937)*

See diary entry for February 11, 1936, for description of the excavation of these sloth bones. More sloth bones, apparently not covered by stones, were found nearby at the rear of the cave in divisions C and D. Possibly Bird became uncertain whether the sloth bones were placed there by humans. He never published this evidence.

Classifications

The faunal specimens from Palli Aike Cave have AMNH catalogue nos. 41.1/1892 and 41.1/1891, the first for materials from the upper part of the deposit, the latter for bones from the lower part of the debris. In comparison with the other excavations, Palli Aike Cave produced a much larger sample of faunal materials (2,000 to 3,000 specimens). The faunal specialist Thomas Amorosi has prepared a presence/absence tabulation (table 14) of the species found in the various excavation units. Bird marked the bones with the letter *P* followed by the numbers 1 to 42. The table defines these field labels according to their positions within the excavation.

The heaviest concentrations of *Mylodon* (giant sloth) remains occur with the field numbers P34, P35, and P36, which correspond to the surface of the ash layer at the back of the cave (fig. 39). This is near the location of the stones over the sloth cache described by Bird. With the exception of less than five sloth bones in the 42 to 48 in. level, all sloth bones (in excess of 150 specimens) are found below 48 in.

The *Onohippidium* (horse) remains are labeled with numbers P22, P24, P25, P31, and P36. These labels represent locations mainly within the C and D units, below 54 in. The horse specimens are found at the surface of the ash layer, or

Table 14. Faunal Remains, Palli Aike Cave

Level/Layer	Excavation Unit (feet indicate distance from mouth of cave)	Field Label	Taxa			
			Mollusca	Aves	Rodentia	Lagomorphen
Top to 6″	all	P1			×	×
6 to 12″	all	P2	×	×		
18 to 24″	C, D	P3		×	×	
24 to 30″	D	P4	×	×	×	
30 to 36″	C	P5		×		
	E	P6	×		×	
36 to 42″ (P25 is 36″ to S of A)	E	P7		×		
	C	P8				
	D	P9				
	B	P25				
42 to 48″	E	P10				
	C	P11				
	D	P14		×		
	B	P15				
48 to 54″ (P23 is 48″ to S of A)	C, D (35′ to R)	P12		×		
	C (25 to 35′)	P18		×		
	C (25 to 35′)	P19				
	D (25 to 35′)	P20		×	×	
	D (20 to 25′)	P23		×		
54 to 60″ (P21, 22 are 54″ to S of A)	C, D	P13		×		
	C, D (35′ to R)	P17				
	C (25 to 35′)	P21		×		
	D (25 to 35′)	P22		×		

Taxa							
Carnivora	Mustelidae	Felidae	Couidae	Camelidae	Onohippidium	Mylodontidae	Unidentified Mammal
	×	×	×				
			×				
			×				
×			×				
							×
			×				
			×	×			×
				×			×
			×				×
				×	×		×
							×
			×	×		×	×
			×			×	
			×				
	×		×	×		×	×
			×	×		×	×
						×	×
			×	×			×
				×			×
			×				×
				×		×	×
			×	×			×
			×	×	×	×	×

Table 14. *(continued)*

Level/Layer		Excavation Unit *(feet indicate distance from mouth of cave)*	Field Label	Mollusca	Aves	Rodentia	Lagomorphen
60″ to S of A		C, D (35′ to R)	P16				
Surface of Ash (S of A) and Stones at Base of Wall		S of A (near fire)	P24				
		trench (20 to 25′)	P26				
		C (35′ to R) wall base	P34				
		wall base	P35				
		stones (C, D 35′ to R)	P36				
Ash Layer	Upper Half	C (20 to 35′)	P27				
	Upper Half	D (20 to 35′)	P28				
	Upper 3rd	C, D (35′ to R)	P30				
	Middle 3rd	C, D (35′ to R)	P31				
	Lower Half	C, D (20 to 35′)	P29				
	Lower 3rd	C, D (35′ to R)	P32				
Below Ash Layer		D (35′ to R)	P37				
		Trench (20 to 35′)	P38				
		D (20 to 35′); C, D (35′ to R)	P39				
		C (20 to 35′)	P40				
Cave Floor		C, D (20′ to R)	P41				
Position Uncertain Mainly S of A			P42		×	×	

S = Surface.
A = Ash layer.
R = Rear of cave.

Taxa							
Carnivora	*Mustelidae*	*Felidae*	*Couidae*	*Camelidae*	*Onohippidium*	*Mylodontidae*	*Unidentified Mammal*
				×		×	×
			×	×	×	×	
						×	×
						×	×
				×		×	×
				×	×	×	
			×	×		×	×
				×		×	×
				×		×	
					×	×	
			×			×	×
						×	×
						×	×
						×	×
						×	×
						×	×
						×	×
	×		×	×	×	×	×

Fig. 39. Bones of extinct fauna, mainly sloth, on top of ash layer in back of Palli Aike Cave. *Top:* area C, rear; *bottom:* area D, rear.

within 6 in. above its surface. One specimen is found within the ash layer (P31).

The camelid (guanaco) remains begin approximately 36 to 42 in. into the deposits, and continue down into the ash layer. The carnivore remains, with the exception of the Canidae, occur in the 24 to 30 in. level. The Canidae occur throughout the deposits, becoming scarce near the ash layer. The lagomorphs and rodents occur only in the upper levels, often toward the front of the cave. The avian material is distributed in a bimodal pattern. These remains are encountered in the surface layers, often toward the front of the cave, and in the C and D units from 48 in. down. The shellfish are distributed in the surface layers toward the front of the cave.

HUMAN REMAINS

Locations

When clearing division F of the cave deposit at 18 in. below the surface, five fragments of a child's cranium were encountered (catalogue no. 99.1/772). They were scattered, all at the same level, with nothing to indicate where the body had been placed. No other human bones were found at a corresponding level anywhere else in the cave. One of the pieces, the right maxilla, retains two unworn deciduous molars and has a first permanent molar imbedded below the bone surface. This suggests an age of perhaps 5 or 6 years. The bones had not been burned and have a fresh appearance. This section of the deposit yielded relatively few artifacts but enough to fix the 18 in. level as within Period IV of the local archaeological sequence.

The incomplete remains of a second, older individual (catalogue no. 99.1/773) lay scattered, disordered, and broken close to the cave wall in the C area near the rear of the cave. The body had been cremated when the surface of the floor was formed by the volcanic ash layer. On, and imbedded in, the surface of this ash were bones of guanaco, sloth, and some horse, so if the cremation was not exactly contemporary with these animals it must have been close to that time. Just above the ash surface on the opposite side of the cave, in area D, we found the only example of the fishtail-type point present in Palli Aike Cave. At Fell's Cave, on the Río Chico, these points occurred only in association with horse and sloth.

Among the burned bones [of no. 99.1/773] were pieces of charred, organic material which might have been remains of the brain, for it closely resembled charred brain found with the cremated crania in Cerro Sota Cave. There was also a charred piece of skin about 2 cm long by 1.5 cm wide with fine fur, possibly baby guanaco. The blackened fragments of the cranium when reassembled showed no distortion. The fractures were similar to those of the cremated skulls 99.1/779 and 780 from Cerro Sota Cave, and resulted either at the time of burning or shortly thereafter.

In area D, directly across from division C in the rear section of the cave, while removing material 30 to 36 in. below the surface along the cave wall, we found a 3.5 cm burned section of what was probably a tibia (catalogue no. 99.1/774). Close to it was a similarly burned section of an adult mandible, the incomplete right half and chin, broken at the left incisor socket. The teeth, except for one premolar and one molar root, are missing. The two items are now numbered 99.1/774 and were the only human remains at this level.

About 2 ft. directly below (in division D at 42 to 48 in.), on the surface of the volcanic ash layer and against and near the cave wall (and partially in a recess or pocket in the cave wall), were more cremated bones (99.1/775). It is not improbable that the two burned bones (99.1/774) found between 30 and 36 in. had been brought up from the lower level by some burrowing animal. The nature of burning is the same as for some of the lower ones, but no fracture contacts have been found. More than one body was burned in this area, for there are small sections of two adult mandibles, neither of which matches the mandible section from the 30 to 36 in. level. The balance of the largely fragmentary bones appear to be from one individual, as though the burning had been done successively and as if most of the bones of the first had been deliberately removed. While there are forty or more cranial fragments, there do not appear to be enough good contacts to permit much reassembly.

These bones, from their position on the surface of the volcanic ash, must be closely contemporary with the sloth and horse remains and with 99.1/773. As with that individual, there was again a small charred lump of organic material, possibly brain, with the bone fragments; also, a charred stick 13 mm in diameter by 95 mm long, the only piece of charcoal of any size seen. The [stick's] end structure appears identical with the wood of the barberry (local name, *calafate*), the only wood available today in the region.

From the occurrence of cremation here and at Cerro Sota Cave, it appears that this method of disposal of the dead was the standard practice among Paleo-Indians in the Americas and it may account for the scarcity of their skeletal remains.

Classifications

Dr. Charles Lester originally described the skeletal material from Palli Aike Cave. Dr. Ian Tattersall of the AMNH has corrected and largely rewritten those descriptions, reproduced below.

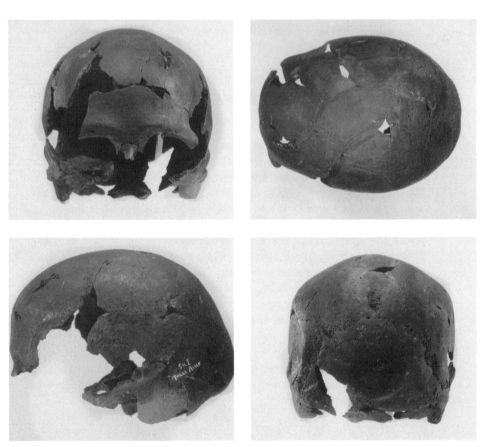

Fig. 40. Skull of Palli Aike individual 99.1/773 (originally no. 1) associated with extinct sloth and horse (not to scale).

Fig. 41. Mandible of Palli Aike individual 99.1/773.

99.1/772

Fragments of cranial vault of immature individual; also fragment of juvenile right maxilla with unworn deciduous premolars and M^1 in crypt.

99.1/773 (originally Palli Aike skeleton 1) (figs. 40 and 41)

Reconstructed partial skull with some loose fragments, lacking face and most of cranial base. Probable female, blackened from fire. Sutural obliteration at an advanced state [thus, old at time of death—ed.]. No evidence of external trauma. Mandible without rami; right incisors and P_1 lost before death; all alveolae present. Lower part of right maxilla with all alveolae present. Left femur missing medial extremities except for epicondyle; diaphysis with well-developed linea aspera. Damaged proximal half of right femur lacking part of neck and parts of diaphysis. Right humerus without head; medial condyle deformed by crystal formation. Partial diaphysis of other humerus. Damaged right radius with separated distal extremities. Left ulna lacking distal end. Right ulna with broken diaphysis and damaged proximal extremity. Charred and damaged distal extremity of left radius. Pieces of heads of two humeri. Piece of ischium with part of acetabulum. Various rib fragments. Part of right proximal end of tibia and other fragments. Numerous other fragments among which can be recognized patella, sternum, manubrium, scapula, and assorted damaged foot bones. Many vertebral fragments, all highly porous and some showing osteoarthritis. Various nonhuman fragments, some possibly guanaco, also bird.

99.1/774

Chin and right half of mandible. One partial root of M_3. Alveolae of four incisors and root of P_4. Fragment of possible tibia. Possibly associated with some remains of 99.1/775 found below it.

99.1/775 (originally Palli Aike skeleton 2)

Fragments of two or more individuals. Numerous skull fragments mainly from vault. Partial juvenile and partial adult mandibles with chins. Fragments of sacrum and damaged vertebral column with moderate osteoarthritis. Partial left maxilla of young adult with roots of M^1; M^3 was apparently in process of erupting. Multiple adult pelvic fragments from ilium, ischium, and pubis. Right radius and ulna; right humerus lacking head. Some carpals, metacarpals, and digits. Partial humural head. A rib. Two femurs with damage by postmortem deterioration and incomplete cremation. Restored complete left femur measures 41.5 cm; charring affects condyles, diaphysis, trochanters, and portion of head. Right femur has well-preserved proximal end and less well-preserved distal end; accurate assessment of length not possible; charring involves the anterior surface of the condyles. See description of the possibly associated skeletal parts with catalogue no. 99.1/774. Associated nonhuman bones, mainly guanaco.

DAILY LIFE

Wednesday, June 3, 1936

Mr. Farrance, *capataz* of the Dickey Section, rode over with us to the cave, which is quite near Pozo del Diablo and is right in a red volcanic cliff, with three lichen-covered crags in front of it. We found two men in residence—probably *pasajeros*—and we were sorry to make them move out, but they really have a right to only one night's stay, just as at the settlements. Mr. F. stayed to lunch—a peon brought his horse over. The cave is about 40 ft. long by 10 ft. wide and quite high, a recent fire hearth in the rear. It's perfectly dry and the floor is covered with sheep manure. Junius started right in to dig a trench back from the entrance—very dusty! So much so, that we put the tent up in a sheltered place further along the cliff. Too dark to work after 5, and we walked over to a small lagoon nearby and chopped a knapsack and two buckets full of ice for water, there being no spring—back in the moonlight. Supper and to bed early for a little reading.

Thursday, June 4

Clear and somewhat windy. The peon brought over some bread and a skin of water—stayed to lunch. The only weed here is green *calafate* and it's hard to make it burn. The digging proves disappointing—not much except scrapers and three knife points. Also, it's only about 3 ft. down before you reach volcanic ash. There may be more artifacts back further, as their fires were near the entrance and there's never much where the fires were.

Friday, June 5

Clear and calm. Mr. Farrance arrived just before lunch and stayed on a while. He's a very nice man—he chopped some wood for us. Very few finds, mostly scrapers.

Saturday, June 6

Cloudy and cold. At the very back of the cave there is a lot of refuse—grass, buried bones, ashes, dried-up skunks—you can imagine the mixture of smells. Junius brought it outside in a bucket and I'd go through it with a trowel—averaged about one specimen per basket. The trench gets deeper as it goes back—about 1.5 m now.

Sunday, June 7

26° before sunrise; at 10:00 against the cliff by the tent it was 30° in the shade and 56° in the sun. A little wind and some snow in the P.M. Sorted specimens and continued my work of yesterday.

This is really a lovely location—the land rises up to the cliff, joining a sort of semicircular bowl. The tent is on the left side, the cave on the right. We look out across a valley covered with tongues of lava, with more volcanic hills beyond. Small patches of snow everywhere. Junius very pleased at finding part of a mortar stone with some red paint still on it; a hard stone and yet somewhat concave from rubbing with other hard stones— undoubtedly the hammer and grinding stones we've been finding. Went out for another supply of ice.

Monday, June 8

Windy and cold in P.M. Tried making a fire outside in shelter of cliff and cooking a *churrasco;* not too successful. Mr. Farrance rode up just as we'd finished—he had some, and also some French toast, which seemed to please him very much. He stayed most of the afternoon and cut some more wood for us. The trench is now down about 4.5 ft. as the old floor has been dipping gradually down, with volcanic ash right below. Found a good many of the triangular [stemless] points; they may be finished specimens, not just points without the notches in yet. Saw a guanaco quite close.

Tuesday, June 9

Rather cold. The peon came over from the section, bringing wood, vegetables, buns, cigarettes, and a roast shoulder of mutton from the Farrances. More triangular points; they all occur in the lower levels. Junius was working at the very back of the cave where the light was poor; so he made an Eskimo lamp with an old plate we'd found, some melted fat and a rag for a wick—very successful!

Wednesday, June 10

Calm, cloudy, and quite warm. In the late afternoon, just as Junius was finishing the work in the cave, he came across some huge bones obviously of a large extinct animal. It was back in the little niche at the far end of the cave; over it had been piled weather-worn stones, which must have been brought from outside, and directly on top of the skeleton were two large slabs of rock. Junius had thought there might be a burial, and so had investigated. The Indians must have piled the stones up on the animal; there is no proof that they killed him—they may have been afraid of him, even though dead, or of his spirit. Junius uncovered a few more bones and even some long, coarse hair! After some discussion as to what to do, we decided to cover him up again, send an airmail to Dr. Wissler, and wait for his answer. They may want to send a man down, or else have us return next summer. It would be fun if they'd send R. T. [Roland T. Bird, Junius' brother, a paleontologist—ed.]! It's a wonderful discovery, the only trouble is that it will probably delay our return home. There's not much doubt that the skeleton is intact; it lies on volcanic ash and it would be wonderful to discover Indian things directly associated with it. As it is, Junius found a fine fragment of a knife right on top. We didn't get to sleep for a long time, talking.

Thursday, June 11

A lovely day. Junius covered the animal over very carefully; anyone digging there would soon be overcome by the dust, which is awful, so I guess he's pretty safe down there! Packed up and under way at 3:30. The car started right off with no trouble at all—most amazing! We lost the way back to the track and were an hour finding it, so at 5:00 we camped, made a fire, cooked supper, went to bed and read.

The following day Junius and Peggy Bird crossed into Argentina, and began a five-month excursion in Patagonia and Chile. Six months later they returned, excavating first at Cerro Soto and Fell's Cave, then at Palli Aike.

Monday, January 11, 1937

The bullock cart (fig. 42) left at 9:00 with all our heavy things—a barrel of water, two sacks of wood, the driver and Pedro. Showers and cold. We left at 11:00 with a light load. Passed the cart just at the Delgado boundary.

Fig. 42. Bullock cart hauling Bird's supplies and Model T up to Palli Aike site.

Went in to see the Farrances and found that poor little Mrs. F. had had a miscarriage Thursday night and the Cruz Roja (Red Cross) had come out for her. Mr. F. was awfully upset, of course, but had heard last night that she was getting along O.K. We stayed to lunch. He seems very skeptical about Mrs. Simpson [Duchess of Windsor—ed.]; says his mother used to say, "if one isn't enough, 100 won't be too many." We got a sheep there and went on, meeting the cart just at the place to turn off to the cave. Had cleared a little. Everything looked very familiar. We went up to the cave and found everything as we left it—place apparently hadn't even been used. Found some points and scrapers at the entrance. Cooked lunch for the driver and Pedro and then Junius put up our stove which he had made in Magallanes (Punta Arenas). Seems to be fine. Put flat stones along the sides. The driver spent the night. The poor oxen were very tired. One is 26 years old and huge, with immense horns.

Tuesday, January 12

High wind all day and cloudy, which is unusual. Miserable working with sifter at entrance of cave. Junius wouldn't let me help. The work goes very fast. Most of the dry, loose dirt goes through or blows away, leaving very little to look over. They found some points, scrapers, etc.—also odds and ends left behind by *pasajeros*—buttons, etc. I fixed up our kitchen which is down near our tent—a very sheltered place. Pedro has his tent just beyond.

Wednesday, January 13

Cloudy, one or two light showers—a little sun and calm. They found many points, etc., one beautiful small black one, a fragment of a baleen comb, with scratched "decorations" on it, etc. Most of the points are the triangular ones—such a large variety of shapes. Junius made some dough-nuts for tea—not rolled, just dropped into fat—very good.

Thursday, January 14

Cloudy and sun—calm until after tea. Work is going very fast in the cave. They're clearing off the top layer on each side of the trench now. Many Patagonian points—many with jagged edges. Scattered fragments of human skulls (in div. F at 18 in.). Junius took a photograph of the cave last evening just at dusk, but the flashpowder didn't seem very strong. Muñeca caught a mouse.

Friday, January 15

Sunny and very warm in A.M.—cloudy in P.M. and calm all day. We classify and pack each batch of things as they come in—already there's an awful lot. Two bird bone beads, two shell and a stone one, fragment of another comb, etc. Junius fixed me such a nice shelf with nails for the pots. Also cut a hole in top of stove, as water boils so slowly on it. I raked the "lawn" getting rid of bones and dead grass. We're using about two gals. of water a day, not counting the wash water.

Saturday, January 16

Cool A.M.—very windy in P.M. Dust so bad at entrance of cave that Junius and Pedro stopped work at tea time. They tried to work again later, but still too windy. Found a pendant made from a sperm whale (?) tooth, similar to the one we found at Yendagaia—the worn edges of the hole show that it was used a lot, and it is a dark amber from age—slightly oval in shape. The first pretty thing we've found. Also some small pieces of a shoulder blade decorated by scratched lines—we fitted most of them together but could get no idea of its size. Junius had an awful time picking out the pieces after he found the first ones. It was partly burned and broken either when digging or on the sifter. Baked two applesauce cakes using our oven on top of the stove with a five-gal. tin over it to keep off the wind. A few days ago a guanaco came and stood on top of the rock wall just beside camp, looked at us, and "yammered" for some time—such a funny noise. Junius got a picture of it.

Sunday, January 17

Half expected the Fells with our mail, or Mr. Farrance, so cooked a special dinner—pea soup, a huge pot roast, steamed chocolate pudding (cooked in with some beans so as not to waste water) with chocolate sauce; and then no one came (fig. 43). It was very windy, but calm and peaceful at our sheltered camp. Quite a lazy day. Junius fixed his goggles, tightened a clutch on the car, and he, Pedro, and Muñeca went after a hare. They saw twenty-one guanacos—four young—very close.

Monday, January 18

Very hot morning—cloudy in afternoon—two Argentine police came by—the track between Mt. Aymond and Palli Aike stations seems to run along this side of the fence. One of them smelled to high Heaven of awful perfume—Muñeca couldn't stand him, but otherwise they were alright. Couldn't understand our camping out this way just to dig up things belonging to dead Indians. The superior officer, an inspector from Gallegos, told us to call him up from the station at Condor if we wanted to cross the border to get down to the camp on the beach at Monte Dinero.

Tuesday, January 19

Awfully windy, as usual. A shepherd came over from the section to see if we needed anything and Junius told him we'd be over tomorrow for meat

Fig. 43. Camp kitchen at Palli Aike, with pet dog Muñeca.

and water. Junius has rigged up such a fine filter for the wash water—a five-gal. tin with holes in the bottom and several inches of sand—the water comes out perfectly clear. Junius shot a hare for Muñeca in the eve.

Wednesday, January 20

Not bad in morning but wind increased until there was a gale blowing. At 3:30, just as we were cranking the car to go over to the section, Mr. Fell, John, and Mr. Campbell arrived. It's good we didn't get off any earlier. They brought specimen bag material from Mrs. Conroy, which was welcome, as I've used just about every available piece of cloth, and a note from her, with no mention of what's happened to our laundry! Mr. Jones returned *North to the Orient* with a very nice note. No mail for us. They brought eggs, milk, and cakes. After tea we showed them the cave and some of the things we've found. I rode with Mr. Fell. Saw an *avestruz* [rhea; *Pterocnemia pennata*] with his brood, at least fifteen—right in the road—such cunning little things. Many golden plover and ducks on the lagoon. We had a fine clean-up at Mr. Farrance's and washed out some clothes. Junius spoke to Mr. Foukes. Had a very good dinner and a nice chat. Filled our barrel with a five-gal. tin and a smaller barrel that Mr. F.

loaned us. Got a fine fat capon. Our bearing burned out again and we just made camp at dusk. Mr. F. had given us a lot of wood, too.

Thursday, January 21

Cloudy, warm, but windy anyway. Sun in afternoon. Sometimes the wind sounds like heavy surf.

Friday, January 22

Very hot—calm and sunny with not a cloud in the sky. A small breeze blowing but it didn't touch our camp—96° in the sun. There wasn't any shade big enough to sit in. We had luncheon over on top of the wall of stone where it was lovely. After tea the wind came up and was an awful nuisance, eddying around in the kitchen as well as up at the sifter. Junius took two levels off divisions A and F and one off divisions B and E, leaving all clear down to 24 in. over whole of cave floor. Found practically nothing. They went without their masks and goggles for the first time.

Saturday, January 23

Cloudy and not too windy, but there were strong gusts up at the cave. We cut all the fat possible off our sheep, divided it up, and salted it well in an effort to keep it in this warm weather. Junius took out divisions C, D, and E between 24 and 30 in.—about the most profitable part of the old debris—found over 100 of the old [triangular] points. First bit of chipping tool (?) associated with old material.

Sunday, January 24

A warm day. Just after lunch the boy from the nearby *puesto* came over again bringing a shepherd from Palli Aike—a little Englishman who seemed very nice. He is interested in Indian things and next winter expects to dig in a shelter on the *estancia* and will write us what he finds. He's very anxious to make the trip down the cordillera with us—says if we'll let him know he'll meet us up north with his two horses. Name's Jackson. Made doughnuts for tea. After he left, just as Junius was going to work on the car bearing, Mr. Foukes, Mr. Farrance, Mr. Will Saunders, Mr. Frazer (acting second at Delgado), and a wool buyer arrived. We certainly were surprised! They brought us letters, Christmas cards, and magazines—and also cakes and jelly from Mrs. Donaldson, who's still at the *estancia*. They looked at the cave and at some of the things we've found and then went on. Very pleasant. We had a lovely evening, with our wealth of mail.

Monday, January 25

A calm, warm day. How long our meat will keep in this weather is a question. We've cut it up, salted it, and kept it hanging under canvas, but still . . . Junius worked on the car in the afternoon and we left for North Arm Station after tea; broke down at the first gate—a bolt in the crank case or something. Junius soon fixed it. John had gotten goggles for us in town—also specimen bag material. They'd brought out our laundry and most recent mail, . . . Heard over the radio of the bad floods on the Ohio and Mississippi—so unusually early.

Tuesday, January 26

A lovely morning. Filled our barrel and two tins with water. Mr. Fell gave us some carrots, a large bottle of milk, and some cakes. John [gave] a tin of Pall Mall cigarettes. They start shearing again tomorrow and will finish in about ten days. On the way back picked up some old fence posts for the firewood. Back in time for luncheon. A great gale of wind came up after tea, which swept around the kitchen and tent in strong gusts. Beautiful full moon.

Wednesday, January 27

Another hot day, it's getting to be quite phenomenal. We took lunch up on top of the "wall" where there was some breeze. Junius and I are quite burned—Pedro may be but he doesn't show it! Junius found some pieces of the sloth some distance away from the main part of the skeleton—it looks doubtful whether we'll get the whole thing, after all. Also found a bone tool or weapon, made to be lashed to a handle of some sort, blunt end, use unknown. Also, a very thin awl such as you find further south but which we haven't seen around here. Windy again after tea, but a very warm eve.

Thursday, January 28

Hot again! Just before lunch a wagon drawn by three horses arrived— much shouting by the driver and straining by the horses on the steep slope up to camp. Turned out to be Mr. Farrance's young brother-in-law—such an *awfully* shy boy—two big barrels of water, some wood, and a big loaf of bread—also a sheep. We sent a quarter of the latter back as it would only spoil here. They stayed to lunch. Found more broken sloth bones—and some horse bones and teeth!!! Cold tea, as usual lately. It's lucky we have so much water as the heat makes you awfully thirsty. Washed out a few clothes. Calm, cool evening.

Friday, January 29

Junius has rigged the canvas better, so that besides shielding our meat, it makes a tolerably livable tent for meals, etc. Found more of the thin, highly polished awls. The boy from the *puesto* stopped in bringing a note from Mr. Jackson, with two plugs of tobacco and a large snail shell he'd found on top of one of the hills. A perfect gale after tea. I took movies of Junius working (with Pedro) in their clouds of dust. Pedro's tent blew loose from some of its stakes.

Saturday, January 30

Cloudy for part of the morning, then hot again. Junius finding many broken sloth bones—almost down to main part of skeleton. He made a test pit and found broken bones below the volcanic ash. More of the small bird bone awls. No more stone points. Calm eve—the air so full of smoke that you couldn't see even the nearby hills—there must be a big fire up in the hills. Junius made a table out of the floor of the truck to use for working on the bones.

Sunday, January 31

Cloudy and windy. Junius did a little work up at cave in morning. Pedro washed clothes and I made a steamed pudding. Sunny and calm in afternoon. Junius packing up fragmentary Indian skeleton that he found several days ago, and working on the equally fragmentary sloth bones. Finished the letter to Dr. Wissler in evening—up very late, until midnight!

Monday, February 1

Some wind, but not bad—sunny, but not too hot. I typed Dr. W's [Wissler's] letter in morning. Junius still finding sloth bones—teeth, part of shoulder blade, etc. Pedro's getting good at making arrow points; he spends most of his spare time chipping, very vigorously, with much puffing and blowing. Our meat all went bad yesterday and Junius buried it. It couldn't have been freshly killed. A *bandurria* [ibis; *Theristicus caudatus*] came around in the evening and Junius shot it. Not much meat for such a long bill!

Tuesday, February 2

Pot-roasted the ibis and it was very good indeed—only trouble was that there weren't at least two. Junius found a horse's upper jaw in very bad condition—is shellacking it in position.

Wednesday, February 3

Cloudy, cool, and showers. Junius and Pedro cutting down trench—it's exasperating to see how near we came to things before—i.e., two fireplaces just an inch or so away, both with horse and sloth bones. A shepherd stopped in after lunch, having brought some sheep back to this camp. Says one of the butchers in Magallanes got permission to burn some of the forest on his land up in the *monte* and now it's out of control—hence the smoke.

Thursday, February 4

Cloudy, sun, and showers. Junius and Pedro took out upper half of layer of ash at rear of cave, stage left (div. D) finding a few stone implements as far down as 5 in. in the ash. Sloth bones very scattered and very broken—apparently imbedded in top of ash. Removing earth from beneath ash in trench, finding broken sloth bones, but no chips. One piece of charcoal. We heard a plane in eve, but couldn't see it. (Found out later it was Bianco, returning from Buenos Aires.)

Friday, February 5

Fine day. The cave looks so big now; the layer of ash is very pretty—terracotta, reddish, and a little blue-gray. Junius is leaving the ash in the rear and the main part of the sloth skeleton—till the last. Went over to section after an early supper. Mrs. Farrance not back yet. Mr. Farrance so busy cleaning up the house! Had tea and some very good cake he'd baked himself. Told him, quite casually, about the sloth bones. Got three tins of water and half a sheep. It was dark before we got back, but fortunately one light [of the Model T] was working. Pedro had turned in and even all that noise didn't wake him!

Saturday, February 6

Sloth bones turn up above and below the layer of volcanic ash, as well as imbedded in it, but there is no certain evidence of human occupation below the ash.

Sunday, February 7

Glorious day and not too hot. Junius and Pedro did a little work in the cave and then Pedro took the gun and went off with Muñeca after hares. He wasn't back by dinner time and the Fells hadn't come, so Junius and I had our pot roast and pudding alone. Shortly afterwards Mr. Fell and John arrived bringing two bottles of milk, bread, cakes, lettuce, turnips, and the big drum of water. We showed them the cave and some of the things we've found. John climbed up to top of cliff and let a string down. Between the kitchen and the cave it's 81 ft. high! They stayed to tea and supper. Pedro came back—he'd gone over to the *puesto*. There were six letters for him, so he was very much pleased. We sent a few bones in with the Fells.

Monday, February 8

Cloudy and calm until after tea, when the wind came up and then sun broke through. We had a lovely *puchero* [stew] with all our vegetables.

Fig. 44. Photo of rear of cave. White arrows point to sloth bones imbedded in ash layer.

Tuesday, February 9

Junius has painted a line with whitewash around the cave, showing where the surface was when we started work. Then took pictures of the exposed section, extending across the cave at 35 ft. showing the layer of volcanic ash and the dirt beneath down to the bottom of the cave (fig. 44). Put white paper arrows to show where parts of sloth bones were exposed. Some pieces he found 13 in. above ash. He made a scale drawing of the section, too (fig. 33). Before the ash entered the cave the floor was quite hollow in the middle with the dirt piled up against the sides. I went up with him in the evening while he did some more work. There are places along the wall, about the level of the ash, where there is a strong draft into the crevices of the rock, as though the cave may extend in further. It would be fine to find some mummified sloth! Watched him uncover a pocket in the wall where a child's body had been burned—level with the top of the ash—with sloth bones around it. He took out the paper that we'd left under the big stone with the sloth bones last June and burned it! Very cold night.

Wednesday, February 10

33° when we got up! Cloudy and calm until P.M. The barometer going way down quite fast—when it starts to go up, it'll probably blow like anything. The *puestero* [shepherd] came by to see if we needed meat. Junius taking more pictures as he clears away the ash. More sloth bones, of course. Pedro was telling Junius that the people over at the *puesto* wouldn't believe him when he said we weren't looking for gold, and added, "Such people are so ignorant!"

Thursday, February 11

30° when we got up and ice on the water in the pail. Junius cleared half of rear end of cave, removing a great many stones, all with rounded edges, ranging from size of fist to ones too large for two people to lift, but none too heavy to roll. Finds that no bones are in relative positions. Well-preserved, broken fragments have smooth, rounded edges—many with bones with scratches on surface. Found two large vertebrae with holes plugged with manure, one about on level with top of ash, other on surface of rock cave floor. In neither case was there manure in surrounding earth, although some has been found in other parts. Made diagram of arrangement of some of the bones (fig. 38)—took photos as they were being uncovered (fig. 45).

The only plausible explanation of the way in which these bones and stones are mixed up is that at the time of the eruption which produced the ash, the stones were thrown into the cave with such force that the projecting knobs of lava were ground smooth, the floor debris thrown up against the walls, as visible in the cross section, and the bones scattered, broken, and scratched as found. Originally the floor must have been covered with sloth manure in which were imbedded the bones of animals that had died there. The black portion below the ash, in which are found burned bones, must have been produced by the burning manure, which turned the ash orange-red where the heat was greatest. If that is so, most of the stones must have come in before the ash, and the ash must have been deposited rather rapidly, as it is burned from the bottom upwards to some "depth." Stones also come in with or after the ash, as some are imbedded in, others lying on it. Found two broken, burned bird bones next to unburned sloth bones, imbedded in light brown earth. Any Indian remains, such as a fireplace with bone refuse, would have been knocked west along with all the other bones.

I baked some cookies. Went up to cave with Junius in eve, while he cleared away some more, and darned socks. Very cold.

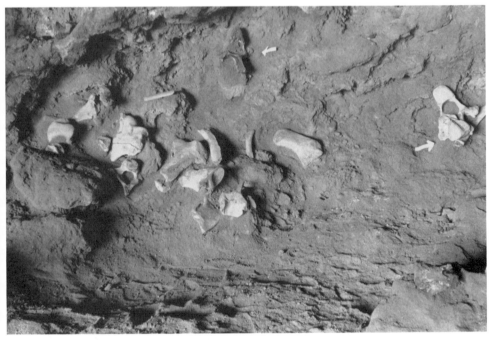

Fig. 45. Sloth bones at rear of cave at end of central trench. This possible cache was covered by stones but contained no articulated bones (see fig. 38).

Friday, February 12

Sunny and coolish—windy and quite cool up at cave. I helped pack some bones. Junius uncovered a big bone at very bottom—about 9 ft. below original surface. He thinks that when the sloths were living here the cave was draughty—there are crevices and holes with a strong in-draught along bottom of wall—the floor was uneven—also, the approach was probably steep, all of which may explain the absence of Indian occupation.

Saturday, February 13

Cool, but sun quite warm at noon. Light showers. Mr. Farrance arrived with some meat and a loaf of bread for us—stayed to lunch. We had beefies [lamb steaks] fried on the stove—very good meat. He was, of course, very much interested in the cave. Just as he was leaving Junius found a small stone, slightly chipped, beside a fireplace, right on the rock floor, under a sloth bone—most satisfactory! It's hard to clear the floor completely as it's rough and covered with a white chalk-like substance, perhaps soda, which is almost as hard as rock. The sparrows are so very

Fig. 46. Dump sifter used by Bird at Palli Aike Cave.

tame; there are almost always eight or more around the kitchen, paying very little attention to us. Pedro out after hares in eve and got a big one— the first thing he ever shot and he was very proud.

Sunday, February 14

Very cold morning—warming up slightly later. Packing bones and Junius and Pedro dug a test pit at entrance to cave and found sloth bones, but in extremely bad condition. Hoped the Fells or Mr. Foukes might come over, but nobody did. In evening Junius and I took measurements with aneroid at center of this crater, on the pampa ridge and bottom of the crater to SW and SE, cliff between camp and cave, cave mouth, etc. Junius made me such a dear Valentine; a gray, heart-shaped arrow point!

Monday, February 15

A cold, cloudy, showery miserable day. Short snowstorm in morning! Shepherd came over from section with half a sheep and some old news-papers for packing. Stayed to lunch and stood around most of afternoon watching whatever was going on. Said Mr. Foukes might come over tomor-row. Junius dug a trench down on east side of cave near entrance—they had taken only the top layers from there before as there were so few things (fig. 46). He found bones well below the ash, all caked up with soda (?) crystals and little of the original bone left. He worked on the plan of the cave in the tent until late.

Tuesday, February 16

Frost on ground when we got up, but turned into a nice, warm day—not too much wind. Hoped Mr. Foukes would come over, but he didn't.

Wednesday, February 17

The carter came over from the section and we sent back with him boxes and bags of specimens and some of our gear—quite a load for the horses. We finished up and started for Dickey Section after supper, with quite a load ourselves. We had one half barrel of water left—how we hated to throw it away! Spent night with Mr. Farrance. Sat up quite late, talking.

Thursday, February 18

Rather cold—showers in morning. In the middle of one downpour Mr. Farrance found the Chilote *mozo* [boy] watering the garden! Left most of our stuff behind and went on with a light load to the settlement. . . .

(from M. Bird 1934–1937)

5. Fell's Cave

GENERAL DESCRIPTION

[Fell's] Cave (fig. 47) or, more correctly, shelter, is in the valley of the Río Chico where the river at one time undercut the canyon wall. The cliff on the southeast side of the canyon shows an outcrop of lava resting on a conglomerate that, in turn, is underlain by a coarse stratified sandstone. At some time in the past the water wore away this sandstone, forming a cave about 28 ft. deep and 36 ft. wide with a ceiling now about 11 ft. above the original floor (fig. 48). This height must have been less at one time, however, since the water did not wear away all the sandstone but left more than a foot of it adhering to the underside of the conglomerate. The recession of the water left a clean, smooth floor of hard clay capping water-deposited sand.

On this [original and lowest] floor the first occupational refuse was found, a layer 3 to 9 in. thick containing many bone fragments, four fire hearths, stone flakes, and artifacts. After this had accumulated, the sandstone adhering to the underside of the conglomerate fell, covering the entire floor with slabs as much as several hundred pounds in weight and effectively sealing the bottom layer. Not until enough of the disintegrating conglomerate had fallen to level the floor somewhat was the cave again reoccupied. This sterile layer ranges from 15 to 20 in. in thickness and represents an uncertain interval of time.

That single, isolated refuse layer is the most significant feature of the site. The fireplaces in it contained broken and burned native horse, sloth, and guanaco bones, with associated artifacts that distinguish the people who hunted these animals as an entirely different group from the later occupants. In all, about 76.5 cubic ft. of this debris was uncovered and examined, or about half the visible total, and from it were recovered 63 stone and 5 bone artifacts, more than 300 chips and flakes, and enough fragmentary bones to fill a twenty-gallon can.

Outstanding among the artifacts are fourteen [J. B. later counted fifteen—ed.] stemmed lance (?) points, of rather rough workmanship. With these there was one poorly made point vaguely suggestive of the Folsom points in outline. There were two cylindrical rubbingstones of coarse, porous lava, 8.2 cm in diameter and about 4.5 cm thick. Of the forty-two scrapers found in this layer, twenty-six are the common, rough, flake, single-edged variety, and the rest are of various shapes and forms, including double-edged and end.

When reoccupation of the cave—represented by the refuse directly above the sterile layer—began, there had been a marked change in the fauna. The sloth and native horse were absent. For food the people depended on birds and foxes and an occasional guanaco. Culturally there had been an equally marked change. The stemmed points were no longer in use. In about 115 cubic ft. of refuse, forming a layer about 10 in. thick, we found no stone points, very few flakes and chips, thirty-six scrapers, and a large quantity of fragmentary and burned fox and bird bones. One roughly made bone point was recovered, a bit of positive evidence that seems to

Fig. 47. Fell's Cave during excavation in 1937. View to southwest across the Río Chico.

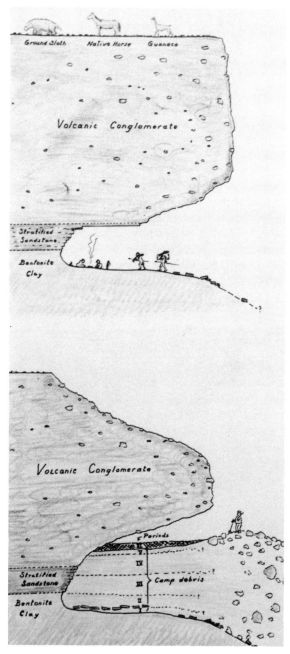

Fig. 48. Fell's Cave 11,000 years ago (*top*) and in A.D. 1936 (*bottom*). Drawings by Junius Bird.

put the reoccupation of the cave as occurring during the bone-point period of Palli Aike.

Above this layer, with no change of structure or line of division, was refuse in which we found evidence of an increase in the proportion of guanacos, and a decrease in the proportion of foxes and birds used for food. The cultural changes were those already noted—bone points replaced by the stemless stone blades, then by the stemmed arrow points.

EXCAVATION INFORMATION, 1936–1937

Bird wrote (1938b: 77) that Fell's Cave was located and selected because arrow points and flakes lay on the surface. It was dug in part to give a new assistant training in preparation to continue the excavations at Palli Aike Cave. In Bird's fieldnotes, the cave is called the Río Chico shelter, or river cave. Bird later named the cave Fell's after the Fell family, owners of the Estancia Brazo Norte (North Arm) where the cave was located.

The cave promised little more than pure exercise, for many tons of stones had piled up against the base of the cliff. The inward slope of the rock suggested a cave, but it was choked almost to the top. A little digging showed that it did go on in and that we could work without moving a yard of stone for every foot of dirt. As barrow after barrow load of dirt and broken bones rattled down the sifter, the little things which, added together, tell their story were picked out and laid aside.

(from Bird 1938a: 269–270)

The Layers

Bird labeled the strata of Fell's Cave with Roman numerals from top to bottom, with I assigned to the layer directly below the surface material. The lowest occupational layer was V. In publications Bird also used Roman numerals to denote time periods in the prehistoric sequence. The oldest of these periods was I, with succeeding periods labeled II, III, IV, and V. Thus the numerals used to denote periods are in the reverse order of those used to label the layers. The excavation in the cave was approximately 9 ft. wide and 20 ft. long, reaching 22 ft. near the bottom (figs. 49, 50, 51, 52, and 53).

Surface Material

Dirt and rocks blending with hard-packed sheep manure. The thickness varied from 18 to 24 in.

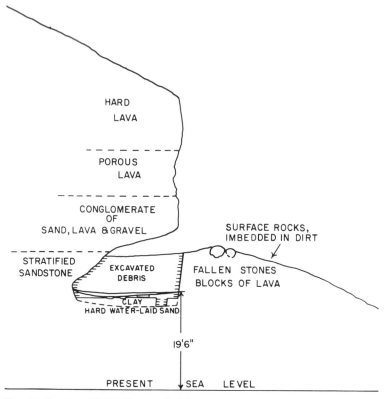

Fig. 49. Profile of Fell's Cave and cliff.

Layer I

Dark earth with many broken guanaco bones and small stones. The approximate thickness is 10 in. or more. The division between this and the lower layer is not distinct.

Layer II

Dark earth with small stones and fewer guanaco bones. The approximate thickness is 10 in. or more. A notable change in earth consistency divides this layer from layer III.

Layer III

Firmly packed dark earth with broken guanaco and fox bones. The approximate thickness varies from 12 to 15 in. There is no distinct division between this and the layer below.

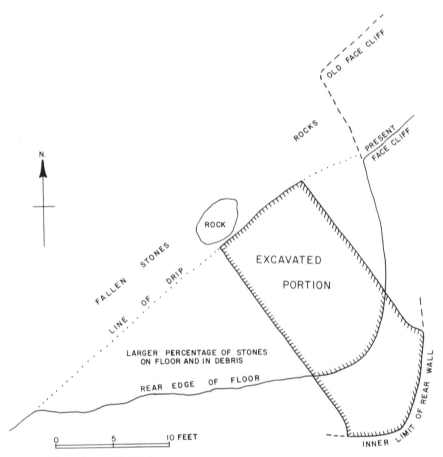

Fig. 50. Plan view of Fell's Cave.

Layer IV

Firmly packed dark earth with more dirt in proportion to artifacts than in the layer above. The approximate thickness varies from 13 to 17 in.

Sterile Layer

A stratum with no human artifacts consisting of slabs of sandstone which fell at the time the place was in use, as they rested on the uppermost bones of layer V below it. The slabs are disintegrated conglomerate rock from the roof of the cave. This barren layer varies in thickness from 15 to 28 in. [Bird

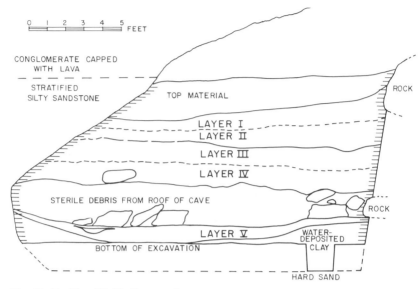

0 1 2 3 4 5 FEET

CONGLOMERATE CAPPED
WITH LAVA

STRATIFIED
SILTY SANDSTONE

TOP MATERIAL

ROCK

LAYER I
LAYER II
LAYER III
LAYER IV

STERILE DEBRIS FROM ROOF OF CAVE

ROCK

LAYER V

BOTTOM OF EXCAVATION

WATER-
DEPOSITED
CLAY

HARD SAND

Fig. 51. Profile of Fell's Cave—view to west.

Fig. 52. Face of west wall of excavation in Fell's Cave. Compare with profile drawing (fig. 51).

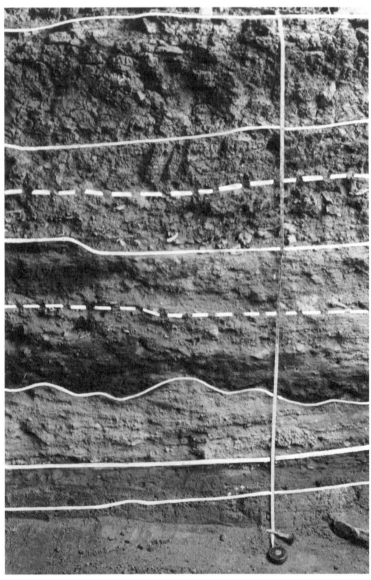

Fig. 53. Detail of west face of excavation at Fell's Cave. Layers highlighted.

wrote (1939*b*: 77), "There is nothing to suggest (in this layer) that we should dig further, except one of the simple rules of archaeology which is to dig beyond what seems to be the bottom"—ed.]. The fallen stones made the floor so rough and irregular that it was unfit for habitation, and it was not until the gradual accumulation of small stones and dirt had leveled it up again that it was [used] once more.

Layer V

The first, or earliest, layer of occupational refuse—soft clayey soil. It varies from 3 to 9 in. in thickness, and contains earth with lithic implements, and bones (figs. 54, 55, and 56). There were also four small fire hearths, and in each case a slight hollow had been made in the floor about 5 in. deep and 2 ft. across. These were full of fine black powder, burned bones, and stone flakes.   *(from Bird 1936–1937 and 1938a: 270)*

Fig. 54. Peggy Bird in Fell's Cave. The chalk line on the ledge 5 ft. above her head shows the original level of the cave floor before excavation began. She is standing on the clay at the bottom of the oldest stratum.

Fig. 55. View over floor of cave toward mouth. Sloth and horse bones in layer V are in situ. See fig. 63.

Fig. 56. View over floor of cave (layer V) to rear. S̀loth and horse bones are in situ. See fig. 63.

Table 15. Distribution of Artifacts from Fell's Cave

Group	Category	Surface	I	II	III	IV	V
					Layer		
Hafted Implements	Ona-type arrow point	–	13	2	–	–	–
	Patagonian-type arrow point	1	11	5	1	–	–
	Small, triangular arrow point	–	2	–	1	–	–
	Small, rudimentary stem	–	1	–	–	–	–
	Old-type, triangular point	–	–	2	20	2[a]	–
	Triangular, concave base	–	1	1	2	–	1
	Fishtail point	–	–	–	–	–	15
	Hafted knife	–	12	5	2	–	–
	Hafted knife, questionable	–	5	2	–	–	–
Knives	Thin, single-edge	–	1	–	2	–	–
	3-sided	–	–	2?	1	1	–
	?, concave base, broad, thin	–	–	1	–	–	–
	Fragment (uncertain)	–	–	–	–	–	3
	Combination knife-scraper	–	–	1	2	–	–
Scrapers	Single-edge, rough flake	11	45	59	36	25	26
	2-edge, large	3	2	2	–	2	1
	2-edge, narrow	–	4	11	1	6	–
	2 points	–	–	–	–	–	2
	Large, rough, circular edge	–	–	1	2	2	6
	Reversed-edge	–	1	–	–	–	1
	End	–	–	–	–	–	6
	Small, hafted	13	26	51	9	–	–
	Unfinished blank	–	1	–	6	1	–
Bolas	Deep groove, flat ends	–	1	–	–	–	–
	Unfinished	–	–	–	1	–	–
	Spherical, fragment	–	1	–	–	–	–
	Lemon-shaped, fragment	–	–	1	–	–	–
	Circular rubbing stone	–	–	–	–	–	2
Bone Implements	Chipping tool	–	12	6	–	–	–
	Bird bone awl	–	–	1	–	–	–
	Solid bone awl	–	1	–	–	–	–
	Lance point	–	–	–	–	1	–
	Bead	–	1	–	–	–	–
	Totals	28	141	153	86	40	63

[a]Found on top surface of layer.   Total of all artifacts = 511.

THE ARTIFACTS

The American Museum of Natural History catalogue places the Fell's Cave artifacts excavated in 1936 and 1937 under the numbers 41.1/1854 to 41.1/1995. Table 15 gives the distributions of the artifacts. Bird supplied small drawings of many of the artifacts to accompany the table (fig. 27 in chapter 3). Bird wrote the following commentaries about types of artifacts in layer V.

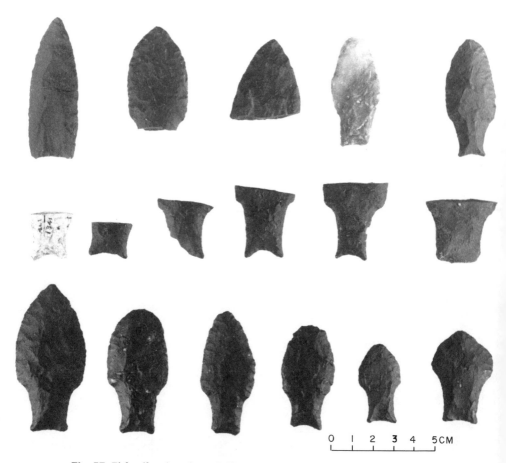

Fig. 57. Fishtail points from Fell's Cave, layer V, associated with extinct sloth and horse. The white stem on the left in the second row is from a low level of Palli Aike Cave.

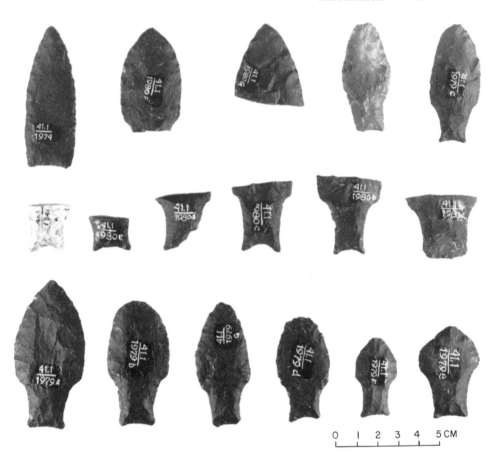

Fig. 58. Reverse side of fishtail points featured in fig. 57.

The Oldest Specimens (Layer V)

"Fishtail" Projectile Points

I recovered fifteen whole and fragmentary examples [of the points] at Fell's Cave and a single stem in Palli Aike Cave (figs. 57, 58). In 1959 four more were found in Fell's Cave by Henry Reichlen and Annette Laming-Emperaire [Emperaire et al. 1963: plate VI]. Subsequently John Fell secured other examples, now displayed in a regional museum in Punta Arenas, Chile [Bird found an additional fishtail point in his excavations in 1970; see fig. 76—ed.]. All of these were found in association with bones of extinct horse [*Parahipparion saldiasi*], giant ground sloth [*Mylodon listai*], and guanaco. . . . If the figures [the radiocarbon dates of approximately 11,000 years] are valid, then the associated projectile points are, at this time, the oldest dated points known in South America. As such, their distribution and characteristics should be of some general interest.

(from Bird 1969a)

Bird's 1969*a* article goes on to review where other such points had been found in Argentina (Estancia Los Toldos site), Uruguay (Department of Flores), and Ecuador (El Inga site). Using six different characteristics, he compares the numerous points from El Inga, near Quito, with the Fell's Cave fishtail points. He notes that the two sites are separated by 4,300 miles, but concludes that "the two lots [of points] create an impression of close identity and cultural unity, much as the widely scattered Clovis and Clovis-like points do in North America." The appearance of a fishtail point near Madden Lake, Panama, led Bird to his final seasons of fieldwork by that lake, where he excavated in search of evidence of early man (Bird and Cooke 1977, 1978).

Discoidal Stones

Two discoidal stones were found in Fell's Cave (fig. 12 in chapter 2), and one in Palli Aike. At Fell's Cave the association with extinct fauna was clear-cut, for they lay directly beneath the fallen rock slabs isolating Period I material from subsequent occupation. In and about the fire hearths bones of giant sloth and horse were abundant, with some of the latter articulated as if from a freshly butchered carcass.

The larger of the two discoidal stones is of vesicular mafic lava. It weighs 1,124 g, varies in diameter from 12.2 to 12.35 cm, is 6.1 cm thick at the center, and thins to 5.5 cm at the rounded edge. This lava might be compared to a Swiss cheese with far more than the usual number of bubbles. After being pecked to shape, the subsequent smoothing touched only the ridges and high points between the bubble spaces. Microscopic examination does not reveal any appreciable differences between the smoothing of sides and edges; consequently, again, surface examination does not help in determining function. Clearly it is unsuited for pigment grinding and has not been used for that purpose.

The second Fell's Cave specimen is of vesicular porphyritic felsic lava; it weighs 476 g, varies in diameter from 8.5 to 8.3 cm, and is 4.2 cm thick at the center, thinning to 3.6 cm at the margin. As with the others, the degree and nature of smoothing on sides and edges are the same. In this case the smoothing has not eliminated the pecking hollows.

The third example is from Palli Aike Cave, roughly 16 mi. eastward from Fell's Cave. While this cave yielded the same cultural record as Fell's, the maximum thickness of the debris formed mainly since the extinction of the horse and sloth amounted to only 54 in. At the entrance, an area subjected to strong wind and other erosion, the accumulation tapered to about 6 in. in thickness. The discoidal stone was found farther in, between 10 and 15 in. below the surface, where the thickness has in places increased to a maximum of 18 in. While there were no readily traceable strata in this part of the accumulation and no horse or sloth bones were in immediate association, such bones were found within a few feet, laterally, in comparable relationship to the cave floor. Thus, while the association with extinct fauna was not as clear-cut as at Fell's Cave, it is a reasonable assumption that the specimen relates to the same period. This is supported by the fact that no similar discoidal stones were, or have since been, found with material of subsequent periods at these or other sites.

The Palli Aike specimen was made from a creamy white welded tuff, the diameter ranging from 7.9 to 8.3 cm. The thickness at the center is 5.2 cm, and the intact side shows little curvature. The surfaces, although somewhat modified by time, retain pecking marks and limited evidence of smoothing on the periphery. Several fragments have broken off, exposing fracture surfaces so irregular that breakage seems more the result of internal weakness or stress rather than knocks or blows. By measuring the volume by displacement before and after restoring the missing portions with plasticine, it was evident that loss by breakage amounts to about 9.5 percent. As the present weight is 354 g, it must have weighed close to 390 g before breakage.

Bird also discussed a fourth discoidal stone found by Professor Osvaldo Menghin at the Los Toldos site in Argentina 310 mi. north of Fell's and Palli Aike caves. It was found in a layer with two probable fishtail points. Bird concluded that the wear pattern on this discoidal stone ruled out its being used for pigment grinding.

A comparison of the four specimens does nothing to resolve the riddle of their function. The marked variations in size and the nature of the materials leave only form and lack of obvious use abrasion as features shared in common. While others will ultimately be found, it will be many years before a large series is available for study. Even then I suspect that they, like the similar disoidal stones of a much later time in the United States, will defy identification.   *(from Bird 1970)*

Scrapers

Large scrapers in a variety of forms (fig. 59) were found in layer V, the oldest, at Fell's Cave. Nos. 1 to 14 are varieties of sidescrapers; nos. 8 to 14 are single-edge rough flakes; nos. 15 to 20 are varieties of endscrapers.

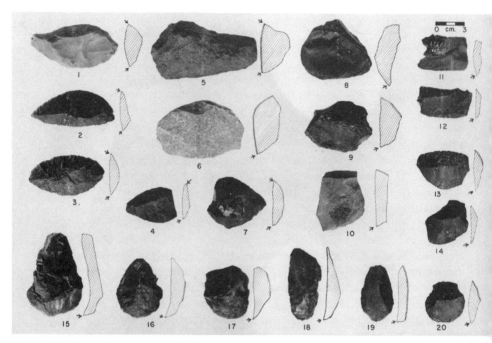

Fig. 59. Scrapers from layer V at Fell's Cave. Nos. 1 to 14 are sidescrapers: (1) rough, two-sided; (2) carefully shaped, two-edged; (3) like 2, but with slight bilateral flaking; (4) double, reversed-edge; (5) heavy, two-edged; (6) heavy, single-edged; (7) two sides to point; (14) rough single-edge flakes. Nos. 15 to 20 are endscrapers of various sizes and forms.

Bone Implements

Four bone fragments (fig. 60, nos. 5–8) which may be the point and shaft parts of flaking tools were found in layer V. Later, when John Fell excavated materials from the lowest stratum, I thought a broken, worked piece he found might fit a small section [that I excavated]. This proved to be the case, as the piece (41.1/1985*b*) does fit it (fig. 60, nos. 8 and 9). A similar worked piece (fig. 61) was found by Emperaire (Emperaire et al. 1963: pl. VII, H2). These two worked pieces were obviously fitted to some shaft or handle, and if they had ends (points) like the known pieces (41.1/1985*a*) and one in Mr. Fell's collection (Fe 238), presently in the Punta Arenas museum exhibit, then they must be [the basal sections] of some type of flaking tool. In that case the missing wooden handles might have been long enough to serve as crutch or extension to transmit pressure from the shoulder or some other part of the body such as Crabtree's flakers used for

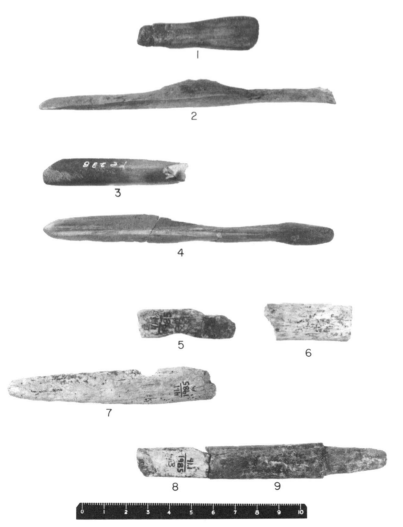

Fig. 60. Bone artifacts from lowest stratum of Fell's Cave. Nos. 1, 2, 3, 4, and 9 were excavated by John Fell. Nos. 5, 6, 7, and 8 were excavated by Bird. Nos. 3 and 7 are points of flaking tools. No. 9 is the basal portion of a flaking tool.

Fig. 61. Three views of the basal portion of a bone flaker, excavated by
H. Reichlen and A. Emperaire at Fell's Cave (Musée de l'Homme, Paris).

removing long blades from obsidian cores. Obviously both known basal
sections broke when under considerable pressure.

Both examples appear to have been made from sloth bones, as the contemporary horse bones do not have the same structure or outer thickness,
while some sloth bones do. Also, there is no evidence of marrow cavity—
only the porous internal bone as in whale and sloth. The only source of
comparable bone from horse would have to be the rib bone.

The outer surface of the worked basal fragment excavated by John Fell
retains some longitudinal scratches left by the scraping tool edge used to
shape it. Similar scratches occur on the sections which are clearly flaking
tool tips.

A bone awl (fig. 12 in chapter 2) was also found in layer V.

(from Bird 1969b)

FAUNAL REMAINS

The Horse Remains, a Disconcerting Find

Beneath the [sterile] sandstone [layer] we discover still more bones and among them a type of [fishtail] stone spear point new to us. That is gratifying enough, but when we see that the bones are those of horses, there comes a most disconcerting feeling.

The domestic horse did not exist in the Americas before the Spanish came, and if these bones should prove to belong to an animal introduced by Europeans, all our conclusions on our previous work were wrong. Although I was willing to swear that 400 years was all too short a time to account for all the material we had uncovered, those horse bones gave us momentarily something of a shock [see entries for January 2 to 5 in Daily Life, below—ed.]. The only alternative was that they belonged to a prehistoric relative of the common horse. This ancient horse was known to live in South America in times long past, but so far as I knew no one had proved that it still existed when even the earliest people lived here. Without special training in paleontology it was not for me to identify these bones, but it was apparent they were of smaller, stockier animals than those used in Patagonia today. Later examination proved that we had found the first evidence that this ancient horse was hunted and eaten by the early natives of South America. *(from Bird 1938b: 77)*

Classifications

The faunal specimens from Fell's Cave have AMNH catalogue nos. 41.1/1993 (layer V) and 41.1/1994 (layers I to IV). They are marked with field labels F1 to F8, which indicate the following locations within the excavation:

F1: Layer I, area against cave wall
F2: Layers I and II, area away from cave wall
F3: Layer II, area against wall
F4: Layer III
F5: Layer IV (above rockfall from roof)
F6: Layer V (material in and near fireplace 2)
F7: Layer V (material in and near fireplace 3)
F8: Layer V, general

Figure 62 shows the locations of some of the larger bones of extinct fauna in layer V. Faunal specialist Thomas Amorosi has made the following tentative classifications.

Aves

Material: 1 thoracic vertebra, 1 innominate, 9 humeri, 1 coracoid, 2 ulnae, 1 tibiotarsus, 1 fercula.

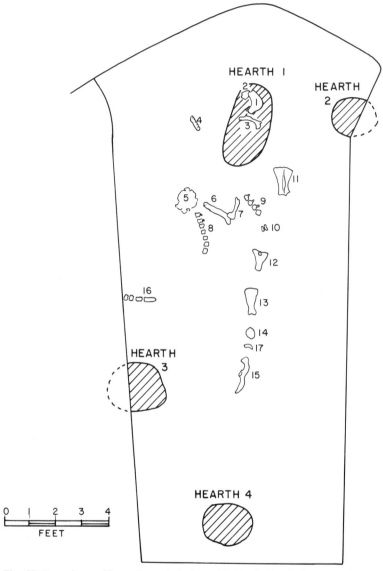

Fig. 62. Locations of hearths and sloth and horse bones in layer V of Fell's Cave: (1) horse mandible; (2) fragment of horse mandible under no. 1; (3) unidentified bone beneath hearth; (4) horse mandible with teeth; (5) fragmented posterior basal portion of horse skull; (6) horse leg bone; (7) adjoining fragments of horse leg bone; (8) neck vertebrae (seven and a half) from horse; (9) crushed horse vertebrae; (10) isolated sloth vertebrae; (11) horse shoulder blade; (12) horse sternum; (13) horse shoulder blade; (14) sloth vertebrae; (15) horse pelvis; (16) horse phalanges; (17) horse tooth.

Distribution: F3—4 humeri, I tibiotarsus, I fercula. F5—I thoracic vertebra, I innominate. F8—I coracoid, 5 humeri, 2 ulnae.

Rodentia

Material: 25 fragmentary crania, 19 mandibles, 5 incisors, 14 molars, I humerus, I radius, I ulna.
Distribution: F3—21 crania, 18 mandibles, 5 incisors, 12 molars. F5—3 crania, I mandible, 2 molars.

Mustelidae

Material: I mandible.
Distribution: F2—I mandible.

Canidae

Material: 4 crania, 3 bullae, 39 maxillae, 65 mandibles, 4 incisors, 2 premolars, 32 canines, 39 molars, 34 tooth fragments, 5 atlases, I axis, 12 cervical vertebrae, 5 thoracic vertebrae, 10 lumbar vertebrae, 2 vertebrae fragments, 16 innominates, 2 scapulae, 3 radii, 5 ulnae, 4 metapodials, I first phalanx, 2 femora, I tibia, I articulated manus.
Distribution: F1—2 maxillae, I mandible. F2—3 crania, I maxilla, 6 mandibles, I incisor, 3 canines, 7 molars, 2 tooth fragments, I atlas, I axis, I cervical verte-bra, I thoracic vertebra, 3 innominates, I scapula, I femur, I tibia. F3—3 max-illae, 3 radii, 4 ulnae, 4 metapodials, I first phalanx, I femur, I articulated manus. F4—2 canines, I molar, 3 tooth fragments, 7 mandibles [J. B. considered that these mandibles were broken for marrow extraction—ed.]. F5—I cranium, 3 bullae, 32 maxillae, 45 mandibles, 3 incisors, 25 canines, 2 premolars, 30 molars, 18 tooth fragments, 4 atlases, 11 cervical vertebrae, 4 thoracic vertebrae, 10 lum-bar vertebrae, 2 vertebrae fragments, 12 innominates, I scapula, I ulna. F8—I maxilla, 6 mandibles, 2 canines, I molar, 6 tooth fragments, I innominate.

Camelidae (Guanaco)

Material: 9 molars, 6 humeri, I metacarpal, 4 calcanea, I astragalus, I metapodial, 2 femora, 2 patellae, 3 tibiae.
Distribution: F6—5 molars, 5 humeri, I calcaneus, I femur, 2 tibiae. F7—I mo-lar, I astragalus, I calcaneus, I metapodial, I tibia. F8—3 molars, I humerus, I metacarpal, 2 calcanea, I femur, 2 patellae.

Onohippidium (Horse) (figs. 62, 63)

Material: 3 cranial fragments, 2 maxillae, 9 incisors, 4 canines, 64 molars, 2 tooth fragments, I atlas, I axis, 7 thoracic vertebrae, I sacral vertebra, I caudal vertebra, I scapula, 2 humeri, I radius, I ulna, 4 carpals/tarsals, I calcaneus, I metatarsal, 3 metapodials, 4 first phalanges, 3 second phalanges, I third phalanx, 3 femora, I patella, 2 tibiae.

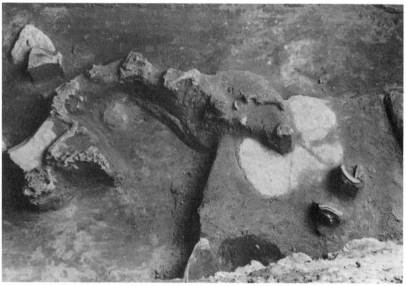

Fig. 63. Details of bones of extinct horse and sloth in layer V. *Top left:* horse mandible and sloth bone; *top right:* horse shoulder blade and sloth vertebra; *bottom left:* horse vertebrae (articulated) and basal rear portion of skull; *bottom right:* sloth bone (*center*), horse tooth, horse pelvis (*left*).

Distribution: F1—1 femur (modern horse on surface). F6—2 molars, 2 tooth fragments, 1 calcaneus, 2 metapodials. F8—3 crania, 2 maxillae, 3 mandibles, 9 incisors, 4 canines, 19 molars, 43 tooth fragments, 1 atlas, 1 axis, 7 thoracic vertebrae, 1 sacral vertebra, 1 caudal vertebra, 1 scapula, 1 humerus, 1 radius, 1 ulna, 4 carpals/tarsals, 1 metatarsal, 1 metapodial, 4 first phalanges, 3 second phalanges, 1 third phalanx, 2 femora, 1 patella, 2 tibiae.

Mylodontidae (Giant Ground Sloth) (figs. 62, 63)

Material: 1 humerus, 1 metacarpal, 1 femur, 1 fibula, 230 skin ossicles.
Distribution: F6—1 metacarpal. F8—1 humerus, 1 femur, 230 skin ossicles.

Fragmentary Material Attributed to Class

Mammalia, large-sized: 27 tooth fragments, 26 cranial, 56 ribs, 99 vertebrae, 299 long bones, 19 flat bones, 12 phalanges, 615 unidentified.
Mammalia, medium-sized: 6 cranial, 6 ribs, 1 vertebra, 6 long bones, 1 metapodial, 2 unidentified.
Mammalia, small-sized: 3 cranial, 1 long bone.
Unidentifiable fragments: 173.

DAILY LIFE

Thursday, December 24, 1936

Clear and windy. Had a hard time getting the old car going. Went to the cave and shifted the kitchen down near our tent. Junius and Pedro went down to the river in the P.M. to another cave [Fell's] and started digging a trench. Many large pieces of stone to be moved. Red sunset—strange rays of light.

Christmas

Junius and I have known each other just five years. He bought me a large box of candy and a cigarette holder. We spent the morning getting Christmas dinner, as John [Fell] was coming over—cream of tomato soup, pot roast, and Wilma Cameron's pudding. It turned out very well—the pudding was a little doughy outside, but fine inside. A terrific gale of wind all A.M., letting up somewhat in P.M.—cloud of dust racing across the valley; the sun was warm, though. After dinner John took us to a lagoon nearby; there is a low rock cliff along one side with several very small caves, some with streaks of red paint at the entrance. Picked up quite a lot of things. Back to *estancia* with John to tea and dinner. John shot two *caiquenes* [geese]—so pretty. After a very good dinner it wasn't hard to persuade us to spend the night, although we hadn't planned to. Listened to the radio— so little Christmas music.

Saturday, December 26

John walked back with us, leading his horse. Followed along the river and did a little collecting at some eroded places. A small cave. Junius shot a big *carancho* [hawk; *Polyborus plancus*]; it measured 5 ft. from one wing tip to the other—looked like an eagle. John had lunch with us and then we all went down to the river [cave]. He went over the sifted dirt. Left after tea. We found one or two old-type [triangular] points.

Sunday, December 27

Pedro washed his clothes and then went over to the *estancia* for the day. Junius and I went down to the *vega* by the river to see what the wind has exposed—found about seventeen more chipped tools—about forty-six in all!—some points, lots of scrapers and the point of a wedge. John came along on his way upriver to see how the rams were—he found a fine bola—the third perfect one from this side of the river. That will be a fine place when it's been eroded more. Pulled a sheep out of the river—very weak. Because of the dry season, the animals spend most of their time in the valley and often get bogged down. Many have died that way. Took some water back in the truck. One of the men from the *estancia* stopped by as we were finishing lunch and John came over on his way home. He'd brought us some more milk. Junius and I [went] down to the river cave [Fell's] to work in the P.M. Showers. Pedro back to supper. Rain in eve.

Monday, December 28

Calm, warm day—a few showers. We all walked over to the cave, taking our pots, etc., along and had lunch over there. The cave gets larger as it goes down—a fine place. A few Ona and Patagonian points, and many triangular ones at bottom. Some dog jaws (?)—five—and bones at bottom—if they *are* dog it should be clear proof the Indians had them long before the whites came. About 6 ft. down a layer of water-laid clay, and below that some buried bones, among them some very large ones. In the evening I washed specimens and Junius shellacked bones.

Tuesday, December 29

A very nice day. A shepherd brought us half a sheep and a bottle of milk. Junius is widening the trench since it is going to be so deep. They took off the top layer, which took most of the day—not much going through the sifter. I made some specimen bags and did some mending.

Wednesday, December 30

Very windy—dust and sand blowing around and it was most disagreeable. Our camp is sheltered and was comparatively calm, but at the cave it was

Fig. 64. View into the mouth of Fell's Cave during excavation, showing the cave entrance, the conglomerate in which the cave has been eroded, and the lava flow overlying the conglomerate. Note the large rocks that have fallen in front of the cave from above. Pedro Ojeda, Bird's assistant, stands beside the cave.

pretty bad. Mr. Fell [John's father] came over, bringing our mail—Christmas card and candy from Sr. Navarro, magazines from home and an airmail from Doris—also Clarence Day's *After All* that she had said she was sending. Such an amusing essay about Mrs. Elsie Clews Parsons. Mr. Fell stayed to lunch—fortunately it was a good one—pea soup, fried beef, rice, and custard. He watched the digging for a while. Many dog (or monte fox) bones. I'm learning quite a lot about anatomy! Junius [went] over to the *estancia* after supper for more provisions, etc. Muñeca went along and caught a mouse. She caught a lizard in the afternoon. Calmish eve (fig. 64).

Thursday, December 31

If possible, even windier than yesterday, miserable. Not many specimens in this new trench—strange. Awfully hard cooking and eating, with the dirt flying. Especially bad going over the dirt at the foot of the sifter. Your eyes get full of dust. Two men stopped as we were starting supper—the mechanic and shearer on their way to shear at Mr. Hamilton's *estancia*, the Portada, just up the river. They'll all come back from there and finish the shearing here.

New Year's Day, 1937

Cloudy and showers, but not windy. Junius, Pedro, and Muñeca off to shoot young steamer ducks—came back with two. While they were gone, the Fells and Mr. Campbell arrived to spend the day, bringing rhubarb, bread, and milk. They took Mr. C. down to see the river cave. Junius and I washed, classified, and packed specimens in the P.M. The others left after tea.

Saturday, January 2

In bottom layer Junius found a new (to us) type of point, sort of "fishtail," not very sharp point; poorly chipped except for stem. At same level, uncovered skeleton of horse, head squashed by a rock, bones quite scattered. Seem to be European hoofs—but a small, stocky horse with very small, broad head. At same level, part of a large vertebra, which looks very much like that [of sloth] in Palli Aike cave! It certainly would be fun if it were!

Sunday, January 3

Cloudy and showers. A shepherd over from *estancia* and stayed to lunch. Mr. Fell, John, and Mr. C. came to tea, bringing jelly (which Mr. F. had made!), butter, and milk. Junius, of course, said nothing about the big vertebra. Mr. F. more convinced than ever that horse bones we've been finding belong to original American horses—extinct—whose fossil heads he's seen out at Cape Fairweather! John and Junius collected many bones from skeleton of the four-year-old horse nearby to compare with the old ones— latter similar—usually the same width but shorter. More "fishtail" points. Soil at bottom is too damp to sift. Heavy rain in late P.M. and eve—the camp certainly needs it.

Monday, January 4

Windy as ever, but the rain laid the dust somewhat, so it wasn't so disagreeable. John brought us another quarter sheep. Another point, and a fragment of a large, strange jaw. Junius dug a test pit and found sand 19 in. below floor level, water-deposited, with some of the iron sand usually associated with gold—he washed out a plate full, but found no gold. Junius [went] over to *estancia* in eve for more provisions.

Tuesday, January 5

Windy again. Cardenas, the shepherd, came by and Junius asked him to ask John to come over sometime (he wanted to tell him about the sloth).

Junius took pictures from the top of the cliff on the other side of the river—wading through that cold water in the cold wind—from the jutting-out point of the cliff looking down where the cave is. And [he took] many time exposures of the horse and sloth bones as they lie in position on their little piles of earth. The rest of the trench is excavated on down about a foot to the floor. There are four different fire hearths at that level. John and Mr. Fell came over just before we left in eve and were very much interested in what Junius had to tell. Junius lifted the large, round sloth bone while they were there, so we have witnesses as to its association with the horse bones.

Wednesday, January 6

Not so windy—no whitecaps on lagoon in front of cave. Junius spent most of day covering one side of the shellacked horse and sloth bones with pieces of burlap soaked in a paste of plaster and water, which soon hardens, forming a "cast" for the bones, so that even the most delicate ones can be moved. The two sets of vertebrae he packed all together in two long packages. There are a few bones, not horse or guanaco and apparently too small for sloth, which may be still another extinct animal. We just can't understand the presence of the horse bones so far down. They couldn't be Spanish ones, even from a shipwreck, for Magellan came by here in 1520 or 1521 and there are four entirely different cultures [lithic complexes] above them, not counting the Tehuelches, who apparently did not use this place. The "Ona" arrow [points] are in the first 10 in.—and when Musters was here, the Indians—Tehuelches—used no arrows and knew nothing of them. The last mention of Onas is by Father Faulkner, who says they were on both sides of the Straits in his time, before 1740. The bones don't seem to belong to the extinct species, which we believe had toes instead of hoofs.

Thursday, January 7

Cloudy and calmer. The bullock cart came over for the twelve bags of bat manure from the first cave and also took some of our gear over. John came over to lunch. At the last minute Junius found several more small bones of the sloth and one large one. There wasn't time to dry it, so he covered it with greased paper, applied the burlap and plaster over that, and lifted it out—worked very well. Junius and Pedro cut *calafate* and made a fence to keep sheep out of the hole. We've used the last of our tea, meat, salt, vegetables, and hardtack—which, by the way, is very good soaked and then fried in fat. Packed up at the camp and just as we were loading the truck it began to pour. Didn't get off until almost 7:00 P.M., but when we reached the *estancia*, they insisted that we had plenty of time to have a bath; it did feel so good! Mr. Campbell still here.

Friday, January 8

A gale of wind all day—the strongest yet; the houses shook at times and the clouds raced across the sky so fast you could hardly see their shadows on the hills. Junius had all the bones and specimens out in the toolshed, sorting, tracing, and repacking them.

(*from M. Bird, 1934–1947: 329–335*)

EXCAVATIONS BY JOHN FELL AND THE FRENCH MISSION

In 1952 Junius Bird asked John Fell to secure a carbon sample from the lowermost deposit at Fell's Cave. Fell soon wrote Bird (Fell 1952) that when he was cleaning debris in the cave, the French paleontologist José Emperaire and his wife, archaeologist Annette Laming, arrived. The Emperaires made a small test excavation in the cave, but never published the results. In their publication on later work in Fell's Cave (Emperaire et al. 1963: 170) they noted that this first test "allowed us to recover the basic aspect of the evidence noted by Bird." John Fell assisted them, and made this brief description in a letter (1952) to Bird:

> The Frenchman cleaned a meter or so down so as to get a clear outline of your layers; he worked with his wife and myself, through all the layers finding some scrapers in all, three points in [period] three, four bone points in [period] two, no points in [period] one, but horse and sloth bones in a bad state of preservation— owing to a fire that came down through all the layers, but no carbon worth taking out—and the French did not seem interested in it.

The French publication (Emperaire et al. 1963: 190) includes a schematic plan view indicating where the Fell and Emperaire excavations took place. Figure 65 published here is based on that plan and on Junius Bird's notes from his work there in 1969–1970. The Emperaire plan has a skewed north arrow and José Emperaire's 1952 excavation is incorrectly dated 1953.

Shortly after the Emperaires left, John Fell removed a carbon sample from the lowest deposit in the cave (chapter 2). He found, among other artifacts, a worked bone object (fig. 60, no. 9) which Bird recognized as fitting together with a bone specimen (41.1/1985*a*) excavated three decades earlier. Fell's excavations in the back and front of the cave occurred sporadically through 1958. Their purpose was to obtain artifacts for his collection and for the museum in Punta Arenas. A record and classification (made by Bird) of those artifacts is on file in the Junius Bird Laboratory of South American Archaeology at the AMNH. Bird noted in his diary (1969–1970*a*, January 5), and wanted it on public record, that John Fell had recognized the richness, if not the antiquity, of Fell's Cave before anyone. In fact, before Bird arrived in 1936, Fell had dug in the slope in front of the cave. Fell then reported finding some small (Ona) points and some larger ones of basalt.

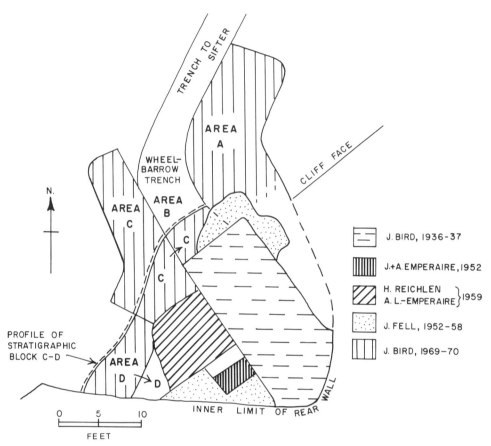

Fig. 65. Plan view of Fell's Cave depicting areas excavated by different investigators.

In 1958 the Emperaires returned to Chilean Patagonia and made test excavations in the plain between the cliff (where Fell's Cave is located) and the river. José Emperaire considered that a test excavation about 100 m upstream was particularly important. It was a trench at the foot of a shelter named Oosin Aike. The notes on these tests were lost and nothing was published on them. Plans were made to return to the area of the cave in late 1958 or 1959, but José Emperaire was killed by the collapse of his excavation at Riesco Island in Ponsonby Sound in December 1958. His work was carried on in and near Fell's Cave by his wife Annette Laming-Emperaire and Henry Reichlen. Between March 20 and 25, 1959, they examined several sites near Fell's Cave, including the Oosin Aike shelter, which, it turned out, did not contain early archaeological levels.

Between March 25 and April 15 they investigated a block of debris in Fell's Cave. That excavation was located southwest of Bird's 1936–1937 excavation and between John Fell's excavations and the cave's entrance (fig. 65). The published results of this work by A. Laming-Emperaire and H. Reichlen (J. Emperaire et al. 1963) describe artifacts and faunal remains in stratigraphic relationships similar to those found by Bird.

When Bird returned to the cave for further work in 1969, he noted in his diary (1969–1970, December 15):

> The Emperaires and Reichlen dumped the material they moved from the inside of the shelter on top of the location where I had my dump sifter years ago. They did not sift, trusting their troweling for recovery of artifacts. As the dirt has washed and blown away, flakes, scrapers, and points are to be found over the dump area.

EXCAVATIONS, 1969–1970

In November 1968 Bird had the opportunity to return, very briefly, to Fell's Cave to work with an NBC film crew making a television documentary, *The First Americans*. This visit to the cave after several decades stimulated him to pursue further research there. He was particularly interested in excavating the deposits remaining in the cave, and in obtaining a series of samples for pollen analysis and for radiocarbon dating.

Thus thirty-three years after the first excavations, on December 15, 1969, Bird renewed work at Fell's Cave (fig. 66). The investigation was completed in February 1970.

Bird (1969–1970*b*, December 15) described his excavation strategy:

> After studying the situation, I decided that there were several things to be taken in sequence. The first was to clear out all of the loose dirt and debris left inside the shelter. Secondly, we could deepen the wheelbarrow runway. This would give us an exposure running more or less straight out from the shelter so that we could see the nature of the formation and the strata, where they exist. The third step would be the removal of a section [area C] parallel with John's wheelbarrow runway and that would give us a wide and safe place to bring out the material further in. I do not want to cut out deeper the existing wheelbarrow runway with so much stone exposed in the sidewall. It probably would not hold as a vertical wall and would be dangerous. The final stage of our work, as I see it now, will be to cut a section a few feet wide (from the surface to the bottom of the deposit) parallel to the existing vertical exposure across the deposit. Some of this will lie under the overhang [area D], a little of it just outside of it [south end of area C], but it is from that section that we can anticipate getting fire hearths [for radiocarbon dates] for some are visible in the exposure now. This afternoon we will start building a ramp for the sifter off to the east of the old dump area. Whatever we move and sift this time will then not interfere if someone later wants to excavate the area in front of the shelter.

Fig. 66. Fell's Cave and camp during excavation in 1969 and 1970.

Preliminary Operations

Bird and his crew (Tom Bird, Patricio Núñez, Hugo Yávar, George Duncan, and Patti Fell) spent nearly a week cleaning up the old excavations in the cave, and then switched to preparing the wheelbarrow trench (area B). Bird recorded (1969–1970b, December 24):

> The three of us, Tom, Patricio, and I started cutting down the main trench to the sifter and got rid of one nice boulder by smashing it in part and rolling the rest. We took out 107 barrow loads each loaded to the brim, according to Tom. Most were rock. We sifted samples of the clay but found nothing. . . . One gets about one barrow load of dirt to three of stone, if one is lucky. The job is going well there.

On December 27:

> We started first with the unit that runs into John Fell's old wheelbarrow trench (fig. 67). [We] labeled it A1. . . . It yielded very little, and the same was true of the next layer down that we took out on the slope with lots of rock. Deepening the wheelbarrow trench—the first thing in the morning—[yielded] forty-one loads.

Artifacts from area A have AMNH catalogue nos. 41.2/8115 to 41.2/8121e. They consist of twenty-five specimens: five Ona points, fifteen hafted scrapers, one spear point, one knife point, one blank, and two single-edge scrapers.

Bird's field notebook (1969–1970a) records a description of area C and its excavation:

> This area lies to the west of the old wheelbarrow trench, parallel with it, starting at the large deeply bedded boulder at the north end and running south to the old excavation edge and turning or extending slightly to the west. It was necessary to remove area C because it consisted mainly of fallen rock which threatened to collapse into the wheelbarrow trench (area B) as this was deepened. The extension [of area C] to the west at its south end could not be removed without digging away fill on their western sides.
>
> The subdivision into layers of the fill in area C was entirely arbitrary. Layer 1 consisted almost entirely of rocks, with some dirt thrown from area B by the

Fig. 67. Wheelbarrow trench to east and area A to right of it.

Emperaire group; layer 2, roughly 25 to 40 cm in depth, again was almost entirely
of rock with virtually sterile dirt; the same applies to layer 3 below 50 cm. From it
were thirty-two barrow loads of rock to eight loads of dirt. The dirt color is light
yellowish brown—*café con leche;* only in under the large boulder overhang at
the north end was there dark brown soil, and this did yield Period V material. As it
was a pocket among the fallen rock cleared by Hugo, the material recovered was
marked "Hugo's mine" (HM). It was impossible to separate it (area C, layers 2 to
6) by division as there were openings and holes in among the rocks into which
chips, flakes, and artifacts must have fallen at varying depths. [Area C, layers 2 to 5,
produced only three rough, single-edge flakes (AMNH catalogue nos. 41.2/8122*a*
to 41.2/8122*c*). The material from Hugo's Mine was classified separately as catalogue nos. 41.2/8123*a* to 41.2/8125*f*. It included seven stemmed points and five
scrapers. Area C, layer 6, produced twenty-six artifacts, consisting of one knife,
two stemmed points, and a variety of scrapers (AMNH cat. nos. 41.2/8126 to
41.2/8132*b*).—ed.]

Bird's diary (1969–1970*b*: January 2) records additional data about area C, and
includes one of several elaborate descriptions he made of the removal of large
boulders from the debris:

Today we worked in area C, just west of the Emperaire-Fell wheelbarrow
trench. This area is a mass of fallen rock without any traceable structural strata, so
we have to subdivide it arbitrarily. Many loads of rock have to be moved before
one can scrape together one load of dirt. . . . The inner portion of area C is well
within the protection of the cliff and partially under the overhang. Among the
stones and in the dirt there are lots of guanaco bones, lots of stone chips, some
scrapers, and among these the small flensing tools (hafted scrapers) of the type that
one gets with the Period IV and V projectile points. . . .
    We started work in the morning by removing a large stone about 3 ft. long by
70 or 80 cm on a side—roughly triangular in section. It projected from the face
of the old excavation wall and is to be seen in photographs (fig. 68) we made of
that surface when it was cleaned off and ready for removal. John Fell warned us
against that particular stone when we first came here. It looked as if it would fall at
any time. To prevent this, we propped a large plank up under it and wedged it so
that the plank took the weight. After we had removed all of the overburden and
the rock lay exposed, George rigged the old house jack we had, which is not a
spiral screw jack, but works with a crank and ratchet, and by extending this jack
full length, then by tying ropes to the rock and anchoring the end of the jack with
enough rope secured to the big boulder downhill, when George cranked the jack
to close it, it exerted a lot of pull on the ropes and slid the rock 8 or 9 in. at a
time. The problem was to maintain tension on the ropes and I used an old trick
learned on the *Morrissey* [Captain Bob Bartlett's schooner] years ago—the same
sort of stopknot and short rope used to take the tension on the main halyard when
hoisting sail. After the sails were up you used a short rope and stopknot and then
you can secure the end of the halyards. Well, the rig and system worked very

Fig. 68. Large rock at end of area C. Patricio Núñez and Hugo Yávar remove debris.

well—the big stone slid away from the face of the cut without jarring loose any dirt at all from the edge on which it rested.

Excavation of Stratigraphic Block C–D

By January 7, 1970, the rocky debris of area C had been removed down through level 6 to a rock fall line (RFL), and surface material over area D had been removed. Excavation was about to begin on the stratigraphic block of area D, and area C (southern end) below the RFL. The RFL of layer 7 in areas C and D is not to be confused with the considerably deeper rockfall found by Bird in the excavations decades before. While clearing the wheelbarrow trench, Bird noted (1969–1970b: January 9) that

> in this portion of the shelter not as much of the sandstone had broken off from the ceiling prior to the last [rock]fall as in the area we excavated in 1937. In that area the slabs lay on debris and isolated the debris of Period I. In this part of the shelter [area B] the lower slab [from the ceiling] rests directly on the water-washed clay, the surface of which dips rather steeply towards the interior of the shelter.

A scaffold was rigged for the careful removal of the upper layers, and to avoid the risk of accidentally dislodging debris (fig. 69). Bird wrote (1969–1970b: January 8): "I spent some time on the scaffold recording and marking strata. The mark-

Fig. 69. Scaffold rigged for removal of upper layers.

ing was done just as we did at the Huaca Prieta in Peru, driving in nails and securing a line to them to serve as a guide for the removal of layers" (fig. 70).

Figure 71 presents the plan views of some of the layers of the C–D block excavated by Bird. The irregular southeastern side resulted after the exposed faces of the Emperaire and Fell excavations had been cleaned. On January 9 Bird recorded (1969–1970b) that "while I intend to take out only a minimum amount of debris, it would yield enough C-14 samples for our purpose. The big problem will be in getting enough artifacts to identify the cultural divisions."

The following comments on the layers of the C–D block have been extracted from Bird's diary (1969–1970b) and fieldnotes (1969–1970a). Additional details, particularly concerning the location within layers of specific artifacts, remain unreported here. Figure 72 depicts the strata of the C–D block. The artifact distributions in the stratigraphy are presented in table 16. The artifacts from this excavation are catalogued at the AMNH under nos. 41.2/8133a to 41.2/8336.

Layers 2–6 (Area D)

Clear-cut divisions between some of the layers is difficult if not impossible to trace.

Layer 7

Because of the incorporation of the southern part of area C, the surface of the layer was almost doubled over that of upper layers. A rock fall line (RFL) forms the surface of layer 7 (fig. 72).

Layer 8

The artifacts from this layer were subdivided into the following categories: *capa* 7/8—juncture between layers 7 and 8; *capa* 8c—bones over layer 8; *capa* 8b—a lens of dry debris; *capa* d and e—lower part of layer 8; *capa* f—portion 75 cm wide against cave wall.

Layer 9

An easily traceable stratum through areas C and D. It was separated from layer 10 by a fine, powdery windblown dust.

Layer 10

A loose, fine, sandy-pebbly mixture, light brown in color with small scattered fire hearths. The junction between layers 10 and 11 was somewhat arbitrary.

Layer 11

Slightly darker than layer 10.

Layer 12

A spear thrower contact point and a bone projectile point were found (fig. 74).

Layer 13

Contained two fire hearths, both about 7 or 8 cm deep.

Layer 14

Produced a small fire hearth 4 cm deep. Its southern side was cut off by the eroded and cleaned wall.

Layer 15–16

Has two numbers because 15 is a lens of material on the south side of layer 16.

Layer 16

Produced a small sloth bone, and 44 cm from it at the same level, a fox bone awl.

Fig. 70. Upper strata of C–D block marked by cords on wall.

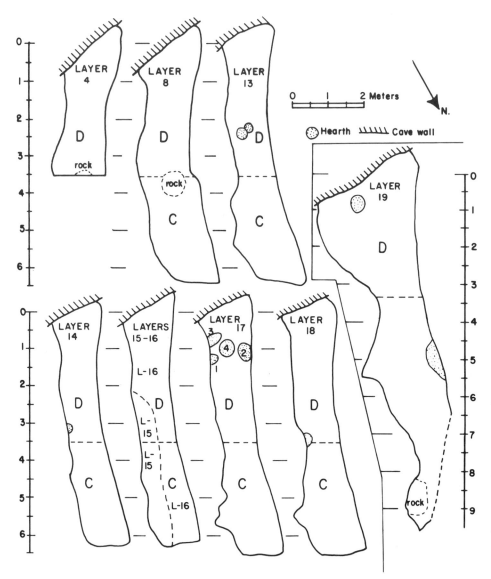

Fig. 71. Plan view of layers in C–D block, 1969–1970 excavation.

Layer 17

Sandy gravel and dirt—quite loose, but firmer than layer 15–16. It is without a clear color or texture change. Several fire hearths here. Hearth 4 lay just below hearths 1, 2, and 3 in a depression 9 cm deep, its bottom reaching almost to the surface of the underlying sterile clay. Such pits could easily have brought up horse and sloth fragments. A horse phalynx was found under the layer's surface 5 cm from the cave wall.

Layer 18–18*a*

18*a* is a lens-shaped deposit combined with layer 18.

Layer 19

Expanded the surface of the excavated debris by nearly one hundred percent by adding undisturbed debris west of area C and debris south of area D by the cave wall. A sloth skull bone fragment and horse metacarpal were found. This layer could be equivalent to the occupation (Period I) before the rockfall of sterile debris so evident in the 1937 trench. There is a fire-blackened area between 4.5 and 5.5 m (fig. 75).

Layer 20

A thin streak only a few cm thick on southwest side. It lay on top of underlying water-laid (sterile) clay. A reworked fishtail point (fig. 76) was found on the surface of layer 20 at 7.33 m. A horse metacarpal was found at 5.25 m.

Layers 21, 21*a*, 22

Sterile.

Radiocarbon Dates

Table 17 presents the radiocarbon dates for samples excavated at Fell's Cave. The first two dates produced were from samples extracted from the lowest part of the occupational debris (Period I) before the excavations in 1969–1970. One was a sample (W-915) secured by John Fell in 1960. It produced an age of 10,720 ± 300 (see The Radiocarbon Dates, chapter 2). The other was a sample (I-3988) removed by Bird in 1968. It produced an age of 11,000 ± 170.

Bird returned to Fell's Cave in 1969–1970 with the intention of securing carbon samples from other strata. More than two dozen samples were taken during the excavation, and nine were sent for processing. The remaining samples, still stored in their original containers, are in the Junius Bird Laboratory of South American Archaeology at the AMNH.

The following additional data about the samples are found in Bird's fieldnotes (1969–1970*a*). All samples were of ash and charcoal from hearths. Measurements give the locations within the layers (see fig. 71).

Table 16. Artifacts from Fell's Cave, 1969–1970

	Layer								
	Area D						Areas C and D		
Group/Category	2	3	4	5	6	7	8	9	10
Points									
Ona, small, barbed		3	6						
Small, triangular			1						
Unidentified, fragment						1			
Patagonian, stemmed		1			5	1	2		
Spear			1				1		
Old-type, stemless, triangular							6	2	1
Fishtail									
Knives									
Hafted		1							
Knife or spear							1	1	
Small, leaf-shaped									1
Single edge (from flake)			1			1	2		
3-edge								2	
Combination knife-scraper	1						1		1
Scrapers									
Rough, single-edge flake	1	6	3	2	9	5	1	1	1
2-edge, large					2		5		2
2-edge, narrow (parallel)				1			1		
2 points									1
2 sides to point	1						2		
1-edge (like 2-edge)		5	1	5	16	7	7	6	4
1-sided, rounded end									5
Large, circular							2	2	2

Layer										
Areas C and D									Position Uncertain	
11	12	13	14	15–16	17ᵃ	18	19	20		Total
										9
										1
										1
									7	16
										2
1	1								5	16
								1		1
										1
										2
										1
1										5
										2
										3
5					26	24	19	24	2	129
2						1			3	15
										2
										1
									2	5
5	8	2	1			2	2		7	78
										5
2		1					1		2	12

Table 16. *(continued)*

Group/Category	Layer								
	Area D						Areas C and D		
	2	3	4	5	6	7	8	9	10
Scrapers									
End					2	1	5		
Reversed 2-edge		1							
Hafted		7	5	4	14	2	10	2	
Fragment, uncertain, misc.			1		1		3	4	
Blank							2		1
Cores					1				
Bolas						1	1		
Bone Tools									
Chipping tool		1				1			
Bird bone awl									
Solid point awl				1					
Bone lance point									
Spear thrower contact point									
Totals	3	25	19	18	46	19	50	22	19

Chips or debitage were found in layers 17 (10 specimens), 18 (73 specimens), and 20 (86 specimens).

| Layer | | | | | | | | | Position Uncertain | Total |
| Areas C and D | | | | | | | | | | |
11	12	13	14	15–16	17ª	18	19	20		
	2			1						11
										1
									11	55
					2					11
3	3									9
3	1									5
1									1	4
1										3
			1		1				1	3
			1							2
	1				2ᵇ					3
		1								1
24	16	4	1	3	31	27	22	25	41	415

ªPolished surface stone.
ᵇCould be awl points.

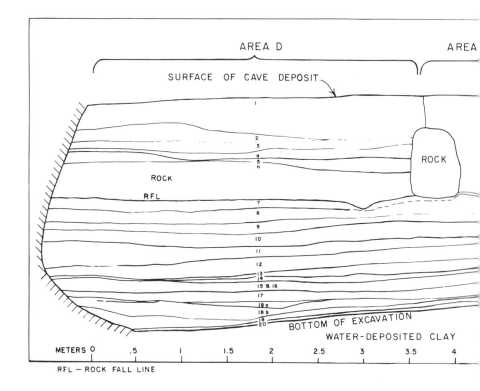

Sample 4

From hearth between 2.6 and 3 m of area D, located 10 cm below the surface of layer 4.

Sample 6

From hearth between 2.18 and 2.7 m just under the surface of layer 8.

Sample 8

Ash from 2.5 m, 11 cm below surface of layer 8.

Sample 3

From small hearth at 4 m entering RFL (rock fall line) in layer 7.

Sample 10

From corner of hearth at 3.6 m, 15 cm below surface of layer 10.

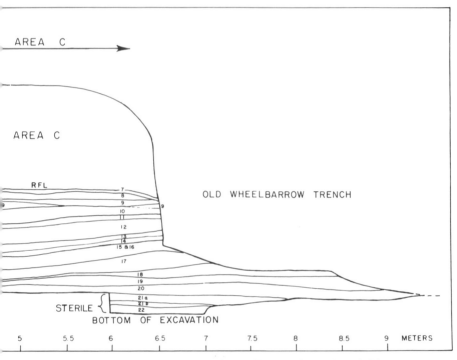

Fig. 72. Profile of C–D block excavated in Fell's Cave by Junius Bird in 1969–1970.

Sample 15

From hearth surrounded by six stones in surface of layer 12 at 2.4 m (fig. 77).

Sample 21

From hearth at 2.65 m, 10 to 14 cm below surface of layer 13.

Sample 18

From hearth at 2.65 m, 10 to 14 cm below surface of layer 13.

Sample 23

From hearth no. 2 at 2.48 m, 7 cm below surface of layer 18.

   The dates from Fell's Cave were used by Bird to estimate the ages of the five periods he established in his 1936–1937 fieldwork (see The Periods, chapter 2). Those dates, along with the artifacts excavated in 1969–1970, were used to classify the layers (excavated 1969–1970) according to the cultural periods:

Fig. 73. Dump sifter used in 1969–1970 excavation. A similar device was used in 1937.

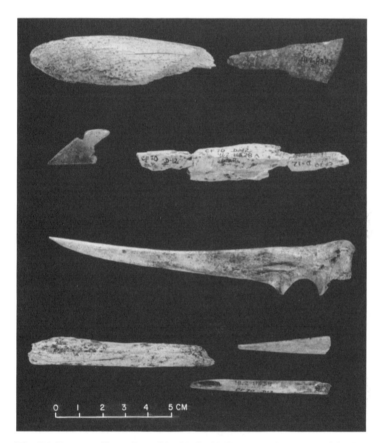

Fig. 74. Bone artifacts found in 1969–1970 excavation (C–D block). *Top row: left*—flaking tool point from layer 7, *right*—flaking tool base from layer 11; *second row: left*—spear thrower contact point from layer 12, *right*—bone spear point from layer 12; *third row:* fox bone awl from layer 16; *fourth row: left*—worked guanaco bone from layer 17, *right*—two bone points, the lower of bird bone, both from layer 17.

Fig. 75. John Fell standing before the excavated C–D block. Layer 19 is exposed.

Period V—Layers 2 to 4
Period IV—Layers 5 to 7
Period III—Layers 8 to 12
Period II—Layers 13 to 17
Period I—Layers 18 to 20

Faunal Remains

The faunal remains from the 1969–1970 excavations were left in Patagonia with the Fell family. Several years later Earl Saxon took the canid and felid remains to England, where they were analyzed by Dr. Juliet Clutton-Brock of the Department of Zoology at the British Museum of Natural History. Her study is published in the following section. Her conclusion that *Canis familiaris* (domestic dog) was present intrigued Bird, who noted in a letter that neither Gaylord

O I 2 3 4 5 CM

Fig. 76. Stone artifacts found in 1969–1970 excavation (C–D block). *Top row (left to right):* stemmed point from layer 5, two hafted scrapers from layer 5, stemmed point from layer 8; *middle row (left to right):* two stemless points from layer 9, two-edge scraper from layer 10; *bottom row (left to right):* two two-edge scrapers from layer 18, a reworked fishtail point from layer 20.

Fig. 77. Fire hearth in layer 12, area D. Stones surround the hearth.

Simpson nor Alfredo Langguth had identified specimens of *Canis* when they had examined the Canidae remains from the 1936–1937 excavations at Fell's Cave. Langguth plans to publish the results of his extensive study in the future. Bird also noted that other bones found in the cave showed no tooth marks or evidence of chewing which might be attributed to dogs. Clutton-Brock responded that gnawed bones can be surprisingly scarce on European and Near Eastern sites, where there certainly were dogs. The canid and felid remains examined by Clutton-Brock were later sent to the American Museum of Natural History. It should be noted that Clutton-Brock's identification is based on teeth alone.

The sloth and ancient horse specimens remain unanalyzed, in Patagonia. However, Bird's fieldnotes (1969–1970a) and diary (1969–1970b) and a list of specimens by Patti Fell give a clear idea of the locations of the extinct fauna within the stratigraphy.

Bird found no sloth or horse down through layer 16, which did contain speci-

le 17. Radiocarbon Dates from Fell's Cave

.	Date	Age	Field No.	Layer	Area	Cultural Period
59	1265A.D. ± 90	685 ± 90	4	4	D	Period V, start of Ona occupation
10	4535B.C. ± 115	6485 ± 115	6	8	D	Period III within period
11	4610B.C. ± 115	6560 ± 115	8	8	D	Period III
38	4790B.C. ± 130	6740 ± 130	3	7	C	Period III
12	6230B.C. ± 135	8180 ± 135	10	10	D/C	Period III, early portion
13	6530B.C. ± 135	8480 ± 135	15	12	D	Period II ends, III starts
15	7080B.C. ± 230	9030 ± 230	21	17	C[a]	Period II within period
14	7150B.C. ± 150	9100 ± 150	18	13	D	
16	8130B.C. ± 160	10,080 ± 160	23	18	D	Period I ends? (II starts?)
15	8770B.C. ± 300	10,720 ± 300	—	(19)		Period I within period
38	9050B.C. ± 170	11,000 ± 170	—	(20)		Period I starts

above ages and dates are based on the 5568 ± 30 C14 half life (not the revised 5,730 figure) and the 1950
dard. Sample I-5138 was immediately below the rock fall line (RFL) which occurred at the close of Period
amples I-5140 and I-5141 were stratigraphically slightly below I-5138, yet their figures are a little younger.
mean of these three must be close to the termination of Period III.
soil and charcoal of sample 21 could not be separated for the analysis. The sample was small and had to be
ed before counting.

mens of fox, *coruro*, guanaco, cats, and birds. Layer 17 produced extinct fauna. Patti
Fell's list records five horse and twelve sloth specimens. Bird's diary (1969–1970b,
January 27) makes the following observations:

> The fourth hearth [of layer 17], which was about an inch below the level of the
> others, had been dug down—a circular hole or depression about 4 in. deep. It was
> jampacked with ash and bits of charcoal tightly packed. In digging that pit at that
> point they had cut down very close to the surface of the first occupation on top of
> the clay. The [horse] foot bone and two other fragments of sloth bone found in
> clearing around the hearth marked the highest occurrence of such remains in the
> deposit. They could easily have been brought up when the hearth was dug. There
> were no other indications on this level, the top of layer 17, of associations with
> extinct animals. There were a few fox bones and a few guanaco, but no artifacts
> which might be ascribed to Period I. With the hearths one might expect much
> more sign of occupation. There were relatively few bones and artifacts. . . .

Bird's notes record numerous specimens of horse and sloth bones in layer 18
along with fox, guanaco, bird, cat, and unidentified bones. Layer 19 contained a
horse metacarpal and the occipital section of a sloth skull along with fox and bird.
Saxon (1979) published a list of faunal specimens from Bird's 1969–1970 excavations. The sloth and horse specimens are erroneously attributed only to layer 19.

The Carnivore Remains Excavated at Fell's Cave in 1970

BY JULIET CLUTTON-BROCK

Fell's Cave is a small rock shelter at Estancia Brazo Norte in the Río Chico Valley on the southernmost tip of Chile. The cave was first excavated by Dr. Junius Bird in 1938 when the remains of the extinct horse, *Onohippidium saldiasi*, sloth, *Mylodon darwinii*, and guanaco, *Lama guanicoe*, were found associated with hearths and human artifacts. Further excavations were carried out in 1970 and yielded a large number of guanaco remains together with the bones and teeth of rodents, canids, and felids. The earliest levels of the cave, cultural units I–III (c. 10,700–6500 B.P.) produced the majority of the carnivore remains, which appear to be replaced by larger numbers of guanaco in the later levels, cultural units IV and V.

I was asked to report on the carnivore remains from Fell's Cave because of my interest in the taxonomy of the family Canidae and in the origins of the domestic dog. I was particularly glad to have the opportunity to examine this material because I hoped it might help with the elucidation of a problem that I have been much intrigued with—the evolution and taxonomic affinities of the Falkland Island "wolf," *Dusicyon australis* (Clutton-Brock 1977). Until it became extinct in about 1880 this enigmatic canid was the only indigenous wild mammal to inhabit the islands, with different races on East and West Falkland Island. The "wolves" fed mainly on birds, especially the goose, *Cloephaga picta*. I found, however, that the canid remains from Fell's Cave could not be closely related to *Dusicyon australis*, but they could be fairly readily differentiated into the three taxa *Dusicyon culpaeus*, *Dusicyon griseus*, and *Canis familiaris*.

The total numbers of elements identified as canid and felid from the five cultural units of Fell's Cave are given in table 18. It was not possible to

Table 18. Canid and Felid Remains from Fell's Cave, Absolute Numbers of Bones and Teeth from Cultural Units I–V

Cultural Unit	Canis familiaris Skull & Teeth	Dusicyon culpaeus Skull & Teeth	Dusicyon griseus Skull & Teeth	Canid Postcranial	Felis cf. colocolo Skull & Teeth	Postcranial
V	–	–	–	4	–	–
IV	–	–	–	5	–	–
III	8	54	–	177	13	45
II	7	25	–	82	6	7
I	3	6	1	13	–	1

identify the postcranial bones of the canids to species, due to their fragmentary state, but as can be seen from the table the majority of the cranial elements could be ascribed to the Colpeo fox, *Dusicyon culpaeus*. It
can be further assumed that the subspecies represented is *Dusicyon culpaeus lycoides*, which is endemic to southern Patagonia at the present
(fig. 78). This is the largest subspecies of *Dusicyon* and the skull is notable
in having an elongated nasal region (snout) without the teeth being larger
than in other subspecies. Also endemic to the region is a smaller species,
Dusicyon griseus, the Argentine gray fox, which is represented by a few
limb bone fragments and one mandibular fragment from the earliest level,
cultural unit I (fig. 79). There is no evidence to suggest the presence at
Fell's Cave of other South American canids such as the bush dog, *Speothos
venaticus*, or the maned wolf, *Chrysocyon brachyurus*, nor do these species inhabit Patagonia at the present day.

   Although most of the canid bones and teeth can be closely aligned with
Dusicyon culpaeus, eighteen tooth and jaw fragments stand out as mor-
phologically separate. These mostly consist of lower carnassial teeth (M_1)
and canines which bear a much closer resemblance to those of the genus
Canis than they do to *Dusicyon*. The lengths of the upper and lower carnassial teeth from Fell's Cave that have been identified as *Dusicyon* and
Canis are given in table 19. If this separation into the two genera is correct, then it is probable that a proportion of the upper teeth and the postcranial elements also belong to *Canis*, although the lack of diagnostic features precludes a definitive separation.

   No member of the genus *Canis* is indigenous to the Patagonian sub-
region, so the implication from its presence in the animal remains from
Fell's Cave is that the first human settlers brought with them the domestic
dog, *Canis familiaris*. Teeth that have been identified as dog are shown in
figure 80, while in figure 81 there is an enlarged view of the lingual side of
a lower carnassial to show the characteristic features of *Canis*. These can
be compared with the drawings in figure 82, which includes the carnassial
tooth of the coyote, *Canis latrans*. The teeth ascribed to *Canis* from Fell's
Cave are much closer to those of the coyote than they are either to recent
comparative material of *Dusicyon* or to the teeth identified as *Dusicyon*
from Fell's Cave. Figure 83 shows drawings of the lingual sides of these carnassial teeth together with a carnassial tooth of the Falkland Island "wolf,"
Dusicyon australis. The carnassial teeth (both upper and lower) of this
canid have unique features that are immediately distinctive, however, and
preclude its presence on the mainland.

   After making the identification of *Canis familiaris* from Fell's Cave, I
received a letter from Professor Alfredo Langguth in Montevideo (dated
June 10, 1977) telling me that he had examined Dr. Bird's material in New
York in 1971–1972 and had identified the canids as *Pseudalopex culpaeus*,

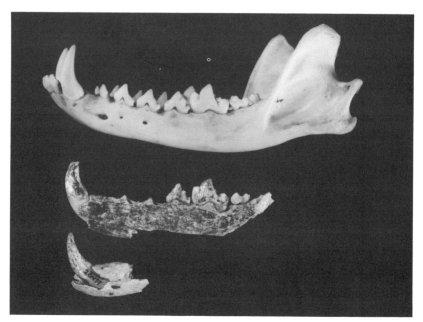

Fig. 78. Mandible of recent *Dusicyon culpaeus* from Tierra del Fuego (*top*) to compare with two left mandibular fragments from Fell's Cave, identified as *D. culpaeus*.

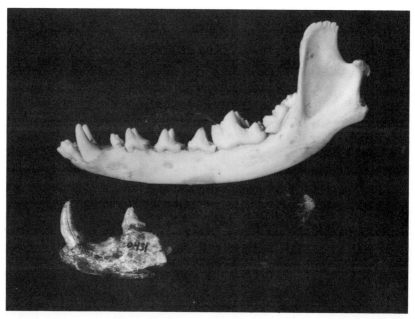

Fig. 79. Mandible of recent *Dusicyon griseus* from Tierra del Fuego (*top*) to compare to the fragment from Fell's Cave, identified as *D. griseus*.

e 19. Lengths of the Carnassial Teeth of *Dusicyon culpaeus* and *Canis familiaris* from Fell's Cave

Number	Cultural Unit	Taxon	Length Upper Carnassial (P^4), mm	Length Lower Carnassial (M_1), mm
204-20	III	D. culpaeus	16.6	
204-20	III	"	17.7	
204-20	III	"	18.0 est.	
203-20	III	"	19.5	
203-20	III	"	18.4	
203-20	III	"	17.5	
203-20	III	"	19.2	
204-21	III	"	17.4	
204-19	III	"	18.3	
204-38	II	"	17.85	
204-37	II	"	17.6	
204-37	II	"	16.3	
204-20	III	"		16.4 (alveolus)
204-21	III	"		16.1
204-21	III	"		18.0 est.
204-21	III	"		17.0
204-37	II	"		16.4
204-37	II	"		17.2
204-37	II	"		17.3
203-19	III	C. familiaris		21.5
203-19	III	"		22.7 est.
204-19	III	"		22.0
203-20	III	"		21.3 est.
204-34	II	"		22.0
204-37	II	"		20.8
204-27	I	"		21.9

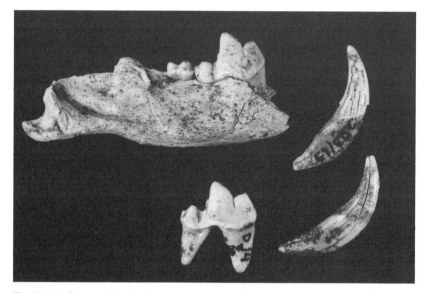

Fig. 80. Right mandibular fragment, two canines, and a lower carnassial tooth from Fell's Cave, identified as *Canis familiaris.*

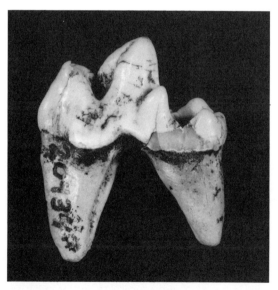

Fig. 81. Lingual view of lower left carnassial tooth (M_1) from Fell's Cave, identified as *Canis familiaris.*

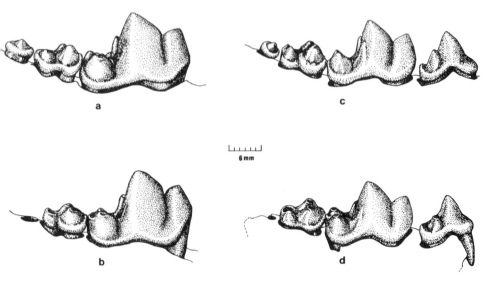

Fig. 82. Labial views of (a) lower right M_1, M_2, M_3, *Canis latrans*, BM(NH) 38.4.1.13; (b) lower right M_1, M_2, *Canis familiaris*, Fell's Cave 20437; (c) lower right P_4, M_1, M_2, M_3, *Dusicyon culpaeus*, BM(NH) 184d; (d) lower right P_4, M_1, M_2, *Dusicyon culpaeus*, Fell's Cave 20421.

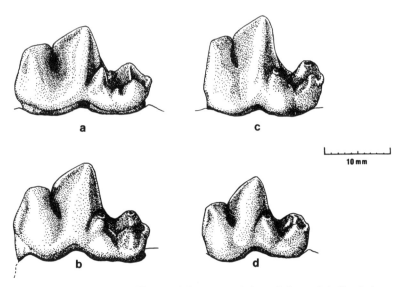

Fig. 83. Lingual views of lower right carnassial teeth from (a) *Canis latrans*, BM(NH) 38.4.1.13; (b) *Canis familiaris*, Fell's Cave 20437; (c) *Dusicyon australis*, BM(NH) 32.3.15.47; (d) *Dusicyon culpaeus*, Fell's Cave 20421.

Pseudalopex griseus, and *Canis avus*. The first two are synonymous with my *Dusicyon* species, but *Canis avus* is a fossil canid which until now has not been equated with the domestic dog. As I have seen no material of *Canis avus* other than that identified by Langguth from Fell's Cave I cannot comment on the origins or affinities of this taxon, but it would seem to be a subject for further research with an important bearing on the time of the first arrival of humans in South America and whether they took the domestic dog with them.

The number of felid remains from Fell's Cave is considerably smaller than that of the canids and as can be seen from table 18 they are restricted to cultural units II and III with one rather dubious identification from unit I. The felid bones and teeth can only be identified on size and it is apparent that they all originate from one rather small species. They have therefore been provisionally ascribed to the locally endemic colocolo, *Felis colocolo*. The lengths of the felid carnassial teeth are given in table 20.

The bones of both canids and felids are much fractured and many have been split longitudinally so that they give every appearance of being the debris from human food. In figure 84 it can be seen that the angle of the mandible from Fell's Cave has been chopped along the base in exactly the same way as the two mandibles from Jaguar Cave in Idaho, North America. These mandibular rami from Jaguar Cave provide evidence for the presence of the domestic dog in North America at the very early date of between 10,000 and 11,000 B.P., and the way that they have been chopped indicates that the little bit of marrow in the corner of the jaw was removed, presumably to be eaten as a morsel of valuable fat (Lawrence 1967).

I am indebted to Dr. E. C. Saxon, who arranged for me to examine the carnivore remains from Fell's Cave that were excavated by the late Dr. Junius Bird in 1970. My thanks are due to Peggy Fell, the owner of the finds, and to Mateo Martiníc of the Instituto de la Patagonia, who arranged for me to have the specimens on temporary loan at the British Museum (Natural History). The drawings in figures 82 and 83 were done by Daphne Hills, Mammal Section, BM(NH).

This report on the carnivore remains from Fell's Cave was first written in 1978 and revised in 1985. Since then radiocarbon dates have been obtained on the accelerator at the Oxford University Research Laboratory on a maxilla and mandible of Canis familiaris *from Jaguar Cave, Idaho. The dates are 3220 ± 80 B.P. (c. 270 B.C.) Lab. no. OxA-922 and 940 ± 80 (c. A.D. 1010) Lab. no. OxA-923. It can therefore no longer be claimed that the canid remains from Jaguar Cave present evidence for the dog in the early Holocene of North America, as stated here. Similarly, until a direct radiocarbon date has been obtained on the canid remains from Fell's Cave the possibility has to be considered that the specimens identified as domestic dog (*C. familiaris*) are intrusive and may postdate the Spanish Conquest of South America.*

Fig. 84. Casts of mandibular rami of domestic dog (*Canis familiaris*) from the Jaguar Cave (*top and middle*) to compare with a canid ramus from Fell's Cave (*bottom*) to show similar butchery along the base of the ramus.

le 20. Lengths of the Carnassial Teeth of *Felis colocolo* from Fell's Cave

Number	Cultural Unit	Taxon	Length Upper Carnassial (P⁴), mm	Length Lower Carnassial (M₁), mm
204-20	III	*F. colocolo*	14.1 est.	
203-21	III	"	12.5	
203-21	III	"	13.35 (alveolus)	
204-37	II	"	12.6	
204-18	III	"		11.85 (alveolus)
204-25	II	"		10.2
204-26	II	"		10.9
204-37	II	"		11.4

Fell's Cave: 11,000 Years of Changes in Paleoenvironments, Fauna, and Human Occupation

BY VERA MARKGRAF

Fifty years have passed since the late Junius Bird first excavated Fell's Cave (fig. 85), located in the southeastern Patagonian basalt plateaus near the Chilean-Argentine border. But today the data obtained from this site still represent one of the most important sequences of man in southernmost South America (Bird 1938b, 1946a, 1951, quoted in Auer 1974; Gradin 1980; Massone 1981). Based on distinct tool and bone assemblages, five cultural phases were distinguished, subsequently dated to encompass the last 11,000 years (Bird 1951). Probably the most exciting find in this sequence was the apparent contemporaneity of early man and extinct fauna, such as the giant ground sloth (*Mylodon*) and native horse (*Onohippidium*), in addition to extant fauna such as guanaco (*Lama guanicoe*). The great abundance of guanaco bones in these early layers and evidence of a substantial reduction of grassland area occurring shortly prior to faunal extinction suggest, however, that the environmental change presented a presumably much greater threat to the grazing population than hunting pressure ("overkill") by Paleo-Indian groups (Markgraf 1985). The pollen record from Fell's Cave added some support to this hypothesis.

This report describes the paleoenvironmental data obtained from pollen analysis of Fell's Cave sediment materials and discusses its significance for our understanding of the general paleoclimatic history of southern South America, in context with faunal extinction and human occupation.

Methods

Eleven samples were selected from the material collected and provided by J. Bird from his excavations in 1936–1937 (samples I, II, III, IV—numbered by Bird) and 1969–1970 (samples D 4, D 13, D 15, D 16, D 19, C 8). These two sets of samples were arranged in chronological order by Bird. For pollen analysis these samples were treated following standard techniques (Faegri and Iversen 1964). Because of substantial amounts of inorganic matter, all samples were treated with hydrofluoric acid to remove silicates. To reduce the organic component in the samples, in this case mostly charcoal particles, samples were treated with potassium-hydroxide followed by acetolysis. With exception of two samples (C 8, IV) all samples had sufficiently high pollen concentration and good preservation to allow counts of 200 (mostly 300) grains per sample. Pollen data are given in percent of total pollen sum, and in pollen concentration per gram sample, using tracer pollen aliquots (*Eucalyptus*, fern spores). The additional in-

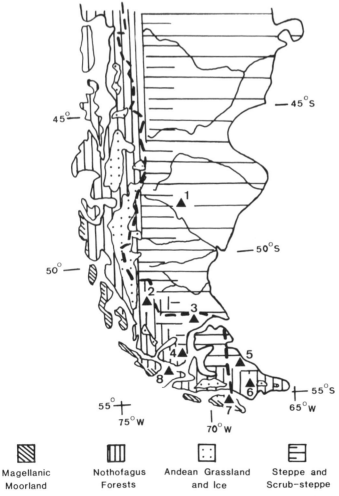

| Magellanic | Nothofagus | Andean Grassland | Steppe and |
| Moorland | Forests | and Ice | Scrub-steppe |

Fig. 85. Map of southern Patagonia and Tierra del Fuego with major vegetation types and site localities mentioned in text: (1) Los Toldos, (2) Mylodon Cave, (3) Fell's Cave, Cerro Sota, and Palli Aike, (4) Puerto Hambre, (5) La Misión, (6) Lago Yehuin, (7) Isla Navarino, (8) Isla Clarence.

formation on pollen concentration proved interesting, because it allowed insight into questions of sediment accumulation *versus* pollen input.

Paleoenvironmental Data

The modern environment of the Fell's Cave area is defined as xeric Patagonian grassland (*Festuca gracillima*—Stipetum, Pisano 1977) under a mean annual precipitation of slightly above 200 mm. Its more xeric components are shrubs, *Adesmia boronoides, Ephedra frustillata, Lepidophyllum cupressiforme, Verbena tridens, Baccharis magellanica,* and more widespread taxa such as *Berberis buxifolia, B. empetrifolia, Empetrum rubrum, Azorella caespitosa,* and *Perezia recurvata* (Pisano 1977; Roig et al. 1981).

The pollen types representing this vegetation are Gramineae, Compositae tubuliflorae (including *Baccharis*-type), *Ephedra,* herbaceous taxa (Caryophyllaceae, Umbelliferae [including *Azorella*], *Acaena,* Cruciferae-type, *Phacelia,* Ranunculaceae, Chenopodiaceae, etc.), shrubby taxa (*Schinus, Verbena, Berberis,* Rhamnaceae), and tree taxa (*Nothofagus, Podocarpus*).

Throughout the Fell's Cave pollen record, Gramineae and Compositae tubuliflorae dominate, reaching together between 70 and 90 percent of the total sum (fig. 86). Herbaceous taxa, *Ephedra,* and *Nothofagus* account for the remaining 30 to 10 percent, while shrub taxa are only represented in traces. According to proportional changes in these types, specifically between Gramineae and Compositae, the record shows a substantial environmental change between 11,000 and 10,000 B.P. At that time Gramineae decrease from over 80 percent to less than 20 percent, while Compositae increase to over 50 percent, *Ephedra* and *Nothofagus* increase to 20 percent and 10 percent, respectively, and shrub types appear. This change is documented in both pollen percent and pollen concentration, indicating that it is an environmental change. This shift can be interpreted as a shift from mesic grassland (under 400 mm mean annual precipitation, Pisano 1977) to xeric grassland (under 200 mm mean annual precipitation, Pisano 1977), which could be due to a decrease in precipitation, or an increase in temperature, or both. Comparison with other regional paleoenvironmental data suggests that a temperature increase is the likely reason for this change, given disappearance of cold taxa such as *Oreobolus* (Moore 1978).

Compared to this paleoenvironmental shift, the younger shifts in the record are far less impressive, most of them seen only in the pollen concentration changes. Thus, for the period from about 9000 to 6000 B.P., when there is good radiocarbon control, Compositae concentration decreased strongly, much more than concentration of the other taxa. This, and the absence of *Ephedra,* suggests a decline of the xeric taxa, perhaps reflecting a return to more mesic conditions with slightly more precipitation.

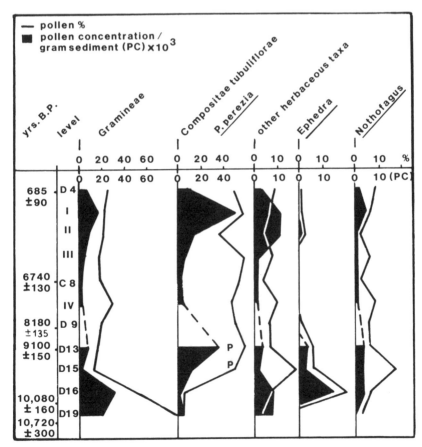

Fig. 86. Pollen diagram of Fell's Cave in percent of total pollen sum and in pollen concentration per gram sediment. The ordering of the samples (stratigraphically) is according to Bird (pers. comm.).

From 6000 B.P. onward radiocarbon control is insufficient to interpret pollen concentration data with much confidence. However, the reoccurrence of *Ephedra* pollen and great numbers of Cruciferae-type grains, most likely an annual taxon, in addition to increased Compositae concentrations, suggests renewed aridity, at least during the last 1,000 years.

Discussion

Previously analyzed paleoenvironmental records from high southern latitudes in South America, which cover the last 11,000 years B.P., include Mylodon Cave (Moore 1978), Puerto Hambre (Heusser 1984), La Misión (Markgraf 1980, 1983), Lago Yehuin (Markgraf 1983), Isla Clarence (Auer 1974), and Isla Navarino (Heusser 1984). Even though the paleoenvironmental resolution is not the same in all these records, all represent the terminal phase of the last glaciation, a time of major paleoenvironmental changes, faunal extinction, and arrival of man. Because these records are from conditions quite different from modern environments (fig. 85), the vegetational history follows a different course in terms of taxa composition and taxa succession through time. Timing, however, and paleoclimatic signal of the respective changes reveal a consistent pattern of changes in this part of the world (Markgraf 1983).

Accordingly, prior to 11,000 B.P. a treeless, herbaceous steppe was the dominant vegetation throughout southern South America between latitudes 50° and 54°S. Cold and dry climates must have prevailed, probably colder than any part of Patagonia today. Between 11,000 and 10,000 B.P. xeric steppe taxa appear in all records (*Berberis, Empetrum, Acaena,* Compositae tubuliflorae, Compositae liguliflorae, *Perezia*) that suggest temperature increase, which in turn enhanced moisture stress. This situation lasted until 8500 B.P., when the different species of *Nothofagus* expanded from their respective, probably small-scale, glacial refugia in the Andean valleys in southern Patagonia and Tierra del Fuego. Forest zonation, resembling the modern zonation, became established at that time. It signifies the establishment of a precipitation pattern and gradient similar to the modern one across the Andes. These climatic conditions remained until nearly the present time, even though differences in the proportion of evergreen versus deciduous *Nothofagus* taxa suggest that the older Holocene (8500 to 6000 B.P.) was somewhat moister and warmer than the younger Holocene (6000 to ?1000 B.P.). In addition, short arid periods interrupted this sequence, between 6000 and 5000 B.P. and since ?1000 B.P.

The Fell's Cave pollen record relates well with this regional paleoenvironmental chronology, even though its interpretation is based solely on shifts in nonarboreal taxa. The temperature increase prior to 10,000 B.P. that appears simultaneously throughout the southern latitudes necessarily has a stronger environmental impact on the more arid, eastern steppe region of Fell's Cave than in the mesic western region. Despite this, the shift from mesic to xeric grassland is also recorded in the west (e.g., in the ground sloth dung samples from Mylodon Cave [fig. 85]). The youngest dung samples (dated 10,800 B.P.) show a shift from Gramineae and herb dominance to Compositae and *Empetrum* dominance (Markgraf 1985), much like the Fell's Cave data. From this it is argued that a substantial reduction in grassland occurred throughout the range of the large herbivore population. This could not have been without consequences for the survival of the grazers (Markgraf 1985). Only the guanaco, apparently less specialized in its forage requirements, managed to survive these problematic times, even though its numbers were greatly reduced at first (Bird 1938a). In view of this forage problem, human predation might represent nothing more than a coup de grace for an animal population already out of equilibrium with its environment (Markgraf 1985).

Given this reduction in mesic steppe environment and animal population, the scarcity of data on human occupation during the following 1,000 years is not surprising. Only by 8500 B.P., when precipitation increased to modern levels and forests became established in the western parts of Patagonia and Tierra del Fuego, did more mesic grassland conditions return to the eastern steppes. This must have been sufficient to bring the guanaco back in greater numbers, as well as human hunters, who are recorded throughout Patagonia (Bird 1946a; Gradin 1980; Massone 1981).

This discussion of paleoenvironmental changes documented in the Fell's Cave section shows the potential of pollen analysis for the interpretation of changes in human occupation and fauna through time. Because of its complexity, this task is quite difficult without a network of regional paleoenvironmental data that establish a background for interpreting specific questions and problems inherent to cave sediments with human and faunal remains.

Most of all I have to thank Junius and Peggy Bird for their interest and help with the material, and many enjoyable discussions on the matter. I thank H. L. D'Antoni for some of the pollen counts, and J. Buckley (Teledyne Isotopes) for his listing of some of the unpublished radiocarbon dates.

6. Cerro Sota Cave

GENERAL DESCRIPTION

Cerro Sota Cave is located on the east side of Cerro Sota hill on North Arm Station [Estancia Brazo Norte] at about lat. 52°3′ S, long. 70°5′ W. The surrounding grassland is a sheep farm pioneered by Mr. William Fell. He and his son John had long known of the cave and kindly gave permission to excavate. The work was started on December 9, 1936, and terminated on December 20, 1936.

The entrance is about 100 ft. above the surrounding pampa at the base of a low lava cliff (figs. 87, 88). Immediately in front, the ground slopes quite steeply, leaving only a small level area for the accumulation of refuse. Loose sand, blown over the crest of the hill from a lagoon on the other side, has piled up at the top of the slope and is held there by a strong uphill eddy. A change of wind sometimes shifts this sand down the hill, but with the recurrence of the westerly winds it is again drawn up into the lee of the cliff. It was noted that the wind which brought the sand up the hill did not carry it quite to the level of the entrance, nor deposit any inside.

As the floor plan shows (fig. 89), the Cerro Sota Cave, in spite of a length of 48 ft. from the drip line to rear, is too narrow to be attractive as a camping place or refuge for more than a very few people at a time. The modern floor surface averaged only 5 ft. in width, although earlier, with a lower floor surface, it had been somewhat wider. The entrance, about 100 ft. above the surrounding pampa, is so small that the interior is only dimly lighted. A crack from the peak of the entrance to the top of the cliff permits some seepage of rain water, but this affects only the outer half of the floor. The inner portion was so completely protected and thoroughly dry that dust masks were required while clearing it.

At the start of excavation the inner part of the cave, which widens somewhat and will be referred to as the inner room, was nearly choked with the naturally mummified bodies of twenty-two sheep, two skunks, a

Fig. 87. View of location of Cerro Sota Cave at base of a low lava cliff.

Fig. 88. Entrance to Cerro Sota Cave before excavation.

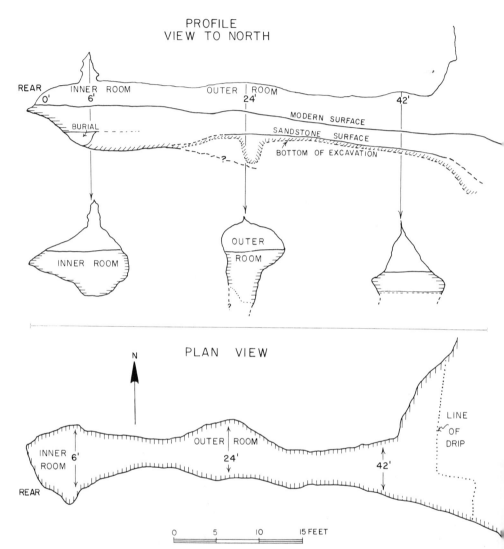

Fig. 89. Profile and plan view of Cerro Sota Cave.

house cat, and an ibis. The sheep had crowded in during a snowstorm and suffocated. Beneath them was a 6 in. thick layer of hard-packed sheep manure covering 8 in. of bat droppings. The most recent Indian artifacts were mixed with, and on top of, the latter. Beneath this the deposit consisted of fine, dry, dark gray dust gradually changing in color to buff at the bottom. Towards the entrance this dust was mixed with an increasing proportion of fine sand. Further down, at and in from the entrance, a deposit of sand, mixed with bits of lava, had become so consolidated that it resembled sandstone. Only sample portions of this were removed, as it contained no bones or anything to indicate the presence of people. Artifacts were scarce, with none deeper than 3 ft. below the surface. Remains of fires occurred between 14 and 30 in., representing the period during which the floor reached and passed the level of maximum cave width, when it was most suitable for use. At 39 in. below the surface of the inner room was a group cremation burial.

In summary, the cave at first was formed in the lava, without a suitable floor, and was unsuitable for occupation by men, and apparently had little attraction for animals. Fine, sandy, windblown dirt piling up against the east side of the hill gradually built up a floor and at the same time must have made it more accessible. Foxes or other animals began to use it, bringing in bone fragments of native horses, guanacos, and sloth, perhaps from nearby Indian camps. Its first native use, as a burial cave, was before the extermination of the horse and sloth. Continued filling with windblown sandy dirt built the floor up to where maximum width made it somewhat more suitable for occupation. At best there was never room enough for more than a few people, perhaps only two or three at a time and then probably only in periods of bad weather. Subsequently, the gradual reduction of head room and floor area made it less desirable, human visits became more infrequent, bats took it over, and with the coming of sheep it was nearly choked up.   *(from Bird 1936–1937)*

EXCAVATION INFORMATION

Bird wrote (1978: 3) that there were no traceable strata below the bat manure and therefore the debris was removed in arbitrary levels of several inches measured from the cave's surface, whether slightly sloping or not. The surface in the inner room and at the cave's mouth was level. Figure 90 describes the composition of the excavated debris at Cerro Sota. Bird suggested that the artifacts from the first 6 in. of the outer room (no. 1) might be contemporary with the artifacts from 6 to 24 in. in the inner room. The artifacts from 6 to 12 in. from the outer room (no. 2) might be contemporary with the artifacts below 24 in. from the inner room.

PLAN VIEW

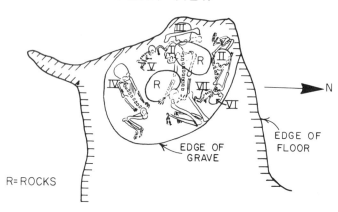

PROFILE - VIEW TO WEST

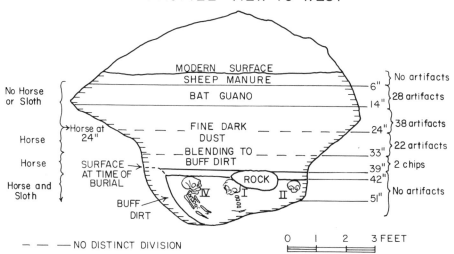

Fig. 90. The group burial in the inner room at Cerro Sota Cave.

THE ARTIFACTS

The number and types of artifacts found are shown in table 21. There are too few to be of use in checking the sequences or establishing periods. All that can be said is that nothing here is contradictory to what was found elsewhere. The steamless point with cement still adhering is the only noteworthy specimen.

21. Artifacts from Cerro Sota Cave

	Inner Room				Outer Room			
	Level				Level		Front of Entrance	
Category	6–15″	15–24″	24–33″	33–42″	1	2	trance	Total
en point, minus stem	–	–	–	–	–	–	1	1
less point (at 24″)	–	–	1	–	–	–	–	1
e, bifacial	–	–	–	–	–	–	1	1
h, single-edge scraper	2	11	5	–	6	6ª	19	49
ed-type scraper	–	–	–	–	–	–	2	2
	24	27	16	2	12	9	–	90
	–	–	–	–	½	½	–	1
merstone, rough	–	–	1	–	–	–	–	1
bone awl	1	–	–	–	–	–	–	1
chipping tool	1	–	–	–	–	–	–	1
battered guanaco long bone	6	1	–	–	–	–	–	7
ed, worked bone	1	–	–	–	–	–	–	1
bead	2	–	–	–	–	–	–	2
Totals	37	39	23	2	18½	15½	23	158

Room 1 = first 6″ beneath sheep manure, corresponding approximately to 6–24″ in Inner Room.
Room 2 = second 6″ beneath sheep manure, corresponding approximately to 24–42″ in Inner Room.
des 1 endscraper and 1 two-sided narrow scraper.

FAUNAL REMAINS

Observations

All through the accumulation, down to the bottom in the inner room, were numerous split and broken, unburned bones such as are found in any Indian camp refuse in the region. They occur not only in the levels where stone flakes and artifacts lay but continued in slightly greater frequency below the oldest artifacts.

The animals represented by bone fragments in the lower two-thirds are mainly guanaco and native horse, with a few fragments of sloth bone. The bones are largely the broken ends and slivers of marrow bones and the smaller ankle and foot bones. Even the marrow-bearing metacarpal bones of the guanaco were broken open, long a common practice among the Indian groups of this region, breakage which seems unlike that produced by carnivores.

In much smaller holes in the same lava formation, holes too small for a person to enter, one finds similar broken and split bones (produced by humans) matching the comparable material on campsites. Clearly, animals have carried them there from the nearby camps and much of what was in the cave must have the same history. As more than seven hundred pieces of horse and guanaco long bones in the inner room lay below the level of occupation and the somewhat earlier cremation, this suggests human presence in the area for an appreciable time before the cremation.

In the upper third of the accumulation the horse and sloth are lacking, and bird and *coruro* bones appear. Mountain lion and fox are rare.

Classifications

The faunal material from Cerro Sota has AMNH catalogue number 41.1/2024. The specimens are marked with the letter C with numbers 1 to 8 which represent the following excavation units:

C1—Inner room, 15 to 24 in.
C2—Inner room, 24 to 33 in.
C3—Inner room, 33 to 42 in.
C4—Inner room, 42 to 51 in.
C5—Inner room, 51 to B (base of rock)
C6—Between inner and outer room
C7—Outer room, level 2
C8—Outer room, level 1

The faunal specialist Thomas Amorosi has tentatively classified the faunal remains as follows:

Aves

Material: 2 innominates, 2 coracoids, 1 humerus.
Distribution: C1—all.

Rodentia

Material: 3 innominates, 1 humerus, 3 femora.
Distribution: C1—all.

Canidae

Material: 2 maxillae, 5 mandibles, 5 canines, 1 axis, 3 innominates, 5 humeri, 2 radii, 4 ulnae, 2 astragali, 1 fragmentary phalanx, 1 femur, 1 tibia.
Distribution: C1—1 skull, 2 maxillae, 4 mandibles, 2 canines, 3 innominates, 3 humeri, 2 radii, 4 ulnae, 2 astragali, 1 phalanx, 1 femur, 1 tibia. C2—3 canines, 1 axis, 2 humeri. C5—1 mandible.

Camelidae (Guanaco)

Material: 1 maxilla, 2 tooth fragments.
Distribution: C1—all.

Onohippidium (Horse)

Material: 3 mandibles, 1 canines (?), 2 molars, 30 tooth fragments, 1 metatarsal, 2 first phalanges, 12 second phalanges, 3 third phalanges, 1 patella, specimens of hair.
Distribution: C1—1 second phalanx (at 24 in.). C2—2 second phalanges. C3—1 mandible, 1 canine, 2 molars, 2 first phalanges, 6 second phalanges. C4—30 tooth fragments, 6 second phalanges, 2 third phalanges, 1 patella. C6—1 mandible, 1 metatarsal (at 28 in.). C7—1 mandible. C8—1 third phalanx.

Horse hair was found in the inner room at a depth of 24 to 33 in. It has AMNH catalogue no. 41.1/2023, and was analyzed by Whitford (n.d.: 4) who classified it as from *Parahipparion saldiasi,* an extinct species. He submitted the following observations to Bird:

> The hairs show a more distinct and more nearly continuous medulla than human hairs. The scales are smoother and more nearly rectangular. The edges of the scales usually show four very sharp and prominent teeth projecting on each side of the hair which causes a very serrate edge to it. The scales are quite uniformly oriented at an acute angle to the longitudinal axis of the fiber. It was very difficult to secure good cross sections but the hairs seem to be very grainy in texture and the medulla is very open. The hairs in most respects show very close structural similarity to the modern horse although the hairs are, as a rule, much finer [when compared with] *Equus kiang, Equus grevyii, Equus zebra, Equus hemionius, Equus berchelli,* Celtic Pony, and Norwegian Horse. In all cases except of the extinct

samples, measurements were made and recorded of the tail, mane, and in some cases of the shoulder hairs. An examination seems to show that hair characteristics from extinct *Parahipparion saldiasi* compare quite favorably with the living *Equus przewalski.* This holds not only for the measurements, but other microscopic characteristics such as shape of scales, scale borders, and medullation.

Mylodontidae (Giant Ground Sloth)

Material: I metacarpal.
Distribution: C4—I metacarpal.

Fragmentary Material Attributed to Class

Aves: I unidentified.
Mammalia, large-sized: 3 cranial, thoracic vertebra, I lumbar vertebra, I unidentified vertebra, I rib, I metapodial, 2 unidentified.
Mammalia, medium-sized: 3 cranial, 2 cervical vertebrae, 2 thoracic vertebrae, 6 caudal vertebrae, I unidentified vertebrae, 5 ribs, 10 long bones.

Bird made field counts of the Cerro Sota faunal remains, and that tabulation has been published (Bird 1983: 63). The collection at the AMNH varies somewhat from the field analysis. For example, several hundred small or splinter fragments are not found among the Museum specimens. They may have been discarded after counting, and never sent to the Museum. The field tabulation also lists a mountain lion mandible (CI) and two horse third phalanges (C2 and C3) not now in the collection. Possible seal remains, a mandible fragment from CI and a tooth from C5, are also not in the collection.

A GROUP BURIAL

Description

At the rear of the cave [there] was a grave containing the cremated remains of three women, three children, and an infant. Their remains were found, crowded together, as the drawings (fig. 90) show, in a hollow scraped in the floor dirt at the rear of the cave. This depression, measuring 4 to 4½ ft. in diameter by a little less than 2 ft. deep, was then lined and packed with grass, and, as the bodies were put in place, more grass was packed between and around, and, presumably, heaped over them. As the hollow was too small to contain the bodies they must have been stacked above the level of the floor. Two rough pieces of lava, each about 2 ft. in diameter, with a number of smaller pieces, were piled on top. At this stage the grass was ignited.

Beneath the stones and where the grass was in contact with the sides of the grave, and below the bodies, a large quantity of the grass was only carbonized, while on top and at places which had better access to air even the bones were completely burned. At the bottom and along the lower part of the forward edge of the grave some grass had not carbonized. Skull VI (catalogue no. 99.1/784), which was partially crushed, and the ends of [some] protruding bones were not burned. Clustered about them were a number of fly pupae cases from which the flies had emerged. None were carbonized and none were found in the carbonized grass which had been in contact with the bodies. The cases were identified as Muscidae by Dr. C. H. Curran, who said the insects were more likely to have been attracted by the rotting or fermenting grass than by the flesh. If they had time to develop before the fire, some should have been found in the charred grass which survived in perfect condition. This indicates that the fire was started while the bodies were fresh and that the burning was intentional. Additional evidence was the presence inside the burned skulls of a shiny, charred substance, the residue of the brains. A similar mass, seemingly the remains of viscera, was found at about the middle of what had been body III (99.1/781).

The unburned head VI was in contact with a small residual portion of several layers of skins or, more correctly, the matted fur from skins, as the skin itself had decomposed. The layer next to the skull had the appearance of baby guanaco and had, sticking to it, matted remnants of human hair. At least two layers of the fur retained red pigment. Whether this had been applied to the fur or the skin could not be determined. At other unburned portions of the burial similar traces of red paint were found, suggesting that the bodies had been wrapped in painted skins or robes. There was nothing to suggest that such paint had been applied to the bodies.

All of the ashes from the cremation, as well as all the dirt in the cave, were sifted but yielded no artifacts or ornaments which might have been associated with the burial. If any were present they might have been destroyed by the fire. Nor were there any artifacts of any kind in proximity to the grave, which seems to mark the first time that the cave was utilized by people. Two unworked stone flakes were found close to the level of the top of the stones before the grave was discovered, flakes which must have been discarded after there was some dirt over the burial.

It is possible that some of the dirt from the hollow was thrown back over the cremation area. If so, it was after the fire had burned out, for none of the bone scraps were scorched, nor was there enough dirt to prevent flies from laying eggs in the rotting, unburned grass. Certainly part of the overlying dirt containing scattered scraps of horse bones accumulated after the cremation for the volume of this material above the level of the grave in both the inner and outer sections of the cave is far greater than the capacity of the hollow.

The horse fur, unrecognized at the time, was found when removing fill lying between 24 and 33 in. below the surface over the grave. With it was some guanaco fur. In both cases the skin had decomposed, leaving the hairs in seemingly original order. These also were studied by Dr. A. C. Whitford, who reported the horse fur to be structurally more similar to fur from the wild horse of Mongolia, *Equus przewalski*, and to a small horse from Norway than to any other living relative.

One cannot keep from wondering about the deaths of seven individuals of such disparate ages: three women, two of whom were elderly, handicapped by the loss of most of their teeth; three children; and an infant. It seems improbable that all should have died of disease so close together as to be burned as a group. Two alternatives exist—that they were all deliberately killed by someone or that they met an accidental death. The latter is a real possibility. At Fell's Cave we found initial occupation debris isolated from the subsequent second period material by slabs of sandstone fallen from the ceiling. Directly under one slab lay the complete articulated foreleg and shoulder of a horse, the bones in their natural positions as if the leg had been freshly butchered, the bones protected by flesh when the slab fell. Below another slab on the same surface were the articulated neck vertebrae and basal skull section of a horse, the skull broken open to remove the brain. While the entire floor area of the shelter was not uncovered, everything else seen suggested that the place was occupied at the time. Whether or not the individuals burned in Cerro Sota were killed by rock fall, it is certain that a real tragedy did occur in the vicinity and that there were enough survivors properly to take care of the dead. And if one cannot prove that the horse brains were eaten by the nearly toothless women, at least it cannot be disproved.

Measurements of Long Bones

The condition of nearly all the [human] bones was such that they could not be moved, so when possible, measurements were taken as they were uncovered.

Skeleton III (99.1/781)
    left femur—14½ to 15 in.
    right femur—approximately 14½ in.
    left humerus—approximately 11¼ in.
    left radius—9½ in.

Skeleton IV (99.1/782)
    right humerus—6½ in.
    right ulna—5⅛ in.
    left ulna—4⅞ in.
    right femur—approximately 8½ in.
    right tibia—7⅛ in.

Skeleton VI (99.1/784)
 right ulna—5⅛ in.

Additional Human Remains

Between 15 and 24 in. below the surface in the inner room were found one adult lower maxillary (?) (99.1/777) with adhering tissue and traces of red paint; one lower maxillary (?) of a child (99.1/778), also with bits of adhering tissue, and a fragment of upper millary (?) from the same individual and one femur, perhaps from the same. These were widely separated. As all of the dirt in the cave was removed and sifted, it is certain that the balance of [these] skeletons was not in the cave. Two finger or toe nails, covered with red paint, came from the same level as the jaw bones.

Skeletal Material

Skeletal material from Cerro Sota Cave is catalogued at the AMNH with the numbers 99.1/776 to 99.1/785. Dr. Charles Lester made the following descriptions, which have been amended and largely rewritten by Dr. Ian Tattersall of the AMNH.

99.1/776

Mandible with all teeth, heavily worn, present. Evidence of gingivitis and possible abscess formation below M_1 bilaterally. The joint surface of the left mandibular condyle is severely deformed, and the left M_2 is badly impacted. Not associated with extinct fauna.

99.1/777

Posterior portion of incomplete right juvenile maxilla with dp, I^2, and partly calcified I crown in crypt. Not associated with extinct fauna.

99.1/778

Juvenile mandible with M_{1-2} in place bilaterally and dm_2 still in place on right. No eruption of M_3. Not associated with extinct fauna.

99.1/779 (originally Cerro Sota skull no. 1) (figs. 91, 92)

Reconstructed partial skull, probably female. Aged individual with advanced stage of cranial suture closure. Other charred skull fragments. Fracture lines of calvaria are postmortem. Left maxilla fairly complete with advanced degree of antemortem tooth loss. Mandible: all teeth posterior to canines lost premortem; heavily worn stumps of both C and right I_2; posterior part of right ramus missing. No antemortem pathology. One lumbar vertebra without inferior articular surface and with much osteoarthritis.

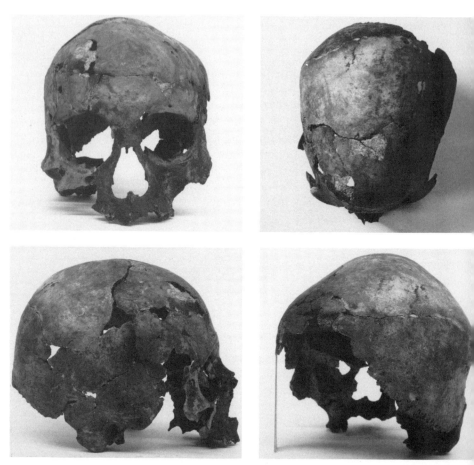

Fig. 91. Four views of skull from skeleton 99.1/779 (not to scale).

99.1/780 (originally Cerro Sota skull no. 2) (fig. 93)

Reconstructed skull of probable female; moderately advanced stage of cranial suture closure; medial orbital walls and internal nasal structure missing; right orbit and maxilla damaged; right zygomatic arch incomplete. Maxillary teeth preserved on left side; all heavily worn. Mandible: right corpus and partial left ramus preserved; totally edentulous.

99.1/781 (originally Cerro Sota skull no. 3) (fig. 94)

Relatively complete cranial vault and base; only parts of upper face preserved including both malars and rim of right orbit. Disassociated maxillary fragments have alveolae with no teeth preserved. Proximal and distal portions of left

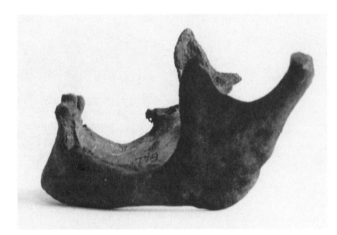

Fig. 92. Mandible of skull from skeleton 99.1/779.

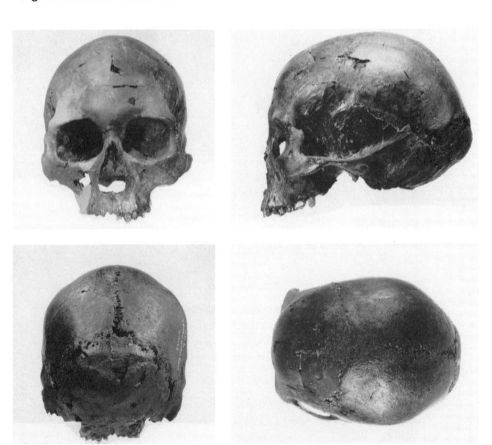

Fig. 93. Four views of skull from skeleton 99.1/780 (not to scale).

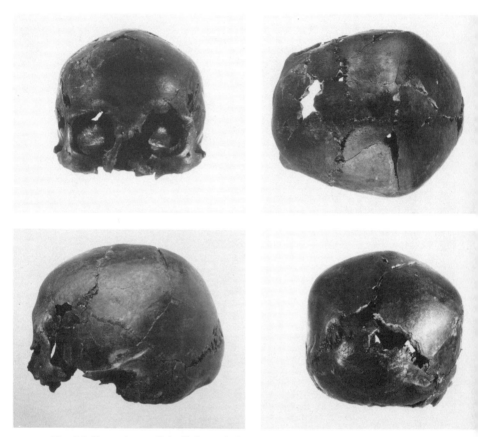

Fig. 94. Four views of skull from skeleton 99.1/781 (not to scale).

humerus. Right radius 24 cm long with considerable osteoarthritic deformity at both extremes.

99.1/782 (originally Cerro Sota skull no. 4)

Numerous cranial fragments, primarily of vault, of child circa 8 yrs. old. Mandible: alveolae or roots for all teeth; partial crown of right M_1 preserved; M_2 in crypt bilaterally. Damaged maxilla, edentulous except for developing teeth deep in crypts. Some fragments of cervical vertebrae.

99.1/783 (originally Cerro Sota skull no. 5)

A few cranial parts of young juvenile including partial mandible with alveolae and calcified crown of one molar. Charred phalanx of older individual.

99.1/784 (originally Cerro Sota skull no. 6)

Badly distorted very thin juvenile skull with partial frontal, parietals, and right temporal; pieces of calvaria with human hair. Badly burned palate and maxilla with alveolae or roots for all teeth; M^2 erupting on left. Mandible complete with alveolae complete for all teeth; left M_1 fully erupted; M_2 in crypt. Several pieces of baby guanaco fur, some with red color, accompany the human remains (see note for catalogue no. 99.1/785, below).

99.1/785 (originally Cerro Sota skull no. 7)

Bird's notes specify that skeletal parts labeled 99.1/785 belong to individual 99.1/784. The remains of the seventh individual, a child in the group cremation burial, have been mislaid, but should have been given catalogue number 99.1/785.

Dentition

In 1981 C. G. Turner II published (with J. Bird) an analysis of the dentition from the individuals found in Cerro Sota and Palli Aike caves. In the article the frequencies of eleven key dental traits are used to compare the Chilean Paleo-Indians with North and South Americans, north Asians, and Europeans. The article's abstract is as follows:

> Teeth of 12 cremated paleo-Indians (11,000 years old) from caves in southern Chile have crown and root morphology like that of recent American Indians and north Asians, but unlike that of Europeans. This finding supports the view that American Indians could easily have been ancestral to most living Indians, that very little dental evolution has occurred, and that the founding paleo-Indian population was small, genetically homogeneous, and arrived late in the Pleistocene.

PROBABLE DATING OF THE DEPOSIT

As has been mentioned, the actual number of artifacts recovered in the cave is very small and most of them are relatively late. Except for the uncertain significance of the cracked bones in the earlier cave fill, this burial marks the first time the cave was utilized by men. At about the same level, at the top of the grave, were two stone flakes, but no tools or weapons. Lacking these, it is impossible to say positively to which culture the burial belonged; thus the relation of the burial to the extinct fauna becomes important. In the dirt over the grave were several fragments of horse bones. As these are also found in the dirt beside the grave down to the bottom of the floor, one might speculate that the earth removed from the hole was thrown back over the grave. However, the earth and bone fragments over the grave were not burned. This, together with the fact that horse bone fragments and even some horse fur were found above the level of the grave and over the entire floor, in a greater volume of dirt than could have been removed from the grave, indicated that the grave was made prior to the extermination of the horse and probably the sloth.

(from Bird 1936–1937: 6–7)

DAILY LIFE

Wednesday, December 9, 1936

A cold wind blowing—hard to get up. Off about 6:00 A.M. Stopped at Comedor Chico to see if they had a spare bearing—no luck, but we did get a very welcome breakfast at Comedor Chico. Sunny, but awfully cold. Stopped at windmill on Mr. Fell's property for water and found front inner tube bulging out, just about to blow up and maybe out. Arrived North Arm at 8:30 and had a second breakfast. Went over the provisions we'd sent out on truck, taking a week's supply. Stayed to lunch; another Bible seller—tall, silent, serious, youngish, English, going around on horseback; was once a cadet on one of the farms. Left for Cerro Sota Cave after lunch—John, Inez, and her husband coming along with a load in their 1917 Ford. So nice and protected along that side of hill. Fixed up kitchen just S of cave—had to put up tent way N, at foot of hill—only flat place. Others left, after helping us. Walked down to river in eve—about ten minutes each way.

Thursday, December 10

Sunny, windy—Junius clearing layer of sheep manure from floor of cave—many dead sheep, two skunks, a cat, and an ibis. Dug a test pit at entrance—charcoal and chips. Made measurements for plan. Work would be impossible without mask. Junius used lantern in eve, working in inner of two "rooms." Rained during the night.

Friday, December 11

Cloudy, sunny, and windy. Junius over to *estancia* before lunch to get wire netting which had been left behind. Set up sieve, which works very well. Two peons stopped by. Inez and Andrew Nicol over in P.M. for tea bringing five-gal. drum of water, cookies, and bottle of milk. Told of Prime Minister Baldwin's speech over radio last night explaining everything that had led up to abdication of King Edward—latter to speak tonight, so I went over with them to hear him. Short but good speech—he has a fine voice—no "English accent." Last words were "God bless you all. God save the King." He is leaving for France to marry Mrs. Simpson. The Duke of York is George VI—will be crowned May 12. I only hope Mrs. S. makes "Mr. Windsor" happy. Later heard speech in Spanish from B.A. [Buenos Aires].

After dinner Inez, Andrew, and I walked over to fence where we met Junius. We walked to next fence, about fifteen min., where car was. On hillside noticed many large blocks of hard lava worn and rounded either by ice or ocean. Inez gave us some jelly. Mr. Fell and John in Magallanes.

Saturday, December 12

Gray and windy. Junius' tooth bothering him. Shepherd brought us some meat—one half a sheep. Junius found a human lower jaw with two very bad teeth—had been growing all crooked, one with an abscess. Made Junius feel much better!

Sunday, December 13

Calm, sun, cloudy, showers. Two peons stopped by. Mr. Fell and John came over to see if Junius wanted to go in town with the Nicols, but his tooth practically O.K. They told us of Mrs. Gallie's death—the Hamilton's elder daughter—she leaves a little boy and a baby. They brought us a bottle of milk. Junius found a large old-type point with part of the shaft cement still sticking to it. Found a vertebra that he's sure isn't horse or guanaco. In eve, went down to river to get twenty gals. of water—we use about three a day. Of course, I went and fell in. Junius brought me a cup of cocoa when I'd gone to bed—the dear.

Monday, December 14

Calm and cloudy: sunny and very warm at lunch time. Found a horse jaw down 19 to 24 in. Practically no stone things all day. We were just turning in when Mr. Fell and John arrived. Brought us more milk—said there was a young fellow at the *estancia* whom they thought would do for us. They start shearing tomorrow.

Tuesday, December 15

Very windy all day; gusts come in the kitchen, making it very disagreeable. The boy came over—he's from Chonchi and his name is Pedro. He's very quiet and *triste* and I think Mr. Fell must have given him quite a lecture before he came over on how to behave! He seems a good worker. Junius found another skull—Pedro cleared out of the cave pretty quickly when he saw it! Also found a horse jaw—thicker than those here now, with the side teeth growing out somewhat differently. Also found several teeth and pieces of teeth. Many cracked horse and guanaco bones, but no chips or scrapers, even.

Wednesday, December 16

Not so windy. Junius found skull of child and small baby. All the bones were covered above and below with grass, which either caught fire accidentally or was intentionally burned so that most of the bones are charred and partially destroyed. A few, at the bottom where the air did not reach, are intact. They must have burned before decomposition set in, for pieces of "sizzled" brain remain in the skulls—one large piece. Also, there are no burned maggot shells in the grass; [there are] a few in the sections that did not burn. Two large stones and some smaller ones had been piled on top. In eve walked down to *vega* in river where we'd been before—found many chipping tools, two wedges and a bola, six *caiquén* [goose] eggs.

Thursday, December 17

Seven bodies in all in the burial, three adults, two children, and two babies [Bird later classified one of the babies as a "child"—ed.]. Mr. Fell, John, Inez, and Andrew over in eve. Last two going to Gallegos tomorrow for Christmas. Brought us about three dozen duck eggs.

Friday, December 18

Finished up work in the cave. Nothing at all in earth outside cave except a few scrapers and part of an arrow point. Apparently in old days the cliff went straight down and cave was too inaccessible to be used. As some sand drifted over hill from lagoon, it became easier to reach and was used a little. Must have been within 250 to 300 yrs.—as horse bones go down all the way. Only very recently that large sand dune has formed, making approach easy. In eve Junius walked over to river to look at rock shelters there. After he left, John arrived with mail. He and I drove over to pick up Junius. Found he'd shot a hare and when he cut off hindquarters for Muñeca found three babies, very much alive! So cunning and so perfectly "finished"—not like puppies. Even have tiny teeth and John says they can fend for themselves almost right away. Junius was so sorry he'd killed the mother. Had to drown them, of course. Largest shelter [later known as Fell's Cave—ed.] looks worth digging in, but there are many loose stones. Will probably work there in a few days, putting in a trench. Read our letters in bed, from Mr. Bird, Dr. Wissler, and the Jaques. Latter sent such an amusing article, "Farewell My Lovely," from *New Yorker* about Model Ts.

Saturday, December 19

Wrapping up bones and specimens in A.M. Junius worked on car in P.M. and until late in P.M. Bearing he made is fine! Finished last of our meat in a pot roast.

Sunday, December 20

Packed up. Left big tent standing—hid small one, provisions, and a few odds and ends in cave and in other small caves. There's one just behind our tent—room for a man to lie down in—full of cracked bones. Such a cunning little mouse comes around the kitchen. A nest of baby birds in a crack in the rock above our tent. Left for *estancia* after lunch. Junius went on almost immediately to hotel at Dinamarquero, where he hoped to catch the mail car to town. He'll have his tooth attended to and come out in the truck Wednesday or Thursday. A Mr. Campbell here—used to buy sheep for San Gregorio Freezer and now has a farm in N. Zealand. Has been away seventeen years and has just come back to see his friends. A nice old man, full of stories.   *(from M. Bird, 1934–1937)*

Junius and Peggy Bird excavated at Fell's Cave (December 24, 1936, to January 8, 1937) and then moved on to Palli Aike, where they had begun excavations the previous year.

7. Mylodon Cave

In view of the association of sloth and horse remains with human artifacts and skeletons in Palli Aike, Fell's, and Cerro Sota caves, it is advisable to reexamine the record of the Mylodon Cave finds. This vast cavern, over 400 ft. wide (fig. 95) at its mouth by 680 ft. deep, is in Chilean territory near Consuelo Cove in Ultima Esperanza Inlet, 125 miles west of Palli Aike Cave. Although the floor is today 520 ft. above sea level, it appears to be a wave-cut cavern formed by the washing away of a conglomerate formation surrounded and capped by a more durable rock. The opening is towards the west-southwest and would have been exposed to constant and severe wave action when sea level coincided with its position.

The great size and the direction it faces make the cave a rather unattractive place to camp. This does not seem to be just a personal reaction but is sensed and admitted by various persons who have been there. Regardless of this, it is spectacular. Although such a formation would attract attention anywhere, it was not the cave but its contents that made it famous.

BACKGROUND

Between 1895 and 1900 pieces of skin and claws, as well as manure of the extinct *Mylodon listai*, a horse's hoof, and numerous bones of both these animals and others were recovered from dry areas on the irregular cave floor. A human skeleton, a few artifacts, some "cut" hay, and signs of "cutting" on the sloth skin and bones were variously interpreted as demonstrating the contemporaneity of man; that he had domesticated the sloths; and, from the fresh appearance of the remains, that this animal might still be living in the recesses of the unexplored mountains. This, as was natural, received considerable attention in papers and periodicals and was discussed in at least forty-eight articles and notices in scientific journals [see bibliography in Emperaire and Laming 1954—ed.]. As the observations of the men who actually worked in the cave were not in agreement, and as the evidence in favor of human association was slight, students concerned with the history of man in America either have omitted all reference to these finds or have quoted the domestication story for what it might be worth. The treatise on *Early Man in South America* by Hrdlička and others (1912) has no reference to the Mylodon Cave, even in the bibliography.

By way of attempting an analysis of the excavations, the material found, and the conclusions reached, we summarize first the chronological record of the actual digging done.

1895

The first discovery of a large piece of sloth skin, "half buried in the dust which had gradually accumulated from the gradual falling away of the roof" (Moreno and Smith Woodward 1899: 144). From this first piece, according to local accounts, a number of sections were cut and it is told that the wife of the man who had found it, becoming annoyed at the stream of visitors it occasioned, all of whom wanted samples without paying for

Fig. 95. Mouth of Mylodon Cave taken from within. Persons at entrance serve as scale.

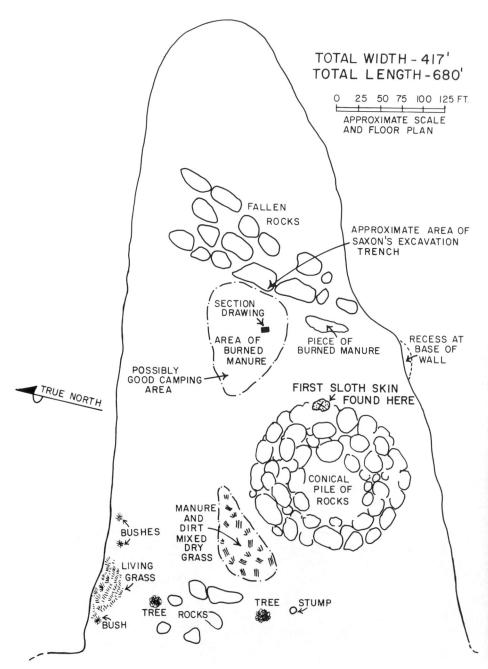

Fig. 96. Drawing of floor of Mylodon Cave.

them, eventually threw it into a bonfire. There are accordingly no records of actual measurements, but, "Dr. O. Nordenskiold recollects that the largest piece of skin he saw which the farm laborers had taken was about 1.5 m (long), this was however not complete in any direction." If any digging was done this first year, it has not been mentioned (fig. 96).

1896

O. Nordenskiold, while in the vicinity, learned of the curious discovery and so visited the cave where he "found some more (2) pieces of the remarkable skin—in one of the crevices of the rock . . . and the large horny sheath of a big claw" (Lönneberg 1899: 150). The references to his visit make it clear that his examination was scarcely more than casual.

1897

F. P. Moreno, while at Consuelo Cove, saw a piece of the sloth skin hanging on a tree, perhaps a remaining portion of the original discovery. Immediately on learning where it had been found he hastened to the spot and made "a few hurried excavations, which gave no further trace of the discovery. I left orders that the search should be continued after my departure; but this once more failed to give any ultimate result. Nothing could be found but modern remains of small rodents—chiefly on or near the surface. . . ." To him belongs the credit of bringing it to the attention of science (Moreno 1899).

1899

Sometime in March, E. Nordenskiold and Borge arrived at Consuelo Cove having come from Sweden with the express purpose "to explore the cave very thoroughly" (Nordenskiold 1900). They stopped work in April, but do not specify the extent of their examinations except for one statement: ". . . I have made extensive excavations in the cave, or rather caves, on the Eberhard farm" (Nordenskiold 1900). He gives the first discussion of the structure of the debris on the cave floor and is conservative in his conclusions, but it must be admitted that for a thorough, extensive study his work leaves much to be desired. The collection secured consists mainly of sloth, horse, and other animal bones, and a few artifacts.

In April, after Nordenskiold had stopped work, R. Hauthal arrived and with four men spent five and a half days digging here and in a smaller cave 3 kilometers to the east. During this time they also visited two other smaller caves. He says, "I must note here that my work was limited to swift excavations because of lack of time, equipment, and sufficient number of peons to make a systematic exploration of all the cave" (Hauthal 1899: 413). Nevertheless, he seems to have secured about the same amount of material as Nordenskiold and Borge, in addition to a fair-sized piece of sloth skin.

1900

A year after his first visit, Hauthal was again in the vicinity. He returned to the cave only to find that in the meantime a lot of digging had been done by men "from the Eberhard farm." This seems to have been the direct result of a growing local conviction that sloth bones and skin had a high commercial value and was probably the source of the collection of skin and bones offered for sale as curios by one of the stores in Magallanes, then [and now] Punta Arenas. There is no record of what was recovered, nor of its final disposition, as far as I know.

Mr. Richard Kruger, of Magallanes, who was on the Eberhard farm at that time, told me that he had been among those who worked in the cave and had seen all the things found from the time of the first discovery. That even he did not see all of them is clear, as he had no knowledge of the dried sloth (?) tongue now in the Salesian Museum in Magallanes. Probably no one person ever saw all that the cave yielded, as it is fairly certain that considerable private prospecting was done.

On his second visit, Hauthal found more sloth and horse bones, but gives no details as to the work. One gathers that it was even less detailed than on his first attempt and that he was greatly depressed by the mining operations which had been carried on in the interval.

This marks the last digging of which there is any published record. As the possibility of further finds of skin seems to have been exhausted, local enthusiasm probably abated at about the same time.

As it stands, the record seems to indicate that the site of this unusual discovery never received the attention it merited, in spite of the widespread discussion and comment which it aroused. The two serious-minded investigators were both of the opinion that they needed a large gang of helpers to accomplish anything, and succeeded only in examining a small portion of the total accumulation. There also seem to be some grounds for accusing Hauthal of being a poor observer.

Most of the dirt moved was turned over by men prompted by the hope of selling what they found, or by idle curiosity. As might be expected, the objects found have been widely scattered and I believe are now divided among collections in Rome, Berlin, Stockholm, Copenhagen, London, La Plata, Magallanes, Santiago, New York, and Los Angeles.

1937

Believing that there was little likelihood of undisturbed stratigraphy, we did not visit the cave until we were about to start home. The present surface of the floor, as can be seen in the photo (fig. 95), resembles some of

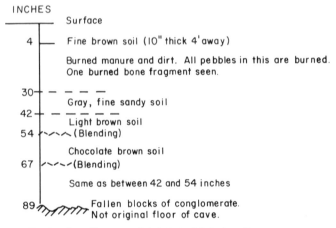

Fig. 97. Section diagram of debris in Mylodon Cave.

the abandoned gold diggings of southern Patagonia. Attention was confined largely to those portions covered with manure, leaving other areas unmolested. As our object was primarily to observe the conditions under which sloth skin and manure had been preserved, we cut back the edge of an old pit to expose an undisturbed section of debris (fig. 97).

(from J. Bird ms. written before 1950)

STRUCTURE OF THE FLOOR DEPOSIT

Nordenskiold gives the following as a characteristic section of the accumulation:

Surface   A few centimeters of sand, gravel, etc.
Layer A   Human occupation; shells, grass, broken guanaco bones
Layer B   Bones of native horses; no proof of human association
Layer C   *Glossotherium* (*Mylodon*) bones and manure
Bottom   Floor of cave

Neither thickness nor total depth of these layers is given.

Hauthal described the structure of the floor deposit in his 1899 and 1901 publications:

The floor, in the anterior part, is covered by a layer of earth (resulting from the decomposition of the sandstone), by stones (cobbles from the conglomerate) mixed with little pieces of boughs, wood, and dry leaves of the trees which form a forest in front of the covern. In this layer I found some broken *Mytilus chorus* shells and some fragmentary guanaco and deer bones. This layer . . . is 1 to 1.5 m thick and shrinks to 1 m at the foot of the little hill.

Further in the interior, in the space halfway between the little hill and the embankment, which divides the cavern, the upper layer is thinner, scarcely reaching some thirty centimeters, increasing . . . to a meter at the foot of the hill. Its material is very heavy, for the great quantity of cobbles which it contains.

Below this layer, continues another of manure of 1.20 meters [1.40 m— 1901] in general thickness. . . .

The manure is very trampled down; in places completely pulverized and very dry; . . . excavating it a dense cloud of very fine dust rises, annoying the workers very much. This is the layer which contains the remains of many and distinct animals; jaws, teeth, claws, parts of skull and other objects. . . . What attracts the attention are the numerous broken bones; some isolated whole bones are found; this breakage I attribute to the hand of man. This layer . . . bore remains of five extinct animals; the greater amount belonged to *Grypotherium* [*Mylodon*].

Towards the rear the layer of manure gradually changes over to ashes and burned earth in a zigzag manner. In some places the ashes are covered by a thin layer of manure. They are not two distinct layers [but are produced by] the action of the fire which spread out [through the dry manure] from the fires of the cave dwellers.

One point which should be emphasized is the impossibility of generalizing about the structure of the floor deposit in a cave of this size. It appears to vary greatly in composition and thickness at different points. The very slight amount of real occupational refuse seems to have been confined to a shallow surface layer on small areas on the outer portion of the floor.

The following section was taken at the point indicated on the plan, where the surface is level; probably the best spot for camping, with the exception of the areas where the shell fragments were found.

No artifact or other sign of human occupation was seen. The 4- to 10-in. layer at the top seems to represent Nordenskiold's layer A and the same on top of it. Below the surface, the earth seemed slightly damp.

RESULTS AND CONCLUSIONS

Apart from the animal remains which formed the bulk of the collections secured, only eighteen items which might be classed as artifacts are recorded from the entire series of excavations (table 22).

Six of Nordenskiold's artifacts came from his layer A, clearly not in association with sloth or horse. The seventh, a bit of twisted thong, together with a small fragment of a human skull, he attributes to his layer C, but without certainty, as he admits that they might have been derived from layer A. Of them he writes: "They cannot be cited as certain proof of the contemporaneity of man and *Grypotherium* [*Mylodon*]" (Nordenskiold 1900).

Hauthal, however, in his first articles refers to *all* of Nordenskiold's finds

Table 22. Artifacts from Mylodon Cave

Category	E. Nordenskiold	Hauthal
Bird bone awl	1	1?
Fox bone awl	–	2
Horse bone awl	–	1
Stone flake, sidescraper?	1	–
Stone flake, unworked	–	3
Leather thong fragment	4	2
Worked bit of leather	–	2
Cord (modern?)	1	–
Totals	7	11

as additional proof of his "hypothesis" that man and the *Mylodon* occupied the cave at the same time. He may have been ignorant of Nordenskiold's observations, but that does not seem likely, as Nordenskiold showed him the things found while still at Ultima Esperanza.

Only two of Hauthal's artifacts, the fox or dog bone awls, have position data. One was found "in the ash . . . at a depth of one meter." The other was "from the layer of manure." If the position of the remaining specimens was known, why was it never mentioned? One of them was purchased in Magallanes with no other information than it came from the cave, yet they are all offered as proof of the contemporary existence of man and the sloth. It is small wonder that little credence was given these claims, although it is now clear that they probably had a good case as far as the fox (and horse) bone awls are concerned. The manner of presentation and the sweeping claims made are regrettable.

The types represented by these artifacts do not serve to place them positively in the chronology indicated by my work. The bird bone awl found by Nordenskiold is so rare among the land people and so common among the canoe users that its presence here with shell refuse suggests that the people who visited the cave subsequent to the extermination of the sloth and other animals belonged to the canoe group.

The fox bone awls might be taken to show that the people of the second land group [Period II] were here while the sloths were still alive, except that they do not exactly match the specimens we have from that period. There is no basis for mentioning more than this.

HUMAN REMAINS

In 1895 Mr. Kruger found a human skeleton at the back of one of the hollows along the base of the south wall. As it was right at the surface of the floor there was no reason to suppose that this person lived at the time of the sloths; in fact, the evidence is to the contrary. Yet, without any discussion of its position it was quoted as proof of man's association with the extinct fauna merely because it was found in the same cave.

As already mentioned, Nordenskiold found a fragment of an immature skull, but had some doubt as to its exact position. The other human bones which have been reported are supposed to have belonged to the first skeleton found, which was not preserved.

SLOTH SKIN

Claims have been made that practically all of the pieces of sloth skin (fig. 98) found show some signs of ancient cutting. Filled with bony ossicles as it is, it cannot be cut without scarring these bones, yet no one mentions whether they are scratched or marked in any way. I have not had an opportunity to examine any of these "cut" edges except in reproductions of photographs, so can add nothing to what has already been said. Hauthal's piece (1899: pl. IV) looks cut, but the ossicles appear undamaged.

Speaking of a piece brought back by O. Nordenskiold, Lönneberg (1899: 153) says: "The anterior and superior margins are freshly cut; the others are old. In some places it looks as if some small rodent had gnawed the edge. . . . The margins of that part of the skin which has covered the leg seem to have been cut by a comparatively sharp instrument, but of course

Fig. 98. Drawing of *Mylodon* by Charles R. Knight.

long ago. There is no doubt, however, that the animal has been killed by man; and that the skin has been taken off and brought to the cave."

Smith Woodward (Moreno and Smith Woodward 1899), describing the section of skin secured by Moreno, states: "One cut border of the skin exhibits distinct indications of freshly dried once fluid matter, which Dr. V. Harley has examined and pronounced to be serum. At one point there is an irregular rounded hole 0.02 m in diameter, which might possibly have been caused by a bullet or dagger; but in any case was probably pierced when the skin was still fresh."

Writing of the piece found by Hauthal, the same author (Smith Woodward 1900) says: "It must have been stripped from the body of the animal by man; but the only distinct marks of tools, which were evidently made when the skin was fresh, are a few indents and small pits on the outer face. The indents must have been made by oblique thrusts of a stick, or a small, blunt, chisel-shaped instrument, and are well shown on Roth's photograph (Hauthal 1899: pl. IV) on the portion marked d,e." He makes no mention of cut edges.

Lehmann-Nitsche (1899: 465–467), describing the *same* skin, writes as follows of the outer edges: "the smooth cuts, it is perceived, comprise, each one, a great space without interruption, certainly made by hand; they have served for removing the skin from the body. . . ." The ossicles along the outer edge are "worn by use and are brilliant, showing that the skin has been employed with some object."

In regard to several small fragments recovered by Hauthal, he adds: "certain of which have been cut from a larger piece; three were found among substances thrown out by the vomit of birds of prey. For us it has no interest to ascertain if they have been torn off by these birds from a larger piece or if they have been picked up loose." He completely dismisses the possibility of the birds of prey having torn them from a carcass, implying that they were first cut by men.

BROKEN OR "CUT" BONE

Considerable difference of opinion was expressed on the interpretation to be placed on the broken sloth bones. Nordenskiold doubted that men were responsible, saying that the bones found at the level of the manure were broken in such a way as to suggest that they had been trampled by sloths. He distinguished between this type of breakage and the intentional fracture of marrow bones in his layer A. Of horse bones, he writes: "I do not dare to say with certainty if . . . they . . . have been worked by man or not." As far as sloth bones are concerned, none could have been broken for marrow as they, like whale bone, have no marrow cavity.

Lehmann-Nitsche, on the other hand, pictures every break as a cut. He describes Hauthal's collection in detail, piece by piece, and adds that Nordenskiold must be mistaken, as his material shows the same cutting as Hauthal's. In all of the discussion, no mention is made of the probability of some fracturing being caused by the fall of rock from the ceiling. Almost none of the bones are burned and the few which are may have been taken from the burned manure.

Such remarks as the following are a fair sample of Lehmann-Nitsche's (1899: 464) deductions:

> One cannot tell with certainty from the remains in what manner the animal has been killed. . . . probably by blows on the head. Once the skin was removed the body has been dismembered. The largest parts were cut in small pieces and eaten with pleasure. They did not leave any more than the attachments of the muscles and the hard tendons.
>
> One is not able to determine with certainty the tool which served for cutting to pieces; indications of blows produced with a cutting instrument cannot be distinguished. These signs of blows and the complete destruction make us assume the use of large stones with sharp corners.
>
> In the feast, the meat has been torn from the bones with the teeth or perhaps with the aid of a small knife. It is not certain that it has been roasted; its flavor has been equal to a herbivore; the flakes of bones from young animals show us that those superior gluttons appreciated tender meat very well.

Although most of his claims are subject to question, there are at least two specimens worth considering. The first of these is a broken skull figured on pl. II, vol. IX, *Revista del Museo de la Plata* (1899) and pl. V, *Proceedings of the Zoological Society of London* (Smith Woodward 1900). Of this, Smith Woodward (1900) says: "[it] exhibits fractures which were almost certainly made when the animal was freshly killed. The cranial roof near the occipital region is battered in four places, . . . the right occipital condyle is partly removed by a sharp, clean cut. There can be no doubt that the animal was killed and cut to pieces by man."

Lehmann-Nitsche (1899: 457) writes: "The two condyles present indications of violence; the right is almost completely cut, acquainting one perfectly that it has been cut with an instrument without edge."

The second specimen, a section of lower jaw, also shown on pl. II of the La Plata report, exhibits the only mark which might be cutting by sawing, although it is not so described. Lehmann-Nitsche says in reference to it (1899: 460): "The portion of the bone, which forms the upper part. . . . has been cut in the form of a sheet in such a way that it is completely separated from the rest of the jaw; but fits perfectly well. It is certain that this sheet has . . . been separated . . . immediately after the death of the animal." Smith Woodward does not include this feature in his remarks on the same object, so it may be only a split.

DOMESTICATION OF THE SLOTH

No one conclusion from the Mylodon Cave discoveries has received more comment than the claim that the natives domesticated the sloth. It has been discredited for several sound theoretical reasons, which need not be repeated at this time, but too little attention has been paid to the incompleteness of Hauthal's observations. Because the story still persists, further comments seem necessary.

First he says: "the entrance [of the cave] is obstructed by great blocks of stone which leave, only at the right, a kind of path, constructed, very probably, by the hand of man." This statement has given rise to the story that the Indians had constructed a wall at the mouth of the cave. On Hauthal's diagram of the cave this path is marked "entrance." The blocks of stone, some of which weigh many tons, have all fallen from the cliff above the cave mouth; there is no resemblance to a wall. Hauthal is wrong in claiming only one entrance; a horse can be ridden through the "obstruction" with no trouble, at about the center of the cave mouth, and an animal, such as a sloth, could pass around or over these blocks at many places.

Another argument which he used was the presence of dried grass in the cave. "At the foot of the little hill, a little higher than the manure, I found much dry hay below the same layer of earth and stones which cover the manure. This hay could have been brought to this site solely by man" (1899).

Smith Woodward speaks of it as "an extensive accumulation of cut hay"; Lehmann-Nitsche as "remains of plants, somewhat rotted."

Hauthal writes: "a heap of dry grass at the edge of the manure layer under about 80 cm of cave roof debris. The fodder could only have been brought here by man since it grows at a brook which flows 1 and 0.5 km from the foot of the cave mouth."

His only other reference to grass in the cave is when writing of the level area east of the little hill: "Here I found dry grass around and over some of the ash heaps up to 15 cm thick which can well be interpreted as old places or couches [of the Indians]." It is worth noting that he does not distinguish this as a different species from his "fodder."

At this time it is difficult to prove or disprove Hauthal's contention that the grass was brought to the cave at the time the sloths were alive. As far as recorded, no one who had opportunity to examine it ever claimed that it had been cut. Moreno seems to have been the first to describe it that way, perhaps because he had found "cut" hay in other Patagonian caves used for bedding by the natives.

While my wife and I were at the cave in 1937, the only place we could find any appreciable amount of dry grass was on the floor where Hauthal found his supposed bedding. Much of it is mixed with the dirt thrown out of the old diggings, but some remains in situ, not visibly in layers or mats, but scattered through the dirt and sand which has accumulated above the sloth remains. Part of it may well have been brought in by the Indians, as it apparently was a practice of theirs.

At the top of the steep slope which rises against the northern wall of the cave, at a height of about 60 ft. above this section of floor, is a patch of live grass about 40 ft. long. Its inner end is 80 ft. inside the cave mouth, and beyond it; as much as 150 ft. inside the entrance are scattered leñadura bushes. This vegetation is supported by a slight seepage of moisture at the base of the wall. The dead leaves, twigs, and grass which eventually slip down the slope probably form the bulk of such remains found on the floor below. As some of the leñadura is at least forty years old, the conditions which support it and the grass must have existed when Hauthal was there, yet when he speaks of the floor debris he attributes the "boughs, wood, and leaves" to the forest growth *"in front of the cave."*

The grass which he found at the rear of the little hill cannot be explained by this but might have been carried there by wind, which is sometimes felt that far back in the cave, or by the rodents *coruros,* whose presence in the cave has been admitted. Their habit of taking grass into burrows, somewhat in the manner of pack rats, has not been mentioned in this connection. In spring one sometimes sees a considerable amount of grass outside their burrows, thrown away when a fresh supply is available.

It is not our intention that these last suggestions be taken too seriously, but in a fair discussion of possible explanations they deserve consideration.

As Hauthal did not note any difference between the "bedding" and the "fodder," we can assume that it was the same type of grass. If so, his assertion that it could not be procured within 1½ kilometers of the cave is a mistake.

His third argument for the domestication theory was his incorrect observation that the manure was confined to one section of the floor which he said marked the confines of a corral. Nordenskiold (1900) remarks on the error of this claim, as he noted manure at other places. From the old diggings it is clear that the animals utilized all the available floor; moreover, no one has ever noted the slightest trace of corral fence or wall, some vestige of which should have been preserved.

Further comment on the domestication hardly seems necessary.

SUMMARY OF EVIDENCE

There is little to be said in summary. The original evidence in favor of man's presence in Mylodon Cave coincident with the now extinct fauna, consisting of a few artifacts and marks on sloth skin and bones, was sound enough to have warranted further investigation. If it had been presented carefully, without including the purely hypothetical, a serious search for additional evidence might have been instigated long ago.

AGE OF REMAINS

There is no reason to suppose that the sloths and horses survived longer in the Ultima Esperanza district than about Palli Aike Cave. Any sound conclusion as to the age of the Mylodon Cave remains should also apply to the other sites which date back to just before the extinction of these animals. Unfortunately, the estimates of age which have been made are based entirely on speculation and range from a few years back to the glacial period.

At the time Bird wrote the above there was no way of determining the age of the sloth remains in Mylodon Cave with any precision. After radiocarbon dating was invented in the late 1940s, Bird was the first to submit samples (of sloth dung) from the cave to Professor Willard Libby's radiocarbon laboratory in Chicago (Bird 1951: 45–46). One sample (C 484) was tested twice, and the two similar results were averaged to produce the date 10,832 ± 400. Bird noted that a recalculation using the Cambridge calculation of the C14 half life would put the date somewhat over 11,000 years. This date was the first solid evidence for the

Fig. 99. A piece of sloth skin with bony ossicles and hair (*right*) and sloth dung (*left*) given to Theodore Roosevelt by the Argentine government. These specimens came from Mylodon Cave.

great antiquity of the sloth remains, and has since been confirmed by numerous other dates on sloth droppings from the cave (Markgraf 1985).

Bird (1951: 46) recorded some information concerning the sample's location, and how it was stored:

> Over a large area on the cave floor is a layer of burned manure up to 30 in. in thickness. Fortunately, the fire did not reach a smaller rocky area and it was there that the 1895–1900 finds were made. In 1937 this appeared to have been completely dug over but some small segments of the manure layer were intact. Although most of this was trampled and compacted by the sloths, some unaltered droppings remained and some specimens of these were submitted to Libby. Because of the disturbed conditions I could not record their position in relation to the former surface and although I believe they were near the top of the manure layer there are no measurements to prove it. After collecting they were packed in a tin box in paper and cotton and, as this box was suitable, they have been stored in it ever since at the museum and have never been on display nor exposed to handling. Before sending the sample to Libby all surfaces were lightly vaccuum cleaned and checked with a low-power microscope for any traces of cotton lint.

At the time Bird was preparing the sample to be sent to Libby, his colleague at the AMNH, Harry Tschopik, proposed the following verse as a cover letter:

Lest you think that my offering is silly,
I make haste to explain—willy-nilly;
These boxes contain
What I saved with great pain—
Examples of sloth dung from Chile.

Deem not this behavior absurd;
There are Pleistocene secrets interred.
These coprolites rare
Will contribute their share
Toward counting past eons for Bird.

TWO ADDITIONAL SPECIMENS

Two specimens, one of sloth dung and one of sloth skin (fig. 99), were given by the Argentine government to Theodore Roosevelt (Mathews 1915), who gave them to the AMNH. These items came from the Mylodon Cave, and were given to Roosevelt by Francisco P. Moreno, then director of the Museo de La Plata.

Editor's Postscript

Junius Bird's investigations in south Chile, beginning in the 1930s and taken up again in the late 1960s, define a ten-thousand-year cultural sequence characterized by five prehistoric periods, distinguished by types of projectile points and other artifacts. These periods are summarized in chapter 2, and have been dated with a series of radiocarbon samples from Fell's Cave. The sequence has stood the test of time and been confirmed through the independent excavations in Fell's Cave by John Fell and by the Emperaires and Henry Reichlen. In recent years the Instituto de la Patagonia has continued archaeological research in the area. These investigations have been reviewed by Mauricio Massone (1981), who continues to use the five periods established by Bird as his basic chronological and cultural framework.

Bird's concern with the early human occupation of the Americas continued throughout his life. He was particularly interested in the question of the dispersion of early hunters from north to south throughout the Americas. Finds of early projectile points from Middle and South America (Bird 1969a; Schobinger 1973; Bird and Cooke 1977 and 1978) were central to a definition of his viewpoint. Bird used fishtail and fluted points found in Central and South America to suggest that the early hunters had close cultural connections, even though the points were distributed over a very wide area. In an attempt to clarify the matter further, he went to Panama for his final seasons of fieldwork. He and Cooke (1977: 7) commented on the critical importance of Central America:

> Since the first finds of paleoindian projectile points with the remains of extinct animals in the United States in the 1920s, much information has been acquired about the life of the humans that made these efficient tools in North America. Meanwhile, in a less complete way, the expansion of megafauna hunters from the Pleistocene into the extremes of South America, where they had already arrived by 9000 B.C., has been documented. Nevertheless, in Central America, so few cultural remains belonging to the paleoindian period have been found that each find, each small piece of

evidence, deserves consideration. This area is of critical archaeological importance if we want to interpret correctly the relationship between the dispersed early artifacts found in South America, and if we want to investigate accurately the chronology and nature of the migrations that brought the paleoindians to that continent. Thus there is the necessity to study stratified sites in Central America.

Bird was unable to find the stratified sites in Central America, even after several years of fieldwork in Panama. His analysis with Cooke (1977: 27–28) of the fluted and fishtail points from Central America concludes as follows:

> During the last five or six years the discussion has intensified about the date of the human occupation of America, about the existence of migrants in the south before the development of fluted points, and about the existence of a sudden invason of paleoindians into the southern continent between 10,000 and 9000 B.C. (Bryan 1973; Lynch 1974; MacNeish 1976). We believe that the similarity between the artifacts that we have described with the other dated specimens in North and South America is a good indicator of close technical ties between the three regions. Even if we do not discard the possibility that man had crossed the Americas before about 10,000 B.C. and had been able to arrive in the southern continent before this date, the fact that the principal instrument used to hunt big animals is of a uniform shape and size (in spite of the great differences in available materials) continues to argue, as we see it, for the rapid movement of the technology through two continents. In this case, even if the paleoindians had been preceded by groups that possessed a different lithic technology, we think that the limited Central American evidence still agrees with the theory of a sudden migration of Pleistocene megafauna hunters from farther north around 10,000 to 9000 B.C.

Bird was always concerned with the growing claims that human populations had arrived in North and South America prior to the terminal Pleistocene. He personally visited sites in both continents which, according to their excavators, produced the early data. Until his death in 1982, Bird remained unconvinced by the evidence for an American pre–projectile point occupation. He was always eager to evaluate the latest claims, but continually found the evidence defective in some way or another (Bird 1969c). An example was his response (1965: 262) to Alex Krieger (1964), who argued for a pre–projectile point occupation:

> In proposing a pre–projectile point cultural stage for North and South America, Alex Krieger has cited certain lithic material from Taltal and other Chilean sites as supporting evidence. That this is an erroneous assumption can be shown by available data. As far as the Chilean record is concerned, Krieger and others have been misled by the low level of technology of certain specific artifacts for which false claims have been made.

They have not recognized that these items are a very widespread feature of seemingly unrelated cultures ranging from the Peruvian and Chilean preceramic to the Inca of the sixteenth century.

Bird's point was that relatively primitive stone tools had been clearly associated with late cultures, and one should not assume that simple tools were necessarily very ancient. In other cases, Bird found claims for very early human occupations in the Americas unconvincing for a number of other reasons: poor stratigraphic control, inexact associations, the classification of nonartifacts as artifacts, and the incautious use of dating techniques.

In summary, despite extravagant claims by later workers, it can be seen that it was Bird's excavations by the Straits of Magellan, and his later analyses of the American early man data, that led to major clarifications of questions raised by Charles Darwin (1933: 213), who visited southern South America a century earlier:

Whence have these people [Fuegian Indians] come? Have they remained in the same state since the creation of the world? What could have tempted a tribe of men leaving the fine regions of the North . . . to enter one of the most inhospitable countries in the world? Such and many other reflections must occupy the mind of every one. . . .

Bibliography

All unpublished manuscripts, fieldnotes, and letters listed below are on file at the Junius Bird Laboratory for South American Archaeology at the American Museum of Natural History in New York City.

AUER, V.
1974 "The Isorhythmicity Subsequent to the Fugeo-Patagonian Ocean Level Transgressions and Regressions of the Latest Glaciation." *Annales Academiae Scientiarum Fennicae* 115: 1–88.

BELL, ROBERT E.
1965 *Archaeological Investigations at the Site of El Inga, Ecuador.* Quito: Casa de la Cultura Ecuatoriana.

BENNETT, WENDELL C.
1936 "Excavations in Bolivia." In *Anthropological Papers*, Vol. 35, Pt. 4. New York: American Museum of Natural History.

BIRD, JUNIUS
1936–1973 Unpublished fieldnotes on sites north of the Straits of Magellan.
1938a "Antiquity and Migrations of the Early Inhabitants of Patagonia." *Geographical Review* 28(2): 250–275.
1938b "Before Magellan." *Natural History* 41(1): 16–79.
1946a "The Archaeology of Patagonia." In *The Marginal Tribes*, 17–29, *Handbook of South American Indians*, Vol. 1, ed. Julian H. Steward. Bulletin 143, Bureau of American Ethnology. Washington, D.C.: Smithsonian Institution.
1946b "The Alacaluf." In *The Marginal Tribes*, 55–79, *Handbook of South American Indians*, Vol. 1, ed. Julian H. Steward, Bulletin 143, Bureau of American Ethnology. Washington, D.C.: Smithsonian Institution.
1951 "South American Radiocarbon Dates." *Memoirs* 8: 37–49. Society for American Archaeology.
1960a "Apéndice 1—Period III Stemless Points from Palli Aike and Fell's Cave." In *La estratigrafía de la Gruta de Intihuasi (Prov. de San Luís, R. A.) y sus relaciones con otros sitios precerámicos de Sudamérica*, ed. Alberto Rex González. Revista del Instituto de Antropología 1: 297–298. Córdoba, Argentina: Universidad Nacional.
1960b Unpublished letter to John Fell, November 10, 1980.
1965 "The Concept of a 'Pre-Projectile Point' Cultural Stage in Chile and Peru." *American Antiquity* 31(2), pt. 1: 262–270.

1969*a*   "A Comparison of South Chilean and Ecuadorian 'Fishtail' Projectile Points." *Kroeber Anthropological Society Papers* 40: 52–71. Berkeley: Kroeber Anthropological Society.
1969*b*   Unpublished notes on bone objects excavated by John Fell and loaned to the AMNH for reproduction.
1969*c*   Oral history on tape with Junius Bird, conducted by Dr. Shirley Gorenstein, in the Junius Bird Laboratory for South American Archaeology, AMNH, New York City. Also on deposit at the Department of Anthropology, Smithsonian Institution, Washington, D.C.
1969–1970*a*   Unpublished fieldnotes of work at Fell's Cave in 1969–1970.
1969–1970*b*   Unpublished diary of fieldwork at Fell's Cave in 1969–1970.
1970   "Paleo-Indian Discoidal Stones from Southern South America." *American Antiquity* 35(2): 205–209.
1975   "Fieldwork in south Chile for AMNH by Junius and Peggy Bird." Unpublished ms.
1977   Unpublished letter to Juliet Clutton-Brock, May 20.
1978   "Paleo-Indian Cremation Burials in Palli Aike and Cerro Sota Cave in South Chile." Paper delivered at the Society for American Archeology, Tucson, Arizona, May 2–8. Published in Spanish translation in 1983.
1980   "Investigaciones arqueológicas en la Isla Isabel, Estrecho de Magallanes." *Anales del Instituto de la Patagonia* 2: 75–87. Punta Arenas, Chile.
1983   "Enterratorios paleo-indios con cremación en las cuevas de Palli Aike y Cerro Sota en Chile Meridional." *Anales del Instituto de la Patagonia* 14: 55–63. Punta Arenas, Chile.
BIRD, JUNIUS B., AND RICHARD COOKE
1977   "Los artifactos más antiguos de Panama." *Revista Nacional de Cultura* 6: 7–31. Instituto Nacional de Cultura, Panama.
1978   "The Occurrence in Panama of Two Types of Paleo-Indian Projectile Points." In *Early Man in America—from a Circum-Pacific Perspective*, ed. A. L. Bryan, 263–272, Occasional Paper No. 1, Department of Anthropology. Edmonton: University of Alberta.
BIRD, MARGARET (PEGGY) MCKELVY
1934–1937   Unpublished journal of trip to South Chile.
1938   "Christmas in Patagonia." *Junior League Magazine* 25(4): 46–47, 71–74.
BRYAN, ALAN L.
1973   "Paleoenvironments and Cultural Diversity in Late Pleistocene South America." *Quaternary Research* 3: 237–256.
CLUTTON-BROCK, JULIET
1977   "Man-Made Dogs." *Science* 197: 1340–1342.
COOPER, JOHN M.
1917   *Analytical and Critical Bibliography of the Tribes of Tierra del Fuego and Adjacent Territory.* Bureau of American Ethnology, Bulletin 63. Washington, D.C.: Smithsonian Institution.

COPPINGER, R. W.
1883   *Cruise of the "Alert."* London: W. S. Sonnenshein and Co.
CRABTREE, DON E.
1970   "Flaking Stone with Wooden Implements." *Science* 169: 146–153.
DARWIN, CHARLES
1886   *A Naturalist's Voyage: Journal of Researches . . . during the Voyage of H.M.S. "Beagle" round the World . . . .* London: J. Murray.
1933   *Charles Darwin's Diary of the Voyage of H.M.S. "Beagle"*, ed. Nora Barlow. New York: Macmillan.
EMPERAIRE, JOSÉ, AND ANNETTE LAMING
1954   "La grotte du Mylodon (Patagonie Occidentale)." *Journal de la Société des Américanistes* Nouvelle Série 43: 173–206. Paris.
EMPERAIRE, JOSÉ, ANNETTE LAMING-EMPERAIRE, AND HENRY REICHLEN
1963   "La grotte Fell et autres sites de la région volcanique de la Patagonie chilienne." *Journal de la Société de Américanistes* Nouvelle Série 52: 167–254. Paris.
FAEGRI, K., AND J. IVERSEN
1964   *Textbook of Pollen Analysis.* Copenhagen: Munksgaard.
FELL, JOHN
1952   Unpublished letter to Junius Bird, November 15.
1960   Unpublished letter to Junius Bird, n.d.
GALLARDO, ANGEL
1899   "El Neomylodon Listai." *Anales de la Sociedad Científica Argentina* 47: 257–261.
GONZÁLEZ, ALBERTO REX
1960   *La estratifgrafía de la Gruta de Intihuasi (Prov. de San Luís, R. A.) y sus relaciones con otros sitios precerámicos de Sudamérica."* Revista del Instituto de Antropología, Vol. 1. Córdoba, Argentina: Universidad Nacional.
GRADIN, C. J.
1980   "Sequencias radiocarbónicas del sur de la Patagonia argentina." *Relaciones de la Sociedad Argentina de Antropología* 14: 177–194.
HAUTHAL, RODOLFO
1899   "Reseña de los hallazcos en la cavernas de Ultima Esperanza (Patagonia Austral)." *Revista del Museo de La Plata* 9: 409–418.
1901   "Die Höhlenfunde von Ultima Esperanza in Südwestlichen Patagonien." *Zeitschrift der Deutschen Geologischen Gesellschaft* 53: 570–581. Berlin.
1904   "Die Bedeutung der Funde in der Grypotheriumhöhle bei Ultima Esperanza (Südwestpatagonien) in anthropologischer Beziehung." *Zeitschrift für Etnologie* 36: 119–134.
HESKETH-PRICHARD, H.
1902   *Through the Heart of Patagonia.* New York: D. Appleton and Co.
HEUSSER, C. J.
1984   "Southernmost Land-based Pollen Sequence from the Southern Hemisphere." *Abstracts*, p. 59, American Quaternary Association.

HRDLIČKA, ALES, WILLIAM H. HOLMES, BAILEY WILLIS, FRED E. WRIGHT, AND
CHARLES N. FENNER
1912   *Early Man in South America*. Bulletin 52, Bureau of American Ethnology. Washington, D.C.: Smithsonian Institution.
KRIEGER, ALEX D.
1964   "Early Man in the New World." In *Prehistoric Man in the New World*, ed. J. D. Jennings and E. Norbeck, 23–81. Chicago: University of Chicago Press.
LAWERENCE, B.
1967   "Early Domestic Dogs." *Zeitschrift für Säugetierkunde* 32(1): 44–59.
LEHMANN-NITSCHE, ROBERTO
1899   "Coexistencia del hombre con un gran desdentado y un equino en las cavernas patagónicas." *Revista del Museo de La Plata* 9: 460–478.
LÖNNEBERG, EINAR
1899   "On some Remains of 'Neomylodon Listaii' brought Home by the Swedish Expedition to Tierra del Fuego, 1896." *Svenska Espeditionen til Magellänsländerna* 2(7): 149–170. Stockholm (summarized in A. Gallardo 1899).
1900   "On a Remarkable Piece of Skin from Cueva Eberhart; Last Hope Inlet, Pat." *Proceedings of the Zoological Society of London*, pp. 379–384.
LOTHROP, SAMUEL K.
1928   *The Indians of Tierra del Fuego*. Museum of the American Indian, Contributions, Vol. 10. New York: Heye Foundation.
1932   "Aboriginal Navigation of the West Coast of South America." *Journal of the Royal Anthropological Institute* 63: 229–256.
LYNCH, THOMAS F.
1974   "The Antiquity of Man in South America." *Quaternary Research* 4: 356–377.
MACNEISH, RICHARD S.
1976   "Early Man in the New World." *American Scientist* 64: 361–367.
MARKGRAF, VERA
1980   "New Data on the Late- and Postglacial Vegetation of La Misión, Tierra del Fuego, Argentina." *Proceedings* 4(3): 68–74. International Palynological Conference, Lucknow, India, 1976–1977.
1983   "Late and Postglacial Vegetational and Paleoclimatic Changes in Subantarctic, Temperate, and Arid Environments in Argentina." *Palynology* 7: 43–70.
1985   "Late Pleistocene Faunal Extinctions in Southern Patagonia." *Science* 228: 1110–1112.
MASSONE, MAURICIO
1981   "Arqueología de la región volcánica de Palli Aike (Patagonia meridional chilena)." *Anales del Instituto de la Patagonia* 12: 95–124.
MATHEWS, W. D.
1915   "Ground-Sloth from a Cave in Patagonia." *Natural History* 15: 256.
MAYER-OAKES, WILLIAM J.
1963   "Early Man in the Andes." *Scientific American* 208: 117–128.

Molina, Manuel J.
1967   "El abrigo de Ush-Aiken (Fell's Cave), Río Chico, Chile, Chile." *Anales de la Universidad de la Patagonia San Juan Bosco, Ciencias Antropológicas* 1: 185–219.

Moore, D. M.
1978   "Post-glacial Vegetation in the South Patagonian Territory of the Giant Ground Sloth, Mylodon." *Botanical Journal Linnean Society* 77: 177–202.

Moreno, Francisco P.
1899   "Note on the Discovery of the Miolania and of Glossotherium (Néomylodon) in Patagonia." *Nature* 60(1556): 396–398.

Moreno, Francisco, and A. Smith Woodward
1899   "On a Portion of Mammalian Skin, Named 'Néomylodon Listai,' from a Cavern near Consuelo Cove, Last Hope Inlet, Patagonia." *Proceedings of the General Meeting of the Zoological Society of London* 1: 144–156 (also in Hesketh-Prichard 1902, pp. 301–314).

Nordenskiold, Erland
1900   "Iakttagelser ach fynd, grottor vid Ultima Esperanza y Sydustra Patagonien." *Kongliga Svenska Vetenskaps-Akademiens Handlingar* n. 5. 33(3) (summarized in "La grotte du glossothérium [Néomylodon] en Patagonie." *Bulletin de la Société Géologique de France* [1900]: 29–32).

Pisano, V. E.
1977   "Fitogeografía de Fuego-Patagonia chilena. I. Communidades vegetales entre las latitudes 52 y 56 grados sur." *Anales del Instituto de la Patagonia* 8: 121–250.

Roig, F. A., J. Anchorena, J. Dollenz, O. Faggi, and A. M. Mendez E.
1981   "Carta fitosociológica de la transecta botánica de la Patagonia austral, 1:1, 250,000." London: n.p.

Saxon, Earl C.
1976   "La prehistoria de Fugeo-patagonia: Colonización de un habitat marginal." *Anales del Instituto de la Patagonia* 7: 63–73.
1979   "Natural Prehistory: The Archaeology of Fugeo-Patagonian Ecology." *Quaternaria* 21: 329–356. Rome.

Schobinger, Juan
1973   "Nuevos hallazgos de puntas 'cola de pescado' y consideraciones en torno al origen y dispersión de la cultura de cazadores superiores todenses (Fell 1) en Suramérica." In *Atti del XL Congresso Internazionale Degli Americanisti (Roma 1972)* I: 35–50. Geneva.

Smith Woodward, A.
1899   "The Supposedly Existing Ground-Sloth of Patagonia." *Natural Science* 15(93): 351–354.
1900   "On Some Remains of Grypotherium (Neomylodon) Listai and Associated Mammals from a Cavern near Consuelo Cove, Last Hope Inlet, Patagonia." *Proceedings of the Zoological Society of London* 64–79 (also in Hesketh-Prichard 1902, pp. 315–330).

STOCK, CHESTER
  1925   *Cenozoic Gravigrade Edentates of Western North America*. Washington, D.C.: Carnegie Institution.
TURNER II, C. G., AND J. BIRD
  1981   "Dentition of Chilean Paleo-Indians and Peopling of the Americas." *Science* 212: 1053–1054.
WHITFORD, ALFRED C.
  1939   "Guanaco Fibers." *Textile Research* 10(1): 22–23. U.S. Institute for Textile Research.
  n.d.   "Report on Hairs." Unpublished ms.